Korean Culture in 100 Keywords

Korean Culture  in **100** Keywords

Writers	Cho Yong-hee, Han Yumi, Tcho Hye-young
Translator	Kim Hye-jin
Proofreader	Amy M. Harp

First Printing	July 2017
4th Printing	January 2024
Publisher	Chung Kyudo
Editors	Lee Suk-hee, Han Ji-hee, Kim Sook-hee, Jang Ji-eun
Designers	Cho Hwa-youn, Park Eun-bi

DARAKWON Darakwon Bldg., 211 Munbal-ro, Paju-si
Gyeonggi-do, 10881 Republic of Korea
Tel: 82-2-736-2031 Fax: 82-2-732-2037
(Marketing Dept. ext.: 250~252 Editorial Dept. ext.: 420~426)

ISBN: 978-89-277-3179-5 13710

http://www.darakwon.co.kr
http://koreanbooks.darakwon.co.kr
Visit the Darakwon homepage to learn about our other publications and
promotions.

Korean Culture in 100

외국인 학습자를 위한 한국 문화 100선

Keywords

DARAKWON

　수년 전부터 "한류" 현상이 세계적으로 확산되고 있다. 드라마나 케이팝과 같은 한국의 대중 문화가 전 세계의 젊은이들에게 성공적으로 다가가는 데는 인터넷이라는 매체가 중요한 역할을 하고 있다. 그러나 이 젊은이들이 한국에 대해 알고 있는 일반적인 지식은, 그것이 고전에 관한 것이든 현대에 관한 것이든, 역사나 지리 또는 사회 구조나 문화 예술에 관한 것이든, 대체로 피상적인 경우가 많다. 반면 한국어에 대한 이들의 관심은 날로 커지고 있는데 지금까지 나온 언어 교재들은 대부분이 오늘날 학습자들에게 필요해 보이는 문화에 대한 접근이 많이 제한적이다.

　최근 들어 여러 방면의 한국 문화가 지구촌 어디에서나 어렵지 않게 접할 기회가 점점 더 많아지고 또 이를 통해 한국어에 대한 관심이 높아지고 있는 상황을 생각할 때 이제는 일반적인 언어 교재에서 벗어나 새로운 한국 문화 교재를 개발해야 할 좋은 시기로 보인다. 좀 더 새로운 차원의 것을 요구하고 있는 학습자들의 기대를 충족시킬 수 있고, 한국 문화의 다양한 모습이 골고루 들어있는 교재를 선보여야 할 때인 것이다.

　지난 십여 년간 해외에서 한국어를 가르치고 있는 저자들이 늘 아쉬워했던 것은 진정한 의미의 읽기 교재가 부족하다는 점이다. 독서를 좋아하고 문화에 대한 호기심이 많은 외국인 학습자들은 초급 수준이더라도 각자의 언어 수준에 맞는 읽기 교재를 통해 한국어와 한국 문화를 배울 수 있기를 늘 바라고 있었다. 서점에 고급 수준의 학습자들을 위한 한국어 읽기 교재는 많이 개발되어 나와 있으나 초급 학습자들에게는 문장 구조의 난이도가 높아 접근하기 어렵고, 반면 전설이나 설화, 옛날 이야기 등의 아동용 서적은 문장 구조도 쉽지 않지만, 사용된 어휘들이 시대에 맞지 않거나 외국인 학습자들의 흥미를 끌지 못하여 독서의 즐거움, 배움의 희열을 충족시키기 어려웠다.

　우리는 이런 교육 환경에 대한 고민과 그 동안의 교육 경험을 바탕으로 외국인 학습자들을 위해 "한국 문화 100선"을 중심으로 한 한국어 문화 읽기 교재를 개발하게 되었다. 각 과는 각각의 문화 주제를 다룬 텍스트와 관련 어휘 및 문법이 실려 있고 그 주제를 소개하는 사진을 넣어 한국어 읽기의 즐거움을 배가시켰다. 또한 주제와 내용의 난이도에 따라 별 하나에서 별 세 개까지로 글을 구분하여 표기하였다. 이 책을 통해서 학습자들은 일반 학습 교재에서 배웠던 단어와 표현들이 텍스트 속에서 구체적으로 어떻게 사용되는지 생생하게 체험하게 될 것이다.

　이 교재는 한국어를 배우고 어제와 오늘의 한국 문화를 알고 싶어 하는 한국어 학습자 뿐만 아니라 나아가 한국어와 한국 문화에 관심이 있는 모든 이들에게도 유용한 책이 될 것이다.

　마지막으로 이 책은 프랑스 파리 한국문화원의 강사들이 몇 년간 공동으로 작업한 결과물이다. 교재 집필 과정 내내 응원해 준 학생들에게 고마움을 표한다. 소중한 시간을 내어 함께 고민하며 좋은 의견을 주었기에 이 책이 탄생할 수 있었다. 또 교정을 해 주신 우리의 소중한 분들께도 특별히 깊은 감사의 인사를 전하고 싶다.

조용희, 한유미, 조혜영

The *hallyu* phenomenon has been spread globally for several years. As Korean popular culture genres like televised drama or K-pop approach the youth around the world, the Internet is playing a crucial part as a medium. However, the general knowledge that these young people have about Korea is mostly superficial, be it about classics, the modern times, history, geography, social structure or arts and culture. Meanwhile, their interest in the Korean language is gradually increasing, and most of the language textbooks published so far have a greatly limited approach to culture which seems to be necessary for today's learners.

Nowadays the opportunities are increasing to easily experience various aspects of Korean culture anywhere around the world, which in turn increases the interest in the language. Given the circumstances, now is the time to go beyond general linguistics and develop a new type of teaching materials on culture, which will satisfy the expectations of learners who demand something on a different level. This is the time to present textbooks that have diverse aspects of Korean culture in a balanced manner.

For the past decade, we the authors, as teachers of Korean overseas, have always felt the lack of authentic reading materials. Foreign learners like to read and are highly curious about the Korean culture; even beginners have wanted to learn the Korean language and culture through reading materials appropriate for each level. There are many Korean reading textbooks in the bookstore for advanced learners; yet, they are not so approachable for beginners due to difficult sentence structures. On the other hand, children's books on legends, folk tales or bedtime stories have hardly drawn interest from foreign learners and have failed to offer the pleasure of reading or the joy of learning, due to complex sentence structures or old-fashioned words.

Thus, we have seriously considered the educational environment and used our teaching experiences to develop a reading textbook on Korean culture, focusing on "100 keywords about Korean culture" for foreign learners. Each subject has a text on a different cultural theme together with relevant words and grammar. Photos are inserted to introduce each theme so that the reading can be more enjoyable. The level of difficulty is indicated by asterisks, from one to three. Through this book, learners will have a living experience of how the words and expressions they have studied in general language textbooks are used in a text.

This book will be useful for anyone generally interested in the Korean language and culture as well as serious learners who would like to study the language and know culture past and present.

On a final note, this book is the result of the several years of teamwork by lecturers at the Korean Cultural Center in Paris. We would like to thank our students who have supported us throughout the writing process. This book would not have existed without their helpful feedback. We would also like to send special thanks to those valuable people who have edited the script.

Cho Yong-hee, Han Yumi, Tcho Hye-young

일러두기 이 책의 사용법

이 교재를 구성하는 100개의 단어들은 주로 파리 한국문화원 수강생들을 대상으로 여러 차례의 설문 조사를 통해 선정되었다. 광범위한 분야를 아우르는 100개의 단어들은 프랑스 학습자들뿐만 아니라 전 세계의 한국어 학습자들이 한국이라는 나라를 총체적으로 이해하는 데 도움이 될 뿐 아니라 한국어 학습에 필요한 문화, 역사, 전통, 사회 등등에 관한 핵심 어휘들과 관련 문법을 배우는 데에 필요한 배경지식을 대표할 수 있다는 의견에 따라 선정되었다.

이렇게 선정된 100개의 단어들은 각각 해당 과의 주제가 되어 이 책에는 총 100개의 과가 수록되어 있으며, 큰 여섯 개의 테마로 나눠 수록함으로써 학습자들이 알고자 하는 주제를 쉽게 찾을 수 있도록 했다. 각 장의 테마는 다음과 같다.

- **1 장** 한국의 상징물 (10단어)
- **2 장** 의식주 (12단어)
- **3 장** 지리와 관광 (21단어)
- **4 장** 사회와 일상생활 (19단어)
- **5 장** 역사와 종교 (20단어)
- **6 장** 예술과 문화 (18단어)

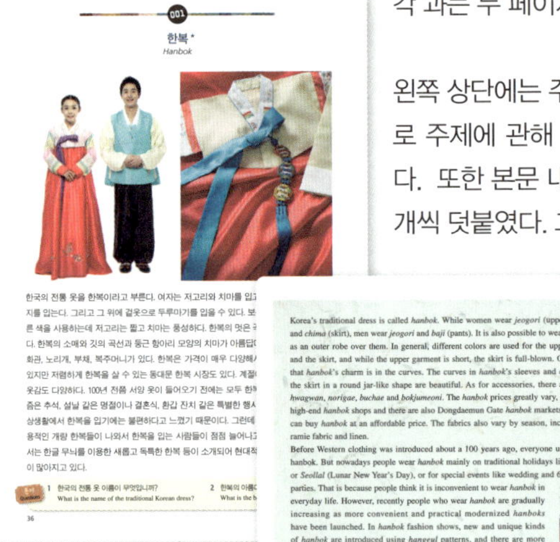

각 과는 두 페이지의 구성으로 되어 있다.

왼쪽 상단에는 주제를 한눈에 알아볼 수 있는 사진이 있고 그 아래로 주제에 관해 꼭 알아야 할 내용을 소개한 한국어 본문을 넣었다. 또한 본문 내용의 이해를 돕기 위한 확인 문제를 각 과별로 두 개씩 덧붙였다. 그에 대한 답은 책 끝에 부록으로 수록하였다.

오른쪽 상단에는 한국어 본문에 대한 영어 번역을 실었다. 이것을 통해 학습자들은 자신들의 한국어 이해도를 스스로 측정할 수 있을 뿐더러, 그동안 이중언어 서적을 바라던 한국어 학습자들의 바람을 해소하는 계기가 되도록 하였다. 하단에는 한국어 본문을 읽는 데 도움이 되는 각 '어휘와 표현'의 영어 번역을 실었다. 주제에 어울리는 작은 사진들을 넣어 학습의 즐거움이 배가되도록 했다.

책 끝의 색인에서는 어휘와 표현에 나온 모든 낱말들을 쉽게 찾을 수 있도록 했다.

각 과에 수록된 한국어 본문은 문장의 난이도에 따라 셋으로 구분해서 그 정도를 ＊별의 개수로 표기해 놓았다.

＊(별 하나)　80～120시간 정도 한국어를 공부한 초급 수준 학습자
＊＊(별 둘)　120～200시간 정도 한국어를 공부한 학습자
＊＊＊(별 셋)　200～300시간 정도 한국어를 공부한 학습자에게 적당하다.

100개의 본문 중에서 ＊는 35개, ＊＊은 47개, ＊＊＊은 18개로 구성돼 있다.

이 책을 접하는 학습자들은 자신들의 언어 수준에 맞는 텍스트를 찾아 읽으며 한국 문화에 대한 지식을 넓힐 수 있을 것이다. 중요한 것은 초급 수준의 학습자라 할지라도 이 책을 통해 읽기의 즐거움과 더불어 한국에 대해 하나하나씩 알아가는 기쁨을 느낄 수 있으리라는 것이다.

끝으로, 한국어 단어 표기 방식은 공식 로마자 표기법을 선택했다. 하지만 예전 표기가 보편화된 단어들은 혼란을 피하기 위해 종전대로 표기하였다. 예를 들면 김치를 *gimchi*가 아닌 *kimchi*로, 택견을 *taekgyeon*이 아닌 *taekkyon*으로 표기했다.

그리고 어휘와 표현에서 동사 어간을 V$_R$로 표기했다.
(예: V$_R$을/ㄹ 만하다　to be worth V-ing)

Notes How to Use This Book

The 100 keywords for this book have been selected through several rounds of surveys with the students at the Korean Cultural Center in Paris, France. The 100 facts address extensive sectors. The facts have been selected because they not only help French and global learners have an overall understanding of the state of Korea, but also represent the background knowledge necessary to study essential words and grammar in learning Korean from various aspects including culture, history, tradition and society.

The 100 keywords thus chosen serve as the topic of each subject. This book has a total of 100 subjects, largely divided in six themes so that learners can easily search the subject they would like to know. The six themes are:

Theme 1: Symbolic Icons (10 Subjects)
Theme 2: Food, Clothing and Shelter (12 Subjects)
Theme 3: Geography and Tourism (21 Subjects)
Theme 4: Society & Daily Life (19 Subjects)
Theme 5: History and Religion (20 Subjects)
Theme 6: Arts and Culture (18 Subjects)

Each subject consists of two pages.

On the upper left side is a photo that can explain the subject at a glance. Under the photo is a Korean text that introduces contents that must be learned regarding the subject. In order to help the learning, two questions are added to check the learner's understanding of the text. The answers are provided in the appendices at the end of this book.

On the upper right side is the English translation of the Korean text. The translation will serve for learners to measure their level of Korean proficiency in terms of understanding; in addition, it will satisfy the need for Korean learners who have long wanted to have a bilingual textbook. On the bottom is the English translation of each Words and Expressions section to help readers understand the Korean text. Small photos that are relevant to each subject are added to provide greater enjoyment.

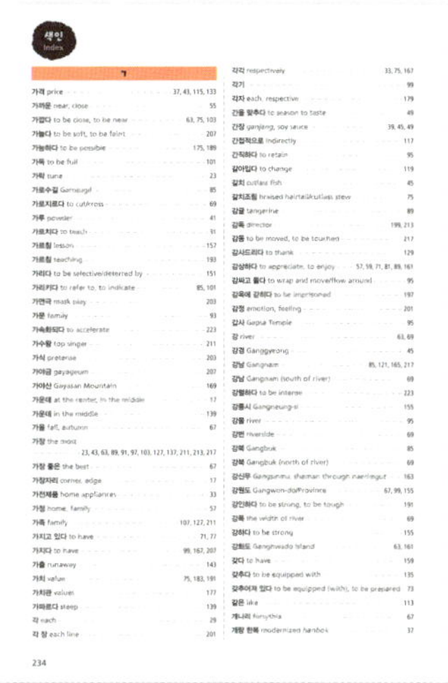

At the end of this book, an index is provided the help learners easily find anything that has appeared under the «Words and Expressions section».

The difficulty of the Korean text under each subject is indicated by the number of asterisk (*), which indicates three different levels as below:

*(One asterisk): Recommended for beginners who have studied Korean for 80 to 120 hours
**(Two asterisks): Recommended for learners who have studied Korean for 120 to 200 hours
***(Three asterisks): Recommended for learners who have studied Korean for 200 to 300 hours

Among the 100 subjects: 35 have one asterisk *, 47 have two asterisks **, and 18 have three asterisks ***.

Learners who read this book can search the texts appropriate for their individual language proficiency and expand their knowledge about the Korean culture. What is even more important is that even beginners of Korean will find the joy of learning facts about Korea one by one, at the same time feeling the joy of reading.

Lastly, the transliterated Korean words in this book follow the official and revised Korean Romanization rules. However, for the words that have been universalized under the old Romanization rules, they have followed the established orthography to avoid confusion; for instance, we have used: *kimchi* over *gimchi*; *taekkyon* over *taekgyeon*. In addition, under the Words and Expressions, V_R indicates a verb stem (e.g. V_R을/ㄹ만하다 means "to be worth V-ing").

차례 Table of contents

Ⅴ 역사와 종교

History and Religion

Ⅵ 예술과 문화

Arts and Culture

부록

Korean Culture in 100 Keywords

외국인 학습자를 위한 한국 문화 100선

I. 상징물
Symbolic Icons

한글 *
Hangeul

한글은 한국의 글자이다. 1443년 조선 시대(1392~1910) 세종대왕(1397~1450)이 발명했다. 그전에는 한자를 사용했지만 백성들은 배우기가 어려웠다. 그래서 세종대왕은 백성들도 쉽게 사용할 수 있도록 새 글자를 만들었다. 그리고 그것을 〈훈민정음〉이라고 불렀다. 훈민정음은 '백성을 가르치기 위한 바른 소리'라는 뜻이다. 처음에는 모두 28자였지만 지금은 자음 14자, 모음 10자로 24자만 남아 있다. 자음은 사람의 발성 기관을 본 따서 만들었다. 모음은 하늘 (●), 땅 (▬), 사람 (▐)의 모양을 본 따서 기본 모음을 만들었다. 과학적이고 독창적인 한글은 외국인들도 쉽게 배울 수 있다.

1 훈민정음은 무슨 뜻입니까?
What does *Hunminjeongeum* mean?

2 세종대왕은 왜 한글을 만들었습니까?
Why did King Sejong the Great create *hangeul*?

Hangeul is the Korean alphabet. It was invented in 1443 by King Sejong the Great (1397-1450) during the Joseon Dynasty (1392-1910). Before the invention, *hanja* (Chinese characters) was used, but it was difficult for the ordinary non-elite people to learn. That is why King Sejong the Great created the new characters for easy use by the people, and the new alphabet was called *Hunminjeongeum*. *Hunminjeongeum* literally means the 'proper sounds to teach the people.' Originally it had 28 letters, but only 24 letters remain at present, consisting of 14 consonants and 10 vowels. The consonants were designed after human vocal organs. The basic vowels are designed after the shapes of heaven (●), earth (▬) and human (▮). Both scientific and unique, *hangeul* can be easily learned by foreigners, too.

어휘와 표현 \ Words & Expressions

한글 *hangeul*, Korean alphabet
글자 letter, character
조선시대 the (era of) Joseon Dynasty
세종대왕 King Sejong the Great
발명하다 to invent
한자 *hanja*, Chinese character
사용하다 to use
V_R지만 V, but
백성 the people
배우기 to learn
어렵다 to be difficult
그래서 so, therefore
쉽게 easily

V_R을/ㄹ 수 있다 can V, it is possible to V
V_R도록 for V-ing, to V
새 글자 new letter
만들다 to make
훈민정음 *Hunminjeongeum*
N(이)라고 부르다 to call N
위한 for
바른 소리 correct/proper sound
N(이)라는 뜻이다 to mean N
처음에 at first, originally
모두 all
자 letter
자음 consonant

모음 vowel
N만 only N
남아 있다 to remain
발성 기관 vocal organ
본 따다 to be designed/modeled after
하늘 heaven, sky
땅 earth, ground
모양 shape
기본 basic
과학적 scientific
독창적 unique
외국인 foreigner

태극기 *
Taegeukgi

태극기는 한국 국기의 이름이다. 1882년에 만들었고 1948년부터 대한민국 국기가 되었다. 가운데에 태극 무늬가 있어서 태극기라고 부른다. 태극은 조화와 균형 속에서 움직이는 우주를 표현한다. 빨간색 윗부분은 양을, 파란색 아랫부분은 음을 상징한다. 음양은 동양 철학에서 서로를 보완하는 기운을 의미한다. 국기의 네 가장자리에 있는 검은색 네 괘는 우주의 하늘(☰), 땅(☷), 물(☵), 불(☲)을 상징한다. 흰색 바탕은 밝음과 순수와 평화를 사랑하는 한국인의 민족성을 표현한다.

1 한국 국기의 이름은 무엇입니까?
What is the name of the national flag of South Korea?

2 태극기에는 무슨 색깔이 있습니까?
What colors are present in *Taegeukgi*?

Taegeukgi is the name of South Korea's national flag. It was made in 1882 and became the national flag of the Republic of Korea in 1948. It is called *Taegeukgi* because there is a *taegeuk* pattern at the center. *Taegeuk* represents a universe that moves in harmony and equilibrium. The upper blue part (of the circle) represents yang, and the lower red part, yin. In Eastern philosophy, yin and yang signify energies that complement each other. The four black trigrams at the four corners of the flag represent the universe's heaven (☰), earth(☷), water(☵), and fire(☲). The white background shows the national trait of Koreans who love brightness, purity and peace.

태극기 *Taegeukgi*	표현하다 to represent, to express	검은색 black (color)
국기 national flag	빨간색 red (color)	괘 trigram
만들다 to create, to make	윗부분 the upper part	하늘 heaven, sky
N이/가 되다 to become N	양 yang	땅 earth, ground
가운데 at the center, in the middle	파란색 blue (color)	물 water
무늬 pattern	아랫부분 the lower part	불 fire
N(이)라고 부르다 to call N	음 yin	흰색 white (color)
조화 harmony	상징하다 to represen/symbolize	바탕 background
균형 balance	동양 철학 Eastern philosophy	밝음 brightness
속 in, inside	서로 each other	순수 purity
움직이다 to move	보완하다 to complement	평화 peace
우주 universe	기운 energy, spirit	사랑하다 to love
	가장자리 corner, edge	민족성 national trait

애국가 ★★
Aegukga

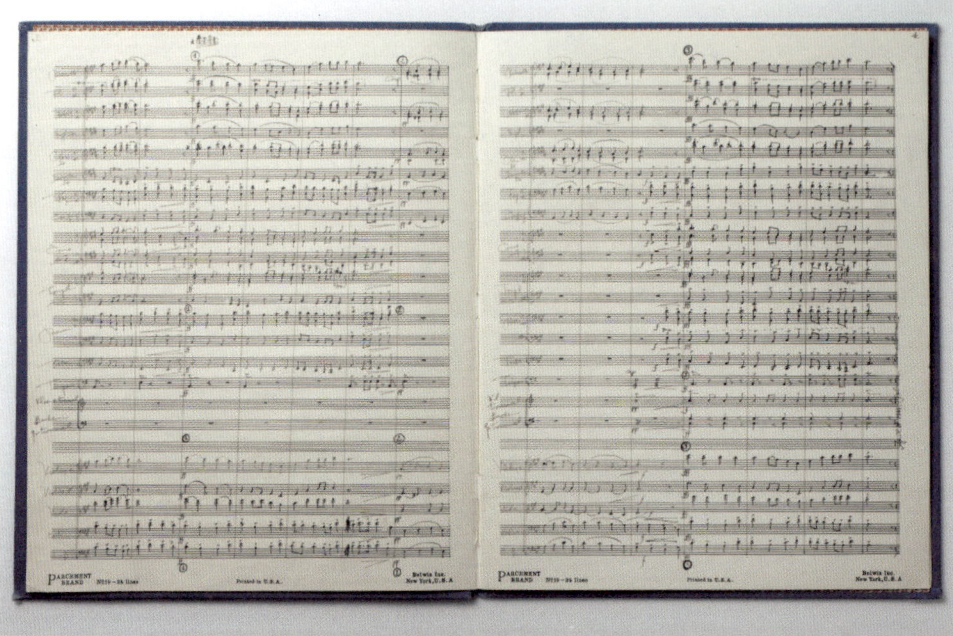

대한민국의 국가는 20세기 초에 안익태가 작곡했다. 국가 이름인 〈애국가〉는 '나라를 사랑하는 노래'라는 뜻이다. 일제 강점기에는 독립을 바라는 한국인들 사이에서 몰래 불리다가 1948년 8월 15일 대한민국 건국을 기념하는 행사에서 공식적으로 채택되었다. 가사는 다음과 같다.

동해물과 백두산이 마르고 닳도록,
하느님이 보우하사 우리 나라 만세
무궁화 삼천리 화려강산,
대한사람 대한으로 길이 보전하세.

1 대한민국 국가의 이름은 무엇입니까?
What is the title of the Republic of Korea's national anthem?

2 애국가는 언제부터 공식 국가가 되었습니까?
Since when *Aegukga* has been the official national anthem?

The national anthem of the Republic of Korea was composed by Ahn Eak-tai in the early 20th century. The anthem's title *Aegukga* means 'a song to love the country.' During the Japanese colonial period, it was secretly sung among Koreans who longed for independence, and later, at the event commemorating the foundation of the Republic of Korea on August 15, 1948, the song was officially adopted as the national anthem. The lyrics are as below:

Until that day when the East Sea's waters run dry and Baekdusan Mountain is worn away,
God protect and preserve the nation; Hurray to Korea.
Three thousand *ri* of splendid rivers and mountains covered with *mugunghwa* blossoms,
Great Korean people, stay true to the Great Korean way forever!

애국가 *Aegukga*

대한민국 Republic of Korea

국가 national anthem

세기 초 early … century

안익태 Ahn Eak-tai

작곡하다 to compose

일본 강점기 the Japanese colonial period

독립 independence

바라다 to hope, to long for

몰래 secretly

불리다 to be sung

V_R다가 V and then

건국 to found a country

기념하다 to commemorate

행사 event

공식적으로 officially

채택되다 to be adopted

동해물 waters of the East Sea

백두산 Baekdusan Mountain

마르다 to run dry

닳다 to wear out

V_R도록 until V

하느님 God

보우하다 to protect and preserve

만세 Hurray

무궁화 *mugunghwa*, hibiscus syriacus

삼천리 three thousand *ri*, (*ri* is an old Korean unit; 3,000 *ri* is approximately 1,200km)

화려강산 splendid rivers and mountains

대한 Great Korea

길이 forever; for a long time

보전하다 to preserve; stay true

무궁화 ★★
Mugunghwa

무궁화는 한국을 상징하는 꽃으로, 꽃말은 '영원히 피는 꽃'이라는 뜻이다. 한국 사람들은 고대부터 무궁화를 하늘 나라의 꽃으로 귀하게 생각했다. 중국에서도 오래전부터 한국을 무궁화의 나라라고 묘사했다. 조선 시대에는 혼례복에 무궁화 수를 놓아서 다산과 풍요를 빌었다. 이렇게 오랫동안 사랑을 받던 무궁화는 현대에 와서 한국의 상징으로 자리 잡았다. 나라의 무궁한 발전과 번영을 기원하는 한국인의 마음을 잘 나타내는 꽃이기 때문이다. 애국가에도 무궁화가 나오고 나라 문장에도 '대한민국'이라는 글자와 함께 무궁화가 그려져 있다. 또한 대통령상, 국회의원 배지에도 무궁화가 활용되고 있다. 그리고 8월 8일은 무궁화의 날로 제정하여 무궁화를 기념하도록 했다.

1 한국을 상징하는 꽃은 무슨 꽃입니까?
What is the flower that represents Korea?

2 무궁화의 꽃말은 무엇입니까?
What does *mugunghwa* mean in the language of flowers?

Mugunghwa (Hibiscus syriacus) is the flower that represents Korea, and in the language of flowers it means 'a flower that blooms forever.' Since the ancient times, Koreans have treasured *mugunghwa* as the flower of heaven. China has described Korea as the country of *mugunghwa* for a long time. During the era of Joseon Dynasty, *mugunghwa* was embroidered on bridal wear, praying for fertility and affluence. Thus loved for a long time, *mugunghwa* was established as a symbol of Korea in the modern times because the flower well shows the heart of Koreans that pray for the infinite development and prosperity of the country. *Mugunghwa* appears in *Aegukga*, and Korea's national emblem also portrays the flower with letters that say 'the Republic of Korea.' *Mugunghwa* is also applied in presidential awards and the badge for the members of the National Assembly. Additionally, August 8 is established as *Mugunghwa Day* to celebrate the flower.

무궁화 *mugunghwa*, hibiscus syriacus
상징하다 to represent, to symbolize
꽃말 the language of flowers
영원히 forever
피다 to bloom
고대 the ancient times
하늘 heaven, sky
귀하게 preciously, highly
생각하나 to think/consider

오래전 a long time ago
묘사하다 to describe
혼례복 bridal wear, wedding clothes
수(를) 놓다 to embroider
다산 fertility
풍요 affluence, richness
빌다 to pray for
현대 the modern times
상징 symbol
자리 잡다 to be established

애국가 *Aegukga*
나라 문장 national emblem
글자 letter
또한 in addition, also
대통령상 presidential award
국회의원 member of the National Assembly, representative
배지 badge
활용되다 to be used/applied
제정하다 to establish

아리랑 ★★
Arirang

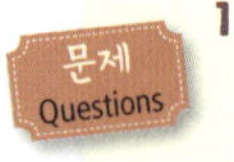

아리랑은 한국의 대표적인 민요이다. 누가 언제 만들었는지 모르지만 한국인이라면 누구나 이 노래를 알고 있다. 지방마다 독특한 정서를 대표하는 아리랑이 있는데 "아리랑 아리랑 아라리요"라는 노랫말이 공통적으로 들어간다. 〈밀양 아리랑〉처럼 멜로디가 경쾌하고 빠른 것도 있고 〈경기 아리랑〉처럼 느리고 슬픈 가락도 있다. 한국인들은 아리랑을 부르며 인생의 '희로애락(기쁨, 노여움, 슬픔, 즐거움)'을 표현했다. 아리랑을 부르며 떠나간 님을 생각하기도 하고 고향에 대한 그리움을 달래기도 했다. 남북한을 합쳐서 약 60여 종의 아리랑이 있는데, 그중 〈정선 아리랑〉, 〈진도 아리랑〉, 〈밀양 아리랑〉이 가장 유명하다. 2002년 월드컵 때에는 아리랑을 응원가로 부르기도 했다. 이처럼 한국적인 감성을 잘 드러내는 아리랑은 2012년에 유네스코 인류무형유산으로 등록되었다.

문제
Questions

1 한국의 대표적인 민요는 무엇입니까?
What is the representative folk song of Korea?

2 한국에서 가장 유명한 아리랑 세 개를 써 보세요.
Write down the three most famous versions of Arirang in Korea.

Arirang is the representative folk song of Korea. Although it is not known who made it or when, all Koreans know this song. Each region has its own version of *Arirang* that includes a unique emotion, but they have the lyrics "Arirang, arirang, arariyo" in common. Some versions like "Milyang Arirang" have a bright and fast melody, and others like "Gyeonggi Arirang" have a slow and sad tune. In the past, Koreans expressed the four feelings of human life (joy, anger, sadness, happiness) as they sang *Arirang*. Singing *Arirang*, some thought of the lover who left, and others comforted their homesickness. There are about 60 versions of *Arirang* altogether from South and North Korea, and "Jeongseon Arirang," "Jindo Arirang," and "Milyang Arirang" are the three most famous. In the 2002 World Cup Games, *Arirang* was used as a cheering anthem to support the Korean national team. Showing Korean sentiments, *Arirang* was inscribed in 2012 on the Representative List of the Intangible Cultural Heritage of Humanity by UNESCO.

아리랑 *Arirang*

대표적 representative

민요 folk song

V_R는/은/ㄴ지 모르다 do not know how/what/if V

누구나 anyone

지방 region, local area

N마다 each N

독특한 unique

정서 emotion

노랫말 lyrics, words

공통적으로 in common

들어가다 to have, to be included

N처럼 like N

멜로디 melody

경쾌하다 to be light/cheerful

빠르다 to be fast

느리다 to be slow

슬프다 to be sad

가락 tune

인생 life

희로애락 (기쁨, 노여움, 슬픔, 즐거움) four human feelings (joy, anger, sadness, happiness)

표현하다 to express

떠나가다 to leave

님 lover

생각하다 to think

V_R기도 하다 V, too (to indicate that two or more actions are done)

고향 home, hometown

N에 대한 regarding/about N

그리움 longing, yearning

달래다 to comfort

남북한 South and North Korea

합치다 to combine, to be altogether

약 about, approximately

N여 종 N types/kinds of

가장 the most

월드컵 the World Cup Games

응원가 cheering anthem

등록되다 to be registered/enlisted

고려청자 ★★★
Goryeo Celadon

고려 시대(918~1392)의 도자기는 푸른빛이 난다고 하여 고려청자라고 불렀다. 옛날부터 중국인들은 '세상에서 제일 훌륭한 물건'이라고 칭찬했다. 화려하고 신비로운 면을 고려와 중국의 귀족들이 좋아했기 때문이다. 처음에는 모양이 단순했지만 점점 발전하여 12~13세기에는 전성시대를 이루었다. 고려청자 중에서 한국을 대표하는 청자는 상감 청자다. 먼저 무늬를 그리고 그 모양 그대로 판 다음에 그 안에 다른 색의 흙을 넣어서 구웠다. 이렇게 만들어진 상감 청자는 여러 무늬가 조화롭게 어우러져 있어 마치 한 폭의 그림 같다. 특히 〈운학 무늬 매병〉이 유명한데, 병의 모양과 구름 사이에서 흰 학이 놀고 있는 하늘빛 청색이 아름답다.

1 고려청자는 무슨 색깔의 빛이 납니까?
What color is the Goryeo celadon?

2 고려청자 중에서 유명한 작품은 무엇입니까?
What is the famous work of Goryeo celadon?

The pottery from the era of Goryeo Dynasty (918-1392) is called Goyreo celadon for its grayish blue-green hue. From the old days, the Chinese praised Goryeo celadon as 'the most remarkable object in the world.' That is because the aristocrats of Goryeo and China liked its glamorous and mysterious side. At first, its shape was simple but it gradually developed to achieve a golden age between the 12th and 13th century. Of all Goryeo celadon, the inlaid (*sanggam*) celadon is the one that most represents Korea. First, designs were drawn and then carved as they were drawn; later, different colored clay was put within (the carved area) before baking. The inlaid celadon thus made looks like a beautiful painting as various designs are in harmony. In particular, 'Celadon Prunus Vase with Inlaid Cloud, Crane Design' is famous; the shape of the vase and the sky blue color in which white cranes are playing among clouds are quite beautiful.

고려청자 Goryeo Celadon
고려 Goryeo Dynasty
시대 era, age, dynasty
도자기 pottery, ceramics, porcelain
푸른빛 bluish/greenish hue
옛날 the old days
세상 world
제일 the most
훌륭하다 to be excellent/remarkable
물건 item, thing
칭찬하다 to praise/compliment
화려하다 to be glamorous/brilliant
신비롭다 to be mysterious

귀족 aristocrat, noble
처음 at first
모양 shape
단순하다 to be simple
점점 gradually
발전하다 to develop
세기 century
전성시대 golden age
이루다 to achieve
대표하다 to represent
상감 청자 inlaid (*sanggam*) celadon
무늬 design, pattern
그대로 as it is
파다 to carve
흙 clay, earth

굽다 to bake
조화롭다 to be harmonious, to be in harmony
어우러지다 to be in harmony
마치 as if, to look like
폭 unit of counting cloth or picture
특히 in particular, especially
운학 무늬 매병 Celadon Prunus Vase with Inlaid Cloud, Crane Design
구름 cloud
희다 to be white
학 crane
놀다 to play
하늘빛 sky blue hue
정색 blue (color)

김치 *
Kimchi

김치는 한국의 대표적인 발효 식품으로 밥과 함께 항상 한국인의 밥상에 올라오는 반찬이다. 김치는 일반적으로 소금에 절인 배추에 무, 파, 마늘, 생강, 고춧가루, 젓갈을 넣고 만든다. 하지만 그 종류는 계절과 지방에 따라 양념과 재료가 다르기 때문에 매우 다양한데 약 300여 종류의 김치가 있다. 그중에서도 배추김치, 깍두기, 총각김치, 열무김치, 오이소박이, 동치미, 깻잎김치는 한국인들이 자주 먹는 김치이다. 고춧가루를 넣지 않고 만든 백김치도 있다. 그래서 백김치는 맵지 않다. 김치로 다른 요리를 만들 수도 있다. 김치찌개, 김치전, 김치볶음밥, 김칫국 외에 생선이나 고기를 넣어서 다양한 요리를 만들 수 있다.

1 김치는 어떤 식품입니까?
What kind of food is *kimchi*?

2 김치로 만들 수 있는 요리는 무엇입니까?
What kinds of dishes can you make with *kimchi*?

Kimchi is a representative fermented food of Korea, and it is always served in a Korean meal together with rice. *Kimchi* is generally made with salted napa cabbage, with added radish, scallion, garlic, ginger, chili pepper powder and salted seafood. But the types greatly vary as the seasonings and ingredients differ by season and region, and there are about 300 types of *kimchi*. Among them, *baechu kimchi, kkakdugi, chonggak kimchi, yeolmu kimchi, oisobagi* (cucumber *kimchi*), *dongchimi* and *kkaennip kimchi* are kinds of *kimchi* that Koreans eat very often. There is also *baekkimchi* made without chili pepper powder, so it is not spicy. You can also make other dishes with *kimchi*. Besdies *kimchi jjigae, kimchi jeon*, fried rice with *kimchi*, and *kimchi* soup, it is also possible to make diverse dishes adding fish or meat.

김치 *kimchi*
대표적 representative
발효 식품 fermented food
N와/과 함께 together with N
항상 always
밥상 meal, table, diet
올라오다 to serve
반찬 side dish
소금 salt
절인 pickled, salted
배추 napa cabbage
무 radish
파 scallion
마늘 garlic
생강 ginger
고춧가루 chili pepper powder
젓갈 salted (pickled) seafood
넣다 to add
만들다 to make

종류 type, kind
계절 season
지방 region
N에 따라 by N
양념 seasoning
재료 ingredient
다르다 to be different
V_R기 때문에 because V
매우 very
다양하다 to be diverse, to vary
약 about, approximately
배추김치 *baechu* (napa cabbage) *kimchi*
깍두기 *kkakdugi* (Korean radish *kimchi*)
총각김치 *chonggak* (chonggak radish) *kimchi*
열무김치 *yeolmu* (young radish) *kimchi*

오이소박이 *oisobagi* (cucumber *kimchi*)
동치미 *dongchimi* (water-based radish *kimchi*)
깻잎김치 *kkaennip* (seaseme leaves) *kimchi*
자주 often
V_R지 않다 do not V
백김치 *baekkimchi* (white *kimchi*)
맵다 to be hot/spicy
다른 different
V_R을/ㄹ 수도 있다 can/may V
찌개 *jjigae* (stew)
전 *jeon* (pancake)
볶음밥 fried rice
국 soup
N 외에 besides N
생선 fish

비빔밥 ★★
Bibimbap

흰밥 위에 여러 가지 야채와 고기를 넣어서 고추장과 함께 비벼 먹는 음식을 비빔밥이라고 한다. 재료에 따라 색깔과 맛이 다양한 음식인데 모양과 색깔이 아름다워서 옛날부터 화반이라고 불렀다. 비빔밥은 각 재료들의 맛이 조화를 이루는 음식이다. 산채 비빔밥, 육회 비빔밥, 해산물 비빔밥 등 재료에 따라 다른 맛을 낼 수 있다. 비빔밥을 담는 그릇에 따라 다른 맛이 나기도 하는데 뜨거운 돌솥에 담아 먹는 비빔밥인 돌솥 비빔밥도 있다. 비빔밥은 지역에 따라 맛과 모양이 다르다. 지역의 비빔밥 중에서 특히 전주비빔밥이 유명하다. 10월 전주에서는 전주비빔밥 축제가 열린다. 축제 기간 동안 직접 비빔밥을 만들어 볼 수 있다. 또한 건강하고 맛있는 식생활에 대한 다양한 정보도 얻을 수 있다. 이처럼 비빔밥은 한국인들이 집에서 쉽게 만들어 먹을 수 있을 뿐 아니라, 특별한 재료와 함께 특별식으로 즐기기도 하는 건강 음식이다.

1 밥, 야채, 고기를 고추장과 비벼 먹는 한국 음식이 무엇입니까?
What is the Korean food that you eat mixing rice, vegetables and meat with *gochujang*?

2 어느 도시의 비빔밥이 특히 유명합니까?
Which city is particularly famous for *bibimbap*?

Bibimbap is a food that is served with white rice topped with various vegetables and meat, mixing them with *gochujang*. The colors and taste of this food vary by ingredients, and since its shape and colors are beautiful, it was called *hwaban* (lit. flower rice) from the old days. *Bibimbap* is a food in which the flavor of each ingredient is in harmony. It is possible to bring out different flavors by ingredients, such as *sanchae*, *yukhoe*, and seafood. The taste can be different by the bowl that *bibimbap* is put in, and there is a type of *bibimbap* is served in a hot stone pot. *Bibimbap*'s taste and shape differ by region. *Jeonju bibimbap* is especially famous among regional versions. In October, the Jeonju Bibimbap Festival is held in Jeonju. During the period of the Festival, you can personally try and make *bibimbap*. Thus *bibimbap* is not only a food that Koreans can easily make and eat at home, it is also a healthy food that is enjoyed as a special meal with various ingredients.

비빔밥 *bibimbap*

흰밥 white rice

여러 가지 diverse

야채 vegetable

넣다 to add, to put in

고추장 *gochujang* (chili pepper paste)

비비다 to mix

재료 ingredient

N에 따라 by N

색깔 color

맛 taste

다양하다 to be various

모양 shape, form

옛날 old days

화반 *hwaban* (flower rice)

각 each

조화를 이루다 to be in harmony

산채 wild vegetables

육회 *yukhoe* (seasoned raw beef)

해산물 seafood

등 such as, including, etc.

맛을 내다 to season, to bring out flavor

뜨겁다 to be hot

돌솥 stone pot, hot stone

담다 to serve, to put in

특히 particularly, especially

전주 Jeonju

축제 festival

열리다 to open, to be held

기간 period

직접 personally, directly

V$_R$아/어/여 보다 to try V

또한 and, in addition

건강하다 to be healthy

식생활 diet

N에 대한 regarding/about N

정보 information

얻다 to acquire

쉽게 easily

V$_R$을/ㄹ뿐만 아니라 not only V but also…

특별한 special

특별식 special meal/food

즐기다 to enjoy

V$_R$기도 하다 sometimes V happens

건강 음식 healthy food

태권도 *
Taekwondo

전통 무술인 택견과 수박도에서 나온 태권도는 몸과 마음을 수련하는 한국의 대표적인 무술이다. 1988년 서울 올림픽에서 시범 종목으로 채택되었고, 2000년 시드니 올림픽에서 정식 메달 종목이 되었다. 현재는 100여 개 국 이상의 나라에서 태권도를 가르치고 배운다. 처음 태권도를 시작할 때는 흰 띠를 매고, 단이 오르면 차례로 노란 띠, 파란 띠, 빨간 띠, 검은 띠를 맨다. 태권도는 아이들의 신체적 건강뿐만 아니라 사회성 발달에도 도움을 준다. 그래서 한국의 많은 아이들이 태권도를 배우고, 대학생들도 동아리 활동을 통해 태권도를 익힌다.

1 태권도는 언제 올림픽 정식 메달 종목이 되었습니까?
When did *taekwondo* become an official medal event of the Olympic Games?

2 태권도를 시작하는 사람은 무슨 색 띠를 맵니까?
When we first start learning *taekwondo*, what color is the belt we wear?

Taekwondo from the traditional martial arts of *taekkyon* and *subakdo*, is a representative Korean martial art that trains body and mind. It was selected as a demonstration sport in the 1988 Seoul Olympics and became an official medal event in the 2000 Sydney Olympics. At present, *Taekwondo* is taught and learned in more than 100 countries. When you first start, you wear white belt, and as you move to higher ranks, you get to wear in the order of yellow, blue, red and black belt. *Taekwondo* helps the development of children's sociality, as well as physical health. Therefore, many Korean children learn *taekwondo*, and college students learn it through club activities.

태권도 *taekwondo*	N여 about N	아이 child
전통 tradition(al)	이상 more than	신체적 physical
무술 martial art	가르치다 to teach	건강 health
택견 *taekkyon*	처음 first	뿐만 아니라 not only, as well as
N에서 나오다 to come from N	V$_R$을/ㄹ 때 when V	사회성 sociality, social skills
몸 body	흰 띠 white belt	발달 development
마음 mind	매다 to wear, to tie	도움을 주다 help
수련하다 to train	단 rank	많은 many
대표적인 representative	오르다 to move up	배우다 to learn
시범 demonstration	V$_R$(으)면 as V	동아리 club
종목 sport, game	차례로 in order	활동 activity
채택되다 to be selected	노란 띠 yellow belt	N을/를 통해 through N
정식 official, formal	파란 띠 blue belt	익히다 to learn
메달 medal	빨간 띠 red belt	
N이/가 되다 to become N	검은 띠 black belt	

첨단 과학 기술 *
Advanced Science and Technology

한국은 IT 정보 기술이 매우 발달한 나라이다. 한국의 초고속 인터넷 보급률과 속도는 세계 제일이다. 삼성, 엘지와 같은 회사들은 디지털과 가전제품 분야에서 해마다 혁신적인 신기술을 개발하여 세계적으로 인정받고 있다. 한국은 중공업 산업에서도 리더의 역할을 하고 있다. 대우, 현대, 기아, 두산과 삼성 중공업 회사들은 각각 조선, 자동차, 철강 산업 분야에서 첨단 기술을 보유하고 있다. 최근에는 의학 분야에서도 첨단 기술과 고도의 서비스를 인정받아 이를 바탕으로 한 의료 사업이 번창하고 있다.

1 초고속 인터넷 보급률이 제일 높은 곳은 어느 나라입니까?
Which country has the highest penetration rate of super-high speed Internet?

2 한국 회사 이름을 세 개 써 보세요.
Please write down the names of three Korean companies.

South Korea is a country that has highly-developed information technology. The penetration rate and speed of Korea's super-high speed Internet are the best in the world. Companies like Samsung and LG are globally recognized for developing innovative new technologies every year in the sectors of digital and home appliances. Korea is playing the role of leader in heavy industries, too. Heavy industry companies like Daewoo, Hyundai, Kia, Doosan and Samsung possess advanced technologies respectively in shipping, automobile and steel industries. Recently, the medical science sector has been recognized for advanced technology and high degree of services, and the medical business based on them is flourishing.

첨단 advanced, state-of-the-art
과학 기술 science and technology
정보 기술 information technology
매우 very, extremely
발달하다 to be developed/advanced
초고속 super-high speed
보급률 penetration rate
속도 speed
세계 world
제일 the most, the best
삼성 Samsung
엘지 LG
N와/과 같은 like/such as N
디지털 digital

가전제품 home appliances
분야 sector, area
해마다 every year
혁신적인 innovative
신기술 new technology
개발하다 to develop
V_R아/어/여(서) V, so…/ for V-ing
세계적으로 globally
인정받다 to be recognized
중공업 산업 heavy industry
리더 leader
역할 role
대우 Daewoo
현대 Hyundai

기아 Kia
두산 Doosan
각각 respectively
조선 shipbuilding
자동차 automobile, car
철강 steel
보유하다 to have, to possess
최근 recent(ly)
의학 medicine, medical science
고도 high degree (of)
서비스 service
N을/를 바탕으로 based on N
의료 사업 medical tourism business
번창하다 to flourish, to prosper

Korean Culture in 100 Keywords

외국인 학습자를 위한 한국 문화 100선

II. 의식주
Food, Clothing
and Shelter

한복 *
Hanbok

한국의 전통 옷을 한복이라고 부른다. 여자는 저고리와 치마를 입고, 남자는 저고리와 바지를 입는다. 그리고 그 위에 겉옷으로 두루마기를 입을 수 있다. 보통 저고리와 치마는 다른 색을 사용하는데 저고리는 짧고 치마는 풍성하다. 한복의 멋은 곡선에 있다고 할 수 있다. 한복의 소매와 깃의 곡선과 둥근 항아리 모양의 치마가 아름답다. 장식으로는 족두리, 화관, 노리개, 부채, 복주머니가 있다. 한복은 가격이 매우 다양해서 고급 한복 가게들도 있지만 저렴하게 한복을 살 수 있는 동대문 한복 시장도 있다. 계절에 따라 견, 모시, 마 등 옷감도 다양하다. 100년 전쯤 서양 옷이 들어오기 전에는 모두 한복을 입었다. 하지만 요즘은 추석, 설날 같은 명절이나 결혼식, 환갑 잔치 같은 특별한 행사 때에 주로 입는다. 일상생활에서 한복을 입기에는 불편하다고 느끼기 때문이다. 최근에는 편리하고 실용적인 생활 한복들이 나와서 한복을 입는 사람들이 점점 늘어나고 있다. 한복 패션쇼에서는 한글 무늬를 이용한 새롭고 독특한 한복 등이 소개되어 현대적이면서도 세련된 한복이 많아지고 있다.

문제 Questions

1 한국의 전통 옷 이름이 무엇입니까?
What is the name of the traditional Korean dress?

2 한복의 아름다움은 무엇입니까?
What is the beauty of *hanbok*?

Korea's traditional dress is called *hanbok*. While women wear *jeogori* (upper garment) and *chima* (skirt), men wear *jeogori* and *baji* (pants). It is also possible to wear *durumagi* as an outer robe over them. In general, different colors are used for the upper garment and the skirt, and while the upper garment is short, the skirt is full-blown. One can say that *hanbok*'s charm is in the curves. The curves in *hanbok*'s sleeves and collars, and the skirt in a round jar-like shape are beautiful. As for accessories, there are *jokduri*, *hwagwan*, *norigae*, *buchae* and *bokjumeoni*. The *hanbok* prices greatly vary, so there are high-end *hanbok* shops and there are also Dongdaemun Gate *hanbok* markets where you can buy *hanbok* at an affordable price. The fabrics also vary by season, including silk, ramie fabric and linen.

Before Western clothing was introduced about a 100 years ago, everyone used to wear hanbok. But nowadays people wear *hanbok* mainly on traditional holidays like *Chuseok* or *Seollal* (Lunar New Year's Day), or for special events like wedding and 60th birthday parties. That is because people think it is inconvenient to wear *hanbok* in everyday life. Recently people who wear *hanbok* are gradually increasing as more convenient and practical modernized *hanboks* have been launched. In *hanbok* fashion shows, new and unique kinds of *hanbok* are introduced using *hangeul* patterns, and there are more *hanboks* that are both modern and refined.

한복 *hanbok*, traditional Korean dress

전통 tradition(al)

저고리 *jeogori*, upper garment

겉옷 outer robe, overcoat

두루마기 *durumagi*, outer robe over *jeogori* and skirt/pants

짧다 to be short

풍성하다 to be full-blown, ample

멋 charm

소매 sleeve

깃 collar

곡선 curve

둥글다 to be round

항아리 jar

아름다움 beauty

장식 accessory

족두리 ceremonial headgear for women

화관 ceremonial coronet for women

노리개 *norigae*, traditional accessory for women

부채 *Buchae*, fan

복주머니 *Bokjumeoni*, lucky pouch

가격 price

매우 very, greatly

다양하다 to be diverse, to vary

고급 high-end, high quality

저렴하다 to be inexpensive/affordable

동대문 Dongdaemun Gate

견 silk

모시 ramie fabric

마 linen

옷감 fabric

서양 옷 Western clothing

명절 traditional holidays

결혼식 wedding (ceremony)

환갑 age of 60

잔치 party, festival

특별하다 to be special

행사 event

주로 mainly

일상생활 everyday life

불편하다 to be inconvenient

느끼다 to think/feel

최근 recently

편리하다 to be convenient

실용적이다 to be practical

생활 한복 daily *hanbok*, contemporary *hanbok*

점점 gradually

늘어나다 to increase

패션쇼 fashion show

무늬 pattern

이용하다 to use

새롭다 to be new

독특하다 to be unique

소개되다 to be introduced

현대적이다 to be modern

세련되다 to be refined

불고기 ★★
Bulgogi

불고기는 한국을 대표하는 음식으로 한국 사람뿐만 아니라 많은 외국인들도 좋아하는 음식이다. 옛날부터 한국인들은 고기를 양념에 재워 놓았다가 구워 먹었다. 그 전통이 이어져서 오늘날의 불고기가 되었다. 불고기는 소불고기, 돼지 불고기, 오리 불고기, 오삼 불고기 등 여러 가지 종류가 있다. 불고기 요리 방법은 다음과 같다. 얇게 썬 소고기 600g을 양념과 섞는다. 양념은 간장 4 큰 숟가락, 설탕 2 큰 숟가락, 참기름 2 큰 숟가락, 다진 파 1 큰 숟가락, 다진 마늘 1/2(반) 숟가락, 후추 약간을 섞어서 만든다. 고기와 양념을 잘 섞은 후 30분 정도 기다렸다가 뜨거운 프라이팬에 볶는다. 이때 양파, 버섯 같은 야채를 함께 넣고 볶아도 된다. 상추에 불고기를 싸 먹어도 맛이 좋다.

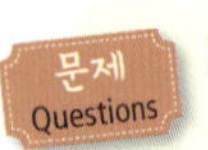

문제
Questions

1 한국을 대표하는 고기 요리는 무엇입니까?
What is the meat dish that represents Korea?

2 불고기 소스는 무엇으로 만듭니까?
What is *bulgogi* sauce made of?

Bulgogi is a dish that represents Korea, which not only Koreans but also many foreigners like. Since the old times, Koreans have marinated meat with seasonings and grilled it before eating. The tradition continued to finally become today's *bulgogi*. There are many kinds of *bulgogi* including beef, pork, duck, squid and pork and others. The *bulgogi* recipe is as follows: Mix 600g of thinly sliced beef with seasoning. The seasoning is made of 4 tablespoons of soy sauce, 2 tablespoons of sugar, 2 tablespoons of sesame oil, 1 tablespoon of chopped scallion, a half tablespoon of crushed garlic, and some black pepper. After you mix the meat and the seasoning, wait for about half an hour and stir-fry it in a hot pan. At this point, you can add and stir-fry vegetables like onion and mushrooms together. It also tastes good to wrap *bulgogi* in lettuce.

불고기 *bulgogi*, marinated meat grilled on a barbecue or stove-top
대표하다 to represent
뿐만 아니라 not only
옛날 old times
양념 seasoning, condiment
재워 놓다 to marinate
굽다 to grill
전통 tradition
이어지다 to continue
요리 방법 recipe

얇다 to be thin
썰다 to slice
그램(g) gram
섞다 to mix
간장 soy sauce
숟가락 spoon
설탕 sugar
참기름 sesame oil
다진 파 chopped scallion
다진 마늘 crushed garlic
후추 black pepper
약간 a little, some

정도 about
뜨겁다 to be hot
프라이팬 pan, skillet
볶다 to stir-fry
이때 at this point
양파 onion
버섯 mushrooms
넣다 to add
V_R아도/어도/여도 되다 can V, it is possible to V
상추 lettuce
싸다 to wrap

003

인삼 ★★
Gingseng

인삼은 뿌리 모양이 사람을 닮아서 인삼이라고 불린다. 옛날부터 인삼을 먹으면 오래 산다고 해서 귀중한 약재로 알려졌다. 땅에 심고 나서 보통 4~6년 후에 인삼을 캐는데 홍삼은 6년 된 뿌리를 수증기에 쪄서 말린 것으로 효능이 가장 좋다. 인삼은 건강 보조 식품으로 다양하게 활용할 수 있다. 인삼 뿌리를 달여 마실 수도 있고, 절편으로 먹을 수도 있고, 가루로 인삼차를 만들어 마시기도 한다. 또 인삼으로 인삼주나 인삼 진액을 만들기도 한다. 찹쌀, 대추, 마늘 그리고 인삼을 닭에 넣어 만든 삼계탕은 특히 여름에 한국인들이 즐겨 먹는 음식이다. 어린 인삼은 샐러드로 먹기도 한다. 또 인삼으로 화장품도 만든다.

문제
Questions

1 6년 된 인삼을 수증기에 쪄서 말린 것은 무엇입니까?
What 6-year-ginseng is grown, steamed and then dried?

2 닭에 인삼을 넣어 만든 음식은 무엇입니까?
What is the food that is cooked by adding ginseng to chicken?

Korean ginseng is called *insam* because the shape of its roots resembles a human ('*in*') form. From old times, it was said that you will live long if you take ginseng, and hence it is known as a valuable medicinal ingredient. Ginseng is dug up generally after 4 to 6 years after it is planted in the ground, and red ginseng, which is made by steaming and drying the roots of 6-year-growth, has the greatest effect. Ginseng is a health supplement and can be used in a diverse manner. You can boil and drink ginseng roots, eat it as honey-sliced pieces, and drink it as ginseng tea using powder. Ginseng is also used to make ginseng liquor or ginseng extract. *Samgyetang* cooked by adding glutinous rice, jujube, garlic and ginseng to chicken, is a food Koreans enjoy especially in summer. Young ginseng is sometimes eaten in salad. In addition, Ginseng is sometimes used to make cosmetics.

인삼 ginseng	심다 to plant	절편 honey-sliced piece
뿌리 root	V_R고 나서 after V-ing	가루 powder
모양 shape	캐다 to dig out/up	진액 extract
닮다 to look alike, to resemble	홍삼 red ginseng	찹쌀 glutinous rice
불리다 to be called	수증기 steam, vapor	대추 jujube
옛날부터 from old times	찌다 to steam	마늘 garlic
오래 long, a long time	말리다 to dry	넣다 to add
V_R는/ㄴ다고 하다 That say that V	효능 effect	삼계탕 *samgyetang*, gingseng chicken soup
귀중하다 to be valuable	건강 health	특히 especially
약재 medicinal ingredient	보조 식품 supplement	즐기다 to enjoy
알려지다 to be known	활용하다 to be used	어리다 to be young
땅 ground, earth	달이다 to boil down	화장품 cosmetics

004

한국의 술 *
Korean Liquor

한국에서 가장 대중적인 술은 소주, 막걸리, 동동주이다. 소주는 투명한 색이고 막걸리와 동동주는 쌀로 만들어 우유 색깔이다. 동동주는 밥알이 위로 동동뜨고 약간 톡 쏘는 맛이 있다. 요즘은 술 종류가 훨씬 다양해졌다. 인삼주는 소주에 인삼을 넣은 것으로, 건강주로 알려져서 가격이 비싼 것도 있다. 과일주는 소주에 과일을 넣어서 만드는데 복분자주, 포도주, 산딸기주 등이 있다. 한국 사람들은 보통 친구 또는 직장 동료들과 함께 술집에 간다. 그래서 술은 사람들과 친해지는 데 중요한 역할을 한다. 삼겹살에 소주 한잔을 마시며 생활의 스트레스를 푼다. 식사와 함께 마시는 술은 반주라고 하고, 술을 마실 때 술잔을 부딪치며 건배사를 하기도 한다. 보통 "건배!"나 "위하여!"라고 하는데 요즘은 매우 다양하고 재미있는 건배사들이 있다.

1 한국의 가장 대중적인 술은 무엇입니까?
What are the most popular liquors in Korea?

2 어떤 건배사들이 있습니까?
In what ways do Koreans toast to celebrate?

The most popular liquors in Korea are *soju*, *makgeolli* and *dongdongju*. While *soju* is clear, *makgeolli* and *dongdongju* have milky colors as they are made of rice. *Dongdongju* has grains of cooked rice floating upward, together with a somewhat tart flavor. These days, the types of liquor have become much more diverse. *Insamju* (ginseng liquor) is made by adding ginseng to *soju*, and since it is known as a healthy alcoholic beverage, there are some expensive kinds. *Gwailju* is made by adding fruits in soju, and there are *bokbunjaju* (Korean black raspberry wine), *podoju* (grape wine) and *sanddalgiju* (wild berry wine) and others. Because Koreans usually go to a bar with friends or colleagues, liquor plays an important role in getting close to other people. People relieve their daily stress drinking *soju* over grilled pork belly. The liquor that we drink over a meal is called *banju* and we sometimes toast when we drink, clinking glasses together. Generally we say "*Geonbae*!" or "*Uihayeo*!," but nowadays there are many ways to toast that are diverse and interesting.

술 liquor, alcoholic beverage

가장 the most

대중적 popular

소주 *soju*

막걸리 *makgeolli*

동동주 *dongdongju*

투명하다 to be clear/transparent

쌀 rice

색깔 color

밥알 grain of rice

동동 뜨다 to float

약간 a little, somewhat

쏘다 to be tart/stringent

종류 type

훨씬 much

다양하다 to be diverse/various

인삼주 *insamju*, ginseng liquor

넣다 to add, to put in

건강주 healthy liquor

알려지다 to be known

가격 price

과일주 fruit liquor/wine

복분자주 *bokbunjaju*, Korean black raspberry wine

포도주 *podoju*, grape wine

산딸기주 *sanddalgiju*, wild berry wine

직장 동료 (work) colleague

술집 bar

친해지다 to make friends with, to be close to

V$_R$는 데 for V-ing, to V

중요한 important

역할 role

삼겹살 pork belly

한잔 a glass of (expression inviting a person to drink)

스트레스를 풀다 to relieve stress

반주 alcoholic beverage over a meal

잔을 부딪치다 to clink glasses with

건배사 toast

건배! Cheers!

위하여! *Uihayeo!* (literally meaning for/to)

매우 very

005

젓갈/젓 ★
Jeotgal/Jeot (Salted Fermented Seafood)

젓갈은 생선이나 생선 내장, 알 또는 조개류 등을 소금에 절인 발효 식품이다. 멸치, 갈치, 오징어, 낙지 등 다양한 해산물로 젓갈을 만든다. 예를 들어 명란젓은 명태의 알로 만들고, 창난젓은 명태의 창자로 만든다. 새우젓은 김치를 담글 때나 삶은 돼지고기를 먹을 때 잘 어울린다. 김치를 담글 때 보통 젓갈을 넣는데 젓갈의 종류에 따라서 김치는 다양한 맛을 낸다. 게장은 게를 간장에 담가 만든다. 조개젓과 어리굴젓도 밑반찬으로 자주 밥상에 오른다. 다양한 젓갈을 즐기고 싶다면 충청남도 강경 젓갈 시장에 가 보자. 거기에서는 수십 종류의 젓갈을 맛보고 젓갈 축제도 볼 수 있다.

문제
Questions

1 생선류 등을 소금에 절인 발효 식품은 무엇입니까?
What is the fermented food that has salted fish and other seafood?

2 가장 유명한 젓갈 시장은 어디에 있습니까?
Where is the most famous *jeotgal* market?

Jeotgal is a fermented food made with salted fish, fish intestines, roe or shellfish. *Jeotgal* is made with anchovies, squid, small octopus and other various seafood. For instance, *myeongranjeot* is made with the roe of pollock, while *changnanjeot* is made with the intestines of pollock. *Saeujeot* (*jeot* made with shrimp) goes well when making *kimchi* or eating boiled pork. *Gejang* is made by marinated crabs in soy sauce. *Jogaejeot* (*jeot* made with shellfish) and *eoriguljeot* (*jeot* made with oysters and chili pepper powder) are often served at the table as basic dishes. If you want to enjoy various types of *jeotgal*, visit Ganggyeong Traditional Slated Fish Market in Chungcheongnam-do. There you can taste scores of *jeotgal* types and see a *jeotgal* festival.

젓갈/젓 *jeotgal/jeot*, salted fermented food
생선 fish
내장 intestine
알 roe
조개류 shellfish
소금 salt
절이다 to pickle, to salt
발효 식품 fermented food
멸치 anchovies
갈치 cutlass fish
오징어 squid
낙지 small octopus
다양한 various, diverse

해산물 seafood
만들다 to make, to cook
명란젓 *jeot* made with pollock roe
명태 pollock
창난젓 *jeot* made with pollock intestines
창자 intestine
새우젓 *jeot* made with shrimps
담그다 to make
삶은 boiled
돼지고기 pork
어울리다 to go well together
N에 따라서 by N, according to N

맛을 내다 to season with
게장 *gejang*, crabs marinated and fermented in soy sauce
간장 *ganjang*, soy sauce
조개젓 *jeot* made with shellfish
어리굴젓 *jeot* made with oysters and chili pepper powder
밑반찬 basic dish, side dish
충청남도 Chungcheongnam-do, South Chungcheong Province
강경 Ganggyeong
젓갈 시장 *jeotgal* market, traditional salted fish market
종류 type
젓갈 축제 *jeotgal* festival

006

김장 ★★
Gimjang (Seasonal Preparation of *Kimchi*)

11월 말이나 12월 초에 한국에서는 많은 양의 김치를 담근다. 이것을 김장이라고 한다. 김장은 야채가 귀한 긴 겨울을 나기 위한 준비 작업이다. 고려 시대 때부터 한국인들은 김장철에 이웃들과 함께 김치를 담그고 나눠 먹었다. 이 풍습은 한국인들의 공동체 의식을 잘 반영한다. 보통 김치를 보관하기 위해서 마당에 큰 독을 여러 개 묻는다. 그리고 김치를 나누어 독 안에 넣고 긴 겨울 동안 조금씩 꺼내 먹는다. 김장 김치는 익는 정도에 따라 맛도 다르다. 요즘은 대부분 아파트에 살기 때문에 김치를 일반 냉장고나 김치냉장고에 보관한다.

문제
Questions

1 김장은 언제 합니까?
When is *gimjang* done?

2 왜 김장을 합니까?
Why do we do *gimjang*?

In late November or early December in Korea, people make a huge quantity of *kimchi*. This is called *gimjang*. *Gimjang* was a preparatory work to get through the long winter when vegetables were scarce. Since the Goryeo Dynasty, Koreans have made *kimchi* during the *gimjang* season together with neighbors, sharing it among themselves. This custom shows the community spirit of Koreans. In general, to store *kimchi*, several large jars are buried in the yard. Then people divide *kimchi* to put in these jars, taking out a small portion to eat during the long winter. *Gimjang kimchi* tastes differently according to the degree of fermentation. Nowadays, people usually live in an apartment unit, so they store *kimchi* in a general or a *kimchi* refrigerator.

김장 *gimjang*
양 quantity
담그다 to make
야채 vegetable
귀하다 to be scarce/precious
길다 to be long
겨울나기 wintering, to get through winter
V_R기 위한 for V-ing, to V
고려 시대 the Goryeo Dynasty
이웃 neighbor

함께 together, with
나누다 to share
풍습 custom
공동체 community
의식 spirit, awareness
반영하다 to reflect
보관하다 to store
마당 yard, garden
독 jar
묻다 to bury
넣다 to put in

조금씩 bit by bit
꺼내다 to take out
익다 to be fermented, to ripen
정도 degree
N에 따라 according to N
대부분 mostly
아파트 apartment (complex or unit)
V_R기 때문에 because V
김치냉장고 *kimchi* refrigerator

007

장독대 ★★
Jangdokdae (Jar Stand)

간장, 된장, 고추장은 한국 음식의 기본양념이다. 발효 식품인 장의 역사는 매우 오래되었다. 콩으로 만드는 간장과 된장은 4~5세기쯤인 삼국 시대부터 만들었고 고추장은 18세기 후반부터 만들기 시작했다. 1~2년에 한 번씩 담그는 이 장으로 음식의 간을 맞추고 맛을 냈다. 이 양념들을 담은 독들을 모아 놓은 곳이 바로 장독대이다. 장독대는 보통 부엌에서 가깝고 그늘진 뒷마당에 두고 항아리 안에는 장 뿐만 아니라 다른 음식들도 보관했다. 장독대는 음식 맛과 가족의 건강을 위해 한국인에게 매우 중요한 곳이었다. 그래서 옛날에는 어머니들이 이곳에 정화수를 떠 놓고 가족들의 건강을 빌기도 했다.

1 한국의 세 가지 기본양념은 무엇입니까?
What are the three basic Korean seasonings?

2 항아리들을 모아 놓은 곳을 뭐라고 부릅니까?
What do you call the place where jars are gathered?

Ganjang (soy sauce), *doenjang* (fermented soybean paste), and *gochujang* (red pepper paste) are the basic seasonings or condiments for Korean food. The *jang* which is a fermented food, has a very long history. People started making *ganjang* and *doenjang* made of soybean from the period of Three Kingdoms of Korea, around the 4th to 5th century; *gochujang* was made from the late 18th century. The *jang* was made once every one to two years, and was used to season or flavor food to taste. *Jangdokdae* is the place where the jars with these seasonings and condiments are gathered together. A *jangdokdae* was generally located in the backyard, close to the kitchen and shaded, and not only *jang* but other foods were stored in these jars, too. The *jangdokdae* was a very important place for Koreans for food favoring and for family's health. That is why mothers long ago would put a bowl of freshly drawn water here and prayed for the family's health.

장독대 *jangdokdae*, jar stand or outer space with jars
간장 *ganjang*, soy sauce
된장 fermented soybean paste
고추장 red pepper paste
기본양념 basic seasoning
발효 식품 fermented food
역사 history
오래되다 to be old
콩 soybean
세기 century

삼국 시대 the period of Three Kingdoms of Korea
후반 late, later
V_R기 시작하다 to start V-ing
한 번씩 once
담그다 to make
간을 맞추다 to season to taste
맛을 내다 to flavor
담다 to contain, to have
독 jar
모아 놓다 to gather, to collect

곳 place, spot
그늘지다 to be shaded
뒷마당 backyard, back of the house
항아리 jar
다른 other, different
보관하다 to store, to preserve
건강 health
옛날 old days
정화수 freshly drawn water
떠 놓다 to put/place
빌다 to pray

008

다례 ★★★
Tea Ceremony

한국의 차 문화는 역사가 오래됐다. 불교의 영향으로 신라 시대와 고려 시대에 특히 발달했다. 차의 종류에 따라서 다기의 형태와 빛깔을 다르게 만들었고 차 문화의 발달로 아름다운 고려청자도 만들어질 수 있었다. 옛날에는 차를 마시는 것이 단순히 음료수를 마시는 게 아니라 몸과 마음을 수련하는 것이었다. 그래서 차 의식이라는 뜻으로 '다례'라고 불렀다. 조선 후기의 대스님인 초의선사(1786~1866)는 차의 백과사전이라고 할 수 있는《다신전》을 썼다. 그는 이 책에서 다례의 기본을 겸손과 덕행이라고 했다. 그리고 색과 향과 아름다움이 조화를 이루었을 때 진정한 차의 맛을 느낄 수 있다고 했다. 차 마시는 예절을 배우고 싶다면 절이나 전통찻집에 가 보자. 요즘은 절이나 전통찻집에서도 다례를 배울 수 있다.

1 한국의 '다례'는 언제 발달했습니까?
When did *darye*, the Korean tea ceremony develop?

2 왜 차 문화를 '다례'라고 부릅니까?
Why do we call the tea culture *darye*?

Korea's tea culture has a long history. Due to the influence of Buddhism, it was developed mostly during the Silla and Goryeo Dynasties. According to the type of tea, the shapes and colors of tea equipments were made differently, and the development of tea culture allowed the beautiful Goryeo celadon to be made. In ancient times, drinking tea was not only about drinking a beverage, but it was about training the body and the mind. Therefore, it was called *darye*, meaning "tea ritual or ceremony". Cho-ui *seonsa* (1786-1866), the great Buddhist monk of late Joseon Dynasty wrote *Dasinjeon*, or the *Book of Korean Tea*, that can be seen as an encyclopedia of teas. In this book, he said that the basics of tea ceremony are humility and virtue. He further said that the true flavor of tea can be felt when the color and the aroma are in harmony. If you want to learn tea etiquette, visit a Buddhist temple or a traditional teahouse where you can learn the tea ceremony.

다례 *darye*, tea ceremony
오래되다 to be old
불교 Buddhism
N의 영향으로 due to the influence of N
신라 시대 the (era of) Silla Dynasty
고려 시대 the (era of) Goryoe Dynasty
특히 especially
발달하다 to develop

다기 tea equipment
형태 shape
빛깔 color
고려청자 Goryeo celadon
단순히 simply, just
수련하다 to train
차 의식 tea ritual, tea ceremony
초의선사 Cho-ui *seonsa*
백과사전 encyclopedia
《나신진》 *Dasinjeon, or the Book of Korean Tea*

기본 basic
겸손 humility
덕행 virtue
향 aroma
아름다움 beauty
조화를 이루다 to be in harmony
진정하다 to be true
느끼다 to feel
예절 etiquette, manners
절 Buddhist temple

009

한옥 ★★

Hanok

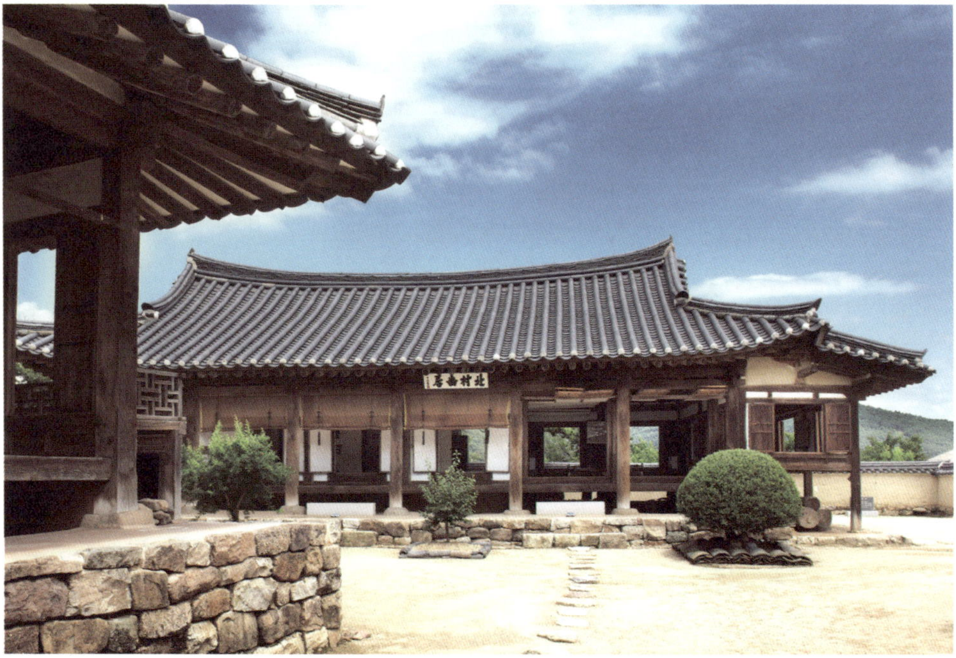

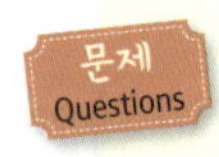

한국의 전통 집을 한옥이라고 한다. 한옥에는 지붕을 기와로 만든 기와집과 볏짚으로 이은 초가집이 있다. 집을 지을 때는 보통 풍수지리설에 따라 자연과 조화를 이룰 수 있도록 지었다. 회색의 기와지붕 선은 근처의 산 모양과 조화를 이루도록 하였고, 집 안은 바람과 햇빛이 잘 통할 수 있도록 만들었다. 큰 한옥에는 안채와 사랑채, 행랑채가 있다. 집 안에 들어갈 때는 디딤돌에 신발을 벗어 놓고 마루를 지나서 들어간다. 온돌은 한옥의 난방 방식으로 한옥의 중요한 특징이다. 서울에는 북촌에 한옥들이 모여 있고 지방에는 하회마을이나 경주, 전주에 한옥 마을들이 남아 있다. 한옥에서 숙박을 해 보는 것도 좋은 경험이 될 것이다.

문제 Questions

1 한국 전통 집을 뭐라고 부릅니까?
What do you call the traditional Korean house?

2 서울에서 한옥이 많이 모여 있는 곳은 어디입니까?
Where in Seoul are the *hanok* buildings clustered?

A traditional Korean house is called *hanok*. There are tiled-roof houses and rice-straw-roofted houses in *hanok*. When a house was built, it was generally built according to feng shui so that it could be in harmony with nature. The curves of gray tiled-roof were to be in harmony with the shape of mountains nearby, and the inside of the house was made to allow wind and sunshine to flow through well. A big *hanok* consists of *anchae* (inner quarters), *sarangchae* (men's quarters), and *haengnangchae* (servants' quarters). When you go inside the house, you must take off your shoes on the stepping stone and enter passing through the *maru*, the wooden floor space. *Ondol* is *hanok*'s heating system, which is an important trait of *hanok*. In Seoul, *hanok* buildings are clustered in Bukchon; outside Seoul, there are *hanok* villages left in Hahoe Folk Village, Gyeongju and Jeonju. It will be a good experience to try and take a lodging at a *hanok*.

한옥 *hanok*
전통 tradition(al)
지붕 roof
기와 tile
기와집 tiled-roof house
볏짚 rice straw
잇다 to plait, to connect
초가집 rice-straw-roof house
짓다 to build
풍수지리설 feng shui
N에 따라 according to N
회색 gray
지붕 roof
선 curve, line

모양 shape
조화 harmony
이루다 to achieve
바람 wind
햇빛 sunshine
통하다 to flow through
V_R을/ㄹ 수 있도록 so that V
안채 inner quarters
사랑채 men's quarters
행랑채 servants' quarters
디딤돌 stepping stone
벗다 to take off
놓다 to place
마루 wooden floor space

지나다 to pass through
온돌 *ondol*
난방 방식 heating system
중요하다 to be important
특징 characteristic, trait
북촌 Bukchon
모여 있다 to be clustered
지방 outside Seoul
하회마을 Hahoe Village
경주 Gyeongju
전주 Jeonju
남아 있다 to remain
숙박 lodging, to lodge, to stay
경험 experience

010

온돌 *
Ondol

온돌은 '따뜻한 돌'이라는 뜻으로 한옥의 전통적인 난방법이다. 부엌에서 요리하는 불의 열기가 방과 연결된 통로를 통해서 방바닥을 따뜻하게 한다. 그래서 부엌에서 가까운 곳이 제일 따뜻하다. 불이 꺼진 후에도 방바닥이 오랫동안 따뜻하다. 지금도 한국의 주택이나 현대식 아파트는 모두 이 온돌 형식을 활용한 바닥 난방으로 이루어진다. 이 온돌 난방을 좋아하는 사람들을 위해서 한국의 호텔에는 온돌방이 따로 있는 곳도 있다.

문제
Questions

1 한옥의 전통적인 난방법이 무엇입니까?
What is the traditional heating method of *hanok*?

2 온돌이 무슨 뜻입니까?
What does *ondol* mean?

Ondol means 'warm (*on*) stone (*dol*),' and it is *hanok*'s traditional heating method. The heat of cooking fire from the kitchen makes the room floors warm through the passages connected to each room. That is why the place nearest to the kitchen is the warmest. The room floors remain warm for a long time even after the fire is extinguished. Even now, both in Korean houses and modern apartments, floor heating is done using this *ondol* format. For people who like this kind of *ondol* heating, some Korean hotels have separately prepared *ondol* rooms.

온돌 *ondol*
따뜻한 warm
돌 stone
N(이)라는 뜻이다 to mean N
한옥 *hanok*
전통적인 traditional
난방법 heating method
부엌 kitchen
불 fire
열기 heat
연결되다 to be connected

통로 passage
N을/를 통해서 through N
방바닥 room floor
따뜻하게 하다 to heat up, to make warm
가까운 near, close
곳 spot, place
제일 the most
꺼지다 to be extinguished
후 after
오랫동안 for a long time

주택 house
현대식 modern
아파트 apartment
형식 format
활용하다 to apply, to use
난방 heating
이루어지다 to be done
N을 위해서 for N
따로 separately

011

마당 **
Madang (Courtyard)

한옥에서 집과 담 사이에 있는 넓은 공간을 마당이라고 부른다. 일반적으로 나무나 꽃이 있는 정원과 달리 한국식 마당은 빈 공간이다. 집 앞과 뒤에 위치해 있어서 실제 삶이 이루어지는 실용적인 공간이다. 가정에서 중요한 역할을 한다. 이곳에서 아이들이 놀고, 여름에는 돗자리나 평상 위에서 식사를 하기도 한다. 가을에는 야채와 고추 등을 말리고, 김장을 하고 농사일을 한다. 잔치, 제사, 장례식처럼 가정의 큰 행사도 이곳에서 열렸다. 마당이 넓으면 작은 정자를 짓고 그곳에 앉아서 집 밖의 풍경을 편하게 즐긴다. 휴식과 생활의 공간인 마당은 자연과 하나가 되고 싶어 한 한국인들의 정서를 잘 보여 준다.

문제
Questions

1 집과 담 사이에 있는 넓은 공간을 뭐라고 부릅니까?
What do you call the wide space between the house and outside(outdoor) walls?

2 여름에는 마당(의) 어디에서 식사를 합니까?
Where in *madang* do you eat meals in the summer?

In *hanok*, the wide space between the house and the outside(outdoor) walls is called *madang*, or courtyard. Unlike gardens that typically have trees or flowers, a Korean-style courtyard is an empty space. Located in the front and back of the house, it is a practical space where real life takes place.This place played an important part at home. Here children played; in the summer, people ate meals on the mat or the low wooden bench; in the fall, vegetables and red peppers were dried out here, and *gimjang* and farming works were done. Big family events, such as party, ancestral rite and funeral, were all held here. In a *madang*, a pavilion was built for people to sit inside and comfortably enjoy the landscape outside the house. The *madang*, a space of rest and living, showed the sentiment well of Koreans, who wanted to become one with nature.

마당 *madang*, courtyard
한옥 *hanok*
담 wall (outside)
넓다 to be wide
공간 space
가정 home, family
중요하다 to be important
역할을 하다 to play a part/role
이곳 here
놓다 to place
돗자리 mat
평상 low wooden bench
고추 red pepper
등 such as, etc.

말리다 to dry out
김장 *gimjang*
농사 farming
잔치 party, festival
제사 ancestral rite
장례식 funeral
N처럼 like N
행사 event
열리다 to hold
정원 garden
차이점 difference
자연 nature
본 따다 to copy, to model after
산수 landscape, scenery

들 field
감상하다 to appreciate
정자 pavilion
짓다 to build
풍경 landscape, scenery
편하게 comfortably, with ease
즐기다 to enjoy
휴식 rest
생활 living
하나가 되다 to be one with something
정서 sentiment, feelings
보여 주다 to show

012

전통 정원의 아름다움 ★★★
Beauty of Traditional Garden

한국의 전통 정원은 자연을 최대한 보존해서 만든다. 낮은 언덕과 평평한 땅은 그대로 두고, 샘과 개울을 이용해서 연못과 작은 폭포를 만든다. 그리고 연못 앞에 정자를 짓고 그곳에서 책을 읽거나 자연을 감상하였다. 선비들은 정원에서 자연의 순리를 터득하곤 했다. 고궁에서도 전통 정원의 아름다움을 볼 수 있다. 창덕궁 후원은 자연과 조화를 이루는 가장 한국적인 정원이다. 그리고 경복궁의 경회루는 큰 연못 가운데에 누각을 지어서 물 위에서 연못과 멀리 보이는 산을 감상할 수 있도록 했다. 지방에도 아름다운 전통 정원이 많이 남아 있다. 전라도 담양의 소쇄원에는 대나무 숲이 있는데, 이 숲을 따라 들어가면 계곡물이 폭포처럼 흐르는 곳에 정자가 있다. 남해 보길도의 부용동에는 계곡물을 막아 만든 연못 가운데에 정자가 있고, 영양의 서석지에는 기이한 모양의 큰 바위들이 연못에 솟아 있다.

1 한국 전통 정원의 특징은 무엇입니까?
What is the characteristic of a traditional Korean garden?

2 가장 한국적인 정원은 어디입니까?
What garden is the most Korean?

Traditional Korean gardens were made preserving nature as best as possible. Leaving low hills and ground intact, Koreans would make a pond and a small waterfall using a spring and a brook. They built a pavilion in front of the pond to read books or appreciate nature there. *Seonbi*, or Confucian scholars would learn the laws of nature in the garden. We can also see the beauty of traditional gardens in old palaces. The Huwon Garden (Secret Garden) at Changdeokgung Palace is the garden that is the most Korean, in harmony with nature. Gyeonghoeru Pavilion at Gyeongbokgung Palace is a tall building created in the middle of a big pond so that people can appreciate the far away mountains. Many beautiful traditional gardens remain outside Seoul, too. At Soswaewon, Damyang, Jeolla-do, there is a bamboo forest. If you go into the forest, you will find a pavilion at a place where valley streams flow like a waterfall. At Buyong-dong, Bogildo Island, Namhae, there is a pavilion in the middle of a pond created by stopping water from a waterfall; at Seoseokji, Yeongyang, huge rocks in strange forms are rising from a pond.

전통 정원 traditional garden
자연 nature
최대한 as best/much as possible
보존하다 to preserve
언덕 hill
평평하다 to be even/level
땅 ground, earth, soil
그대로 두다 to leave as it is, to leave intact
샘 spring
개울 brook, small stream
연못 pond, lake
폭포 waterfall
정자 pavilion
짓다 to build
감상하다 to appreciate
선비 *Seonbi*, Confucian scholar

순리 flow, law, reason
터득하다 to learn
V_R곤 하다 often V
고궁 old palace
창덕궁 Changdeokgung Palace
후원 the Huwon Garden (Secret Garden)
조화를 이루다 to be in harmony
한국적 Korean
경복궁 Gyeongbokgung Palace
경회루 Gyeonghoeru Pavilion
누각 pavilion, tall building
멀리 far away
지방 region, areas outside Seoul
전라도 Jeolla-do/Province
담양 Damyang
소쇄원 Soswaewon

대나무 bamboo
숲 forest, woods
계곡물 valley streams
흐르다 to flow
남해 Namhae
보길도 Bogildo Island
부용동 Buyong-dong
막다 to stop
영양 Yeongyang
서석지 Seoseokji
기이하다 to be eccentric, to be strange
모양 shape, form
바위 rock
솟아 있다 to rise

Korean
Culture
in 100
외국인
학습자를 위한
한국 문화
100선
Keywords

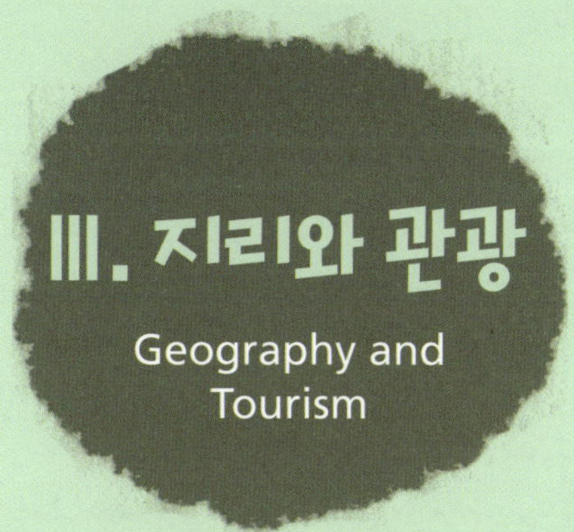

III. 지리와 관광

Geography and Tourism

001

한반도 ★★
Korean Peninsula

한반도는 국토가 남북으로 길게 뻗어 있고 그 모양은 호랑이와 비슷하다. 남북의 길이가 1,100km이고, 동서의 가장 좁은 곳은 216km이다. 반도국이라서 섬이 많은데, 모두 3,600여 개가 있다. 동해에는 울릉도와 동쪽 끝 섬인 독도가 있다. 서해에는 인천국제공항이 있는 영종도, 인삼으로 유명한 강화도가 있다. 그리고 남해에는 한국에서 제일 큰 섬인 제주도가 있다. 한반도는 산이 많아서 국토의 70%가 산이다. 백두산 (2,744m)이 제일 높고 제주도의 한라산(1,940m)이 두 번째로 높다. 동쪽에 있는 태백산맥은 바다와 가깝고 경치가 아름답다. 이 산맥의 북쪽에는 금강산이 있고 그 남쪽에는 설악산이 있다. 남서쪽으로는 낮은 산과 평야가 많고 사이사이에 강물이 흐른다. 그래서 이 지방에서는 벼농사를 많이 한다. 한반도에 특히 중요한 강으로는 북쪽에 압록강(790km)과 두만강(521km)이 있고 남쪽에는 낙동강(525km)과 한강(514km)이 있다.

1 한국은 국토의 몇 퍼센트가 산입니까?
What percentage of Korea's land consists of mountains?

2 한국에서 제일 큰 섬은 무엇입니까?
What is the biggest island in Korea?

The Korean peninsula is a land stretched long from north to south, and its shape looks like a tiger. From the north to the south, it is 1,100km long; the narrowest between east and west is 216km long. Since it is a peninsular state, there are many islands, about total 3,600. In the East Sea, Ulleungdo Island and Dokdo Island are at the eastern end. In the West Sea, there is Yeongjongdo where the Incheon International Airport is located and Ganghwado Island which is famous for ginseng. In the South Sea, there is Jejudo Island, the biggest island in Korea. The Korean peninsula has many mountains which cover 70% of its land. Baekdusan Mountain is the highest (2,744m), and Hallasan Mountain in Jejudo Island is the second highest (1,940m). Taebaeksanmaek Mountains in the east are close to the sea and offer beautiful scenery. To the north of these mountains is Geumgangsan Mountain, and to the south is Seoraksan Mountain. To the southwest, there are many hills and plains, in which rivers flow here and there. That is why this region grows a lot of rice. Among the rivers particularly important for the Korean peninsula, there are Amnokgang River (790km) and Dumangang River (521km) in the north, and Nakdonggang River (525km) and Hangang River (514km) in the south.

어휘와 표현 Words & Expressions

한반도 Korean peninsula
국토 territory, land
남북 North and South
길게 long
뻗어 있다 to stretch
모양 shape, form
호랑이 tiger
비슷하다 to be similar
길이 length
가장 the most
좁다 to be narrow
곳 place
반도국 peninsular state
섬 island
동해 East Sea
오징어 squid
울릉도 Ulleungdo Island
끝 end

독도 Dokdo Island
서해 West Sea, Yellow Sea
인천국제공항 Incheon International Airport
영종도 Yeongjongdo Island
인삼 ginseng
강화도 Ganghwado Island
남해 South Sea
제일 the most
제주도 Jejudo Island, Jeju-do/ Province
퍼센트(%) percent, percentage
백두산 Baekdusan Mountain
높다 to be high
한라산 Hallasan Mountain
두 번째 second
태백산맥 Taebaeksanmaek Mountains

가깝다 to be close
경치 landscape
아름답다 to be beautiful
금강산 Geumgangsan Mountain
설악산 Seoraksan Mountain
남서쪽 southwest
낮다 to be low
평야 plain
강 river
흐르다 to flow
지방 region
벼농사를 하다 to grow rice, to do rice farming
중요하다 to be important
압록강 Amnokgang River
두만강 Dumangang River
낙동강 Nakdonggang River
한강 Hangang River

002

극동 아시아 속의 한국 *
Korea in East Asia

한국은 극동 아시아에 위치하고 있고 삼면이 바다로 둘러싸인 반도이다. 동쪽에는 일본과의 사이에 동해가 있고, 서쪽에는 중국과의 사이에 서해가 있고, 남쪽에는 남해가 있다. 북쪽 국경에는 중국과 러시아가 있다. 이처럼 한반도는 일본과 중국 사이에 있는 반도국이라서 침략을 자주 받았다. 한국은 한국 전쟁(1950~1953) 후에 분단국가가 되었다. 그래서 남과 북 사이에는 38선을 따라 휴전선이 있다. 이와 같은 정치적, 지리적 이유로 한국은 일본, 중국, 러시아, 미국의 동북아시아 국방 정책에 중요한 국가이다.

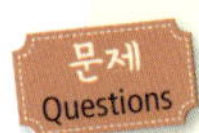

1 한국과 일본과의 사이에 있는 바다 이름은 무엇입니까?
What is the name of the sea between Korea and Japan?

2 한국 전쟁 후에 남한과 북한 사이에 생긴 경계선 이름은 무엇입니까?
What is the name of the boundary between North and South Korea, which was created after the Korean War?

Korea is located in East Asia and it is a peninsula whose three sides are surrounded by water. To the east between Korea and Japan is the East Sea; to the west between Korea and China is the West Sea; and to the south is the South Sea. At the northern borders, there are China and Russia. Because Korea is between Japan and China and is a peninsular state, it was frequently invaded. Korea became a divided state after the Korean War (1950-1953). That is why there is a truce line along the 38th parallel. For such political and geographical reasons, Korea is a state important to the East Asian national defense policies of Japan, China, Russia and the US.

극동 아시아 East Asia
속 in, inside
위치하다 to be located
삼면 three sides
N(으)로 둘러싸인 to be surrounded by N
반도 peninsula
동쪽 east
N와/과 N 사이에 between N and N
동해 the East Sea
서쪽 west
서해 the West Sea

남쪽 south
남해 the South Sea
북쪽 north
국경 (national) border
한반도 Korean Peninsula
반도국 peninsular state
N(이)라서 because (it is) N
침략 invasion
자주 often, frequently
전쟁 war
후 after
분단국가 divided state

N이/가 되다 to become N
삼팔선(38선) the 38th parallel
휴전선 truce line, ceasefire line
정치적 political
지리적 geographical
이유로 for reasons (of), because
동북아시아 Northeast Asia
국방 정책 national defense policy
중요한 important
국가 country, nation, state

계절과 날씨 *
Seasons and Weather

한국에는 사계절이 있다. 봄, 여름, 가을, 겨울이다. 봄은 3월부터 5월까지이고 날씨가 따뜻하고 꽃들이 많이 핀다. 진달래, 개나리, 벚꽃이 산과 들을 뒤덮는다. 여름은 6월부터 8월까지인데 날씨가 덥고 습하다. 6월 말부터 7월 말까지는 장마철이라서 비가 많이 온다. 9월부터 11월에는 덥지도 춥지도 않은 가을 날씨가 계속된다. 이 때에는 높고 푸른 하늘이 아름답고 산에는 나뭇잎이 화려하게 물든다. 그래서 단풍놀이를 간다. 여행하기에 가장 좋은 계절이다. 겨울은 12월부터 2월까지이다. 날씨가 춥고 건조하다. 기온이 영하 10도 이하로 내려가는 추운 날도 있다. 하지만 비가 적게 오고 습하지 않다. 겨울에는 눈도 많이 내려서 동쪽 강원도 지방의 산에서는 스키를 탈 수 있다. 한국은 대륙성 기후지만 요즘은 온난화 현상 때문에 날씨가 조금씩 변하고 있다.

문제
Questions

1 한국에는 몇 개의 계절이 있습니까?
How many seasons does Korea have?

2 한국의 여름 날씨는 어떻습니까?
What is Korea's weather like in the summer?

Korea has four seasons: spring, summer, fall and winter. Spring is from March to May, and the weather is warm and many flowers bloom; azalea, forsythia, cherry blossoms cover mountains and fields. Summer is from June to August, and the weather is hot and humid. It rains a lot from late June to late July because of the monsoon season. From September to November, fall weather continues, which is neither hot nor cold. In this season, the deep blue sky is beautiful and the tree leaves get splendidly colored in the mountains. That is why people leave for a fall foliage picnic, and it is the best season to travel. Winter is from December to February; the weather is cold and dry. There are cold days when the temperature drops to minus 10 degrees Celcius or below. Since it snows a lot in winter, you can ski in the mountains in Gangwon Province in the country's east. Korea has a continental climate but because of the global warming phenomenon, the weather is changing little by little.

사계절 four seasons	V_R지도 V_R지도 않다 neither V nor V	기온 temperature
봄 spring	계속되다 to continue	영하 below zero
여름 summer	높다 to be high, (sky) to be deep	N 이하로 N or less, N or below
가을 fall, autumn	푸르다 blue	내려가다 to go down, to drop
겨울 winter	하늘 sky	날 day
따뜻하다 to be warm	아름답다 to be beautiful	적게 little
꽃이 피다 to blossom	나뭇잎 leaf	동쪽 east
진달래 azalea	화려하게 splendidly, impressively	강원도 Gangwon-do/Province
개나리 forsythia	물들다 to be colored	지방 region, area
벚꽃 cherry blossom	단풍놀이 fall foilage picnic, excusrsion to view autumn colors	대륙성 기후 continental climate
들 field	여행하기 to travel	온난화 현상 global warming phenomenon
뒤덮다 to cover	가장 좋은 the best	때문에 because of
덥다 to be hot	춥다 to be cold	조금씩 little by little
습하다 to be humid	건조하다 to be dry	변하다 to change
말 end		
장마철 monsoon season		

004

한강 *
Hangang River

한강은 한국을 동에서 서로 가로지르는 두 번째로 긴 강이다. 길이가 514km로 서울을 강북과 강남으로 나눈다. 한강에는 다리가 27개 있고 여의도 등 섬이 5개 있다. 한강은 강폭이 아주 넓어서 인상적이다. 한강 다리는 대부분 길이가 1km가 넘는다. 제일 긴 다리는 방화대교로 2,559m이다. 시민들은 한강에서 다양한 여가 생활을 즐길 수 있는데 한강 유람선을 타면 주변의 아파트와 63빌딩, 국회의사당 등을 볼 수 있다. 그리고 수상 스키장, 요트장, 낚시터에서는 시민들이 수상 스포츠를 즐길 수 있다. 또한 한강 공원과 같은 녹지대가 곳곳에 있어서 산책을 하거나 자전거 전용 도로에서 자전거를 탈 수 있다. 강변에는 아름다운 카페들도 많이 있다.

1 한강은 서울을 어떻게 나눕니까?
How does Hangang River divide Seoul?

2 한강에서 제일 긴 방화대교의 길이는 얼마입니까?
How long is Banghwa Bridge, the longest bridge of Hangang River?

Hangang River is the second longest river that runs from Korea's east to west. It is 514km long and divides Seoul into Gangbuk and Gangnam. There are 27 bridges over Hangang River and five islands, including Yeouido Island. Hangang River is impressive because its width is quite extensive. Most of Hangang bridges are over 1km long, and the longest is the Banghwa Bridge at 2,559m. Citizens can enjoy various leisure activities at Hangang River. If you board a cruise ship, you can see nearby apartment complexes, the 63 Building and the National Assembly. You can enjoy water sports at the water skiing sites, marina and angling sites. In addition, because there are green spaces all over such as the Hangang Park, you can either take a walk or ride a bicycle in the bicycle lanes. There are also many beautiful cafés on the riverside.

한강 Hangang River	강폭 the width of river	국회의사당 National Assembly
동 east	넓다 to be wide	수상 스키장 water skiing site
서 west	V_R아서/어서/여서 because V	요트장 marina
가로지르다 to cut/cross	인상적이다 to be impressive	낚시터 fishing/angling site
두 번째 the second	대부분 most of, mostly	스포츠 sport
긴 long	넘다 to be over	즐기다 to enjoy
강 river	제일 the most	N와/과 같은 like N
길이 length	방화대교 Banghwa Bridge	녹지대 green space
강북 Gangbuk (north of river)	시민 citizen	곳곳에 all over, everywhere
강남 Gangnam (south of river)	여가 생활 leisure activities	V_R거나 V or
나누다 to divide	유람선 cruise ship	자전거 전용 도로 bicycle lane
다리 bridge	타다 to ride, to board	자전거 bicycle
여의도 Yeouido Island	V_R(으)면 if V	V_R을/ㄹ 수 있다 can V
등 including, and the like	주변 nearby	강변 riverside
섬 island	63(육삼)빌딩 63 Building	아름나운 beautiful

005

서울의 고궁 ★★
Ancient Palaces in Seoul

살아 있는 한국의 역사를 볼 수 있는 곳 중의 하나가 고궁이다. 서울에 있는 4대 궁으로는 경복궁, 창덕궁, 창경궁, 덕수궁이 있다. 이 고궁들은 화려하고 웅장한 건물을 가지고 있으면서도 그 아름다움이 주변 자연 경관과 조화를 이루고 있다. 그래서 고궁에서 관광과 휴식을 동시에 즐길 수 있다. 경복궁(1395)은 조선 시대 정궁으로 제일 오래된 궁이다. 창경궁(1484)은 대비나 공주를 위한 별궁으로 지어졌다. 아름다운 후원으로 유명한 창덕궁(1405)은 가장 한국적이고 자연 친화적인 궁으로 세계유산에 등록됐다. 덕수궁은 1593년부터 자리 잡은 옛 왕궁터에 근대 유럽식 석조 건물(1909)이 함께 있어서 한국의 전통과 현대를 한자리에서 볼 수 있다. 현재는 덕수궁의 일부가 현대미술관으로 사용되고 있다. 덕수궁 돌담길은 낭만적인 산책길로 유명하다. 이 고궁들은 모두 야간 개장을 하고 있어 밤에도 그 아름다움을 감상할 수 있다.

1 서울의 유명한 4대 궁은 무엇입니까?
What are the four famous main palaces of Seoul?

2 서울에서 가장 자연 친화적인 궁으로 세계유산에 등록된 궁은 무엇입니까?
Which is the palace in Seoul that is the most nature-friendly and listed as a World Heritage Site?

One of the places where you can see the living and breathing history of Korea is an ancient palace. The four major palaces of Seoul are Gyeongbokgung Palace, Changdeokgung Palace, Changgyeonggung Palace, and Deoksugung Palace. While these ancient palaces have splendid and grand structures, their respective beauty is in harmony with the surrounding natural landscape. Therefore, you can enjoy sightseeing and rest at the same time at these ancient palaces. Gyeongbokgung Palace (1395) was the main palace of the Joseon Dynasty, and it is the oldest palace. Changgyeonggung Palace (1484) was built as a royal villa for the queen dowager or princesses. Changdeokgung Palace (1405), famous for its beautiful Huwon Garden, is a palace that is the most Korean and nature-friendly, and it is listed as a World Heritage. Deoksugung Palace was established in 1593. Since modern European stone-built structures were added (1909) to this ancient royal palace site, you can see the traditional and the modern times in one place. Currently, a part of Deoksugung Palace is used as a modern art museum. The stonewall walkway of Deoksugung Palace is famous as a romantic promenade. All these ancient palaces are open at night, so you can appreciate the beauty in the evening.

고궁 ancient palace	경관 landscape, scenery	왕궁터 site of royal palace
살아 있다 to be alive, to be living and breathing	조화를 이루다 to be harmonious	근대 modern
	관광 sightseeing, tourism	유럽식 European
역사 history	휴식 rest	석조 stone, stone-built
경복궁 Gyeongbokgung Palace	정궁 main palace	현대 modern, contemporary
창덕궁 Changdeokgung Palace	대비 queen dowager	한자리 at one place
창경궁 Changgyeonggung Palace	공주 princess	현재 now, currently
덕수궁 Deoksugung Palace	별궁 royal villa	일부 a part of
화려하다 to be splendid	지어지다 to be built	미술관 art gallery
웅장하다 to be grand	후원 Huwon Garden (Secret Garden)	돌담길 stonewall walkway
건물 building, structure		낭만적 romantic
가지고 있다 to have	자연 친화적 nature-friendly	야간 개장 to open at night
아름다움 beauty	세계유산 World Heritage	감상하다 to appreciate
주변 surrounding	등록되다 to be enlisted	
자연 nature	자리 잡다 to be established	

006

서울 남산 *
Namsan Mountain, Seoul

서울 한가운데에 위치한 남산은 시민들의 산책로이고 휴식 공간이다. 걸어서 가거나 케이블카를 타고 정상에 오르면 서울을 한눈에 볼 수 있는 'N서울타워'가 있다. 그 안에는 전망대와 360도로 회전하는 프랑스 식당도 있다. 이 식당은 젊은 연인들이 로맨틱한 프러포즈를 하는 장소로 드라마에도 자주 나온다. 남산에는 식물원, 야생화 공원, 도서관 등 여러 시설들이 골고루 갖추어져 있다. 남산골 한옥 마을에서는 전통문화 체험도 할 수 있고, '한국의 집'에서는 전통 음악과 춤 공연 등을 보고 전통 혼례식도 할 수 있다.

문제
Questions

1 남산에서 서울을 한눈에 볼 수 있는 곳은 어디입니까?
Where in Namsan Mountain can you see Seoul at one glance?

2 남산에서 전통 문화를 체험할 수 있는 곳은 어디입니까?
Where in Namsan Mountain can you experience traditional culture?

Located in the middle of Seoul, Namsan Mountain is a walking trail and a resting place for citizens. If you climb to the top either on foot or by a cable car, there is N Seoul Tower where you can see Seoul at one glance. Inside the tower are an observatory and a French restaurant that rotates 360 degrees. This restaurant appears frequently in TV dramas as a place for romantic proposal by young lovers. In Namsan Mountain, there are various facilities, including a botanical garden, a wild flower garden and a library. At Namsangol Hanok Village, you can experience traditional culture; at the Korea House, you can watch a performance of traditional music and dance and have a traditional wedding ceremony.

남산 Namsan Mountain
한가운데 in the middle of
위치한 located
시민 citizen
산책로 walking trail, promenade
휴식 rest
공간 space
케이블카 cable car
타다 to ride
정상 top
오르다 to climb
V_R(으)면 if/when (subject) V
한눈에 at one glance
V_R를/ㄹ 수 있다 can V

N서울타워 N Seoul Tower
전망대 observatory
360(삼백육십)도 360 degrees
회전하다 to rotate, to turn
젊은 young
연인들 lovers
로맨틱한 romantic
프러포즈를 하다 to propose
장소 place
자주 often, frequently
나오다 to appear
식물원 botanical garden
야생화 wild flower
등 including, and the like

여러 various, many
시설 facility
골고루 well, evenly
갖추어져 있다 to be equipped (with), to be prepared
남산골 한옥마을 Namsangol Hanok Village
전통 tradition(al)
문화 culture
체험 experience
춤 dance
공연 performance
혼례식 traditional wedding ceremony

007

남대문과 남대문시장 *
Namdaemun Gate and Namdaemun Market

조선 시대에 수도로 들어가는 동서남북에 네 개의 큰 대문을 세웠다. 그 문의 이름에는 각각 유교의 4대 가치인 인의예지가 담겨 있다. 사대문 중 남쪽에 있는 남대문의 원래 이름은 '숭례문'이다. 이는 '예를 숭상하는 문'이라는 뜻이다. 남대문은 한국의 국보 1호로 지정될 만큼 그 가치가 높다. 조선 시대부터 남대문 주변에서 물건을 사고 팔면서 시장이 생겼고 지금도 남대문시장은 재래시장이다. 쇼핑가인 명동과 가까워서 젊은이들도 남대문시장을 많이 찾는다. 외국인 여행객들은 남대문시장에서 주로 김과 인삼주 그리고 한류 스타 기념품들을 산다. 남대문시장에는 떡볶이, 어묵, 김밥과 같은 길거리 음식을 먹을 수 있는데 먹자골목의 낙지 볶음, 해물탕, 갈치조림이 특히 유명하다.

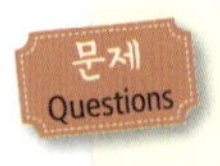

1 남대문의 원래 이름은 무엇입니까?
What is the original name of Namdaemun Gate?

2 남대문시장은 어느 쇼핑가와 가깝습니까?
Which shopping district is Namdaemun Market near?

During the Joseon period, four big gates were established at four cardinal points of entering the capital. The names of these gates contain the four main values of Confucianism, *in-ui-ye-ji* (benevolence, righteousness, propriety and wisdom) respectively. Of these four main gates, the one in the south, Namdaemun Gate had the original name of Sungnyemun, which means 'a gate to revere propriety.' Namdaemun Gate has such a great value that it has been designated as the National Treasure No. 1 of Korea. A market was formed here as people bought and sold goods near Namdaemun Gate from the Joseon Dynasty, and Namdaemun Market remains a traditional market even today. Since it is close to the shopping district of Myeongdong and the tourist attraction of Namsan Mountain, many young people visit Namdaemun Market. Foreign tourists mainly buy dried laver, ginseng liquor and souvenirs like *hallyu* star goods. People can eat street foods at Namdaemun such as *tteokbokki*, fish cake and *gimbap*, and stir-fried *nakji* (small octopus), spicy seafood stew and braised cutlass stew are particularly famous.

남대문 Namdaemun Gate
시장 market
조선 시대 the Joseon Dynasty, Joseon period
수도 capital
들어가다 to enter
동서남북 four cardinal points (north, south, east, and west)
큰 big, large
대문 gate
세우다 to build, to erect
각각 respectively
유교 Confucianism
4대 가치 four main values
인 benevolence
의 righteousness
예 propriety
지 wisdom
담다 contain
남쪽 south
원래 original

숭례문 Sungnyemun Gate
숭상하다 to revere
뜻 meaning
국보 National Treasure
1호 No. 1, the first
지정하다 to designate
V_R을/ㄹ만큼 such…that V
가치 value
주변 nearby
물건 item, goods
팔다 to sell
생기다 to be formed
재래시장 traditional market
쇼핑가 shopping district
명동 Myeongdong
가깝다 to be close/near
V_R아서/어서/여서 since/because V
젊은이 youth, young people
찾다 to visit
외국인 foreigner

여행객 tourist
김 (dried) laver
인삼주 ginseng liquor
한류 *hallyu*, the Korean Wave
스타 star
기념품 souvenir
떡볶이 *tteokbokki*, spicy stir-fried rice cakes
어묵 fish cake
김밥 *gimbap*, Korean dried laver and rice roll
N와/과 같은 such as N
길거리 음식 street food
먹자골목 food alley
낙지 볶음 stir-fried small octopus/octopus minor
해물탕 spicy seafood stew
갈치조림 braised hairtail/cutlass stew
유명하다 to be famous

008

동대문과 근처 시장들 ★
Dongdaemun Gate and Nearby Markets

남대문처럼 동대문도 옛날 수도로 들어가는 큰 대문 중의 하나로 사대문 중 동쪽에 위치하고 있다. 동대문은 인의예지 중 '인'을 상징하는 '흥인지문'이라는 옛날 이름을 가지고 있다. 수도에 오가는 사람들이 많았기 때문에 동대문 주변에 시장이 만들어졌다. 현재 동대문시장은 밤에는 상인들이 물건을 사 가는 도매 시장으로 낮에는 소매 시장으로 24시간 문을 연다. 시장 건물 앞에는 무대가 있어서 주말 밤에는 춤과 노래 공연을 볼 수 있다. 청계천과 동대문 주변에는 의복 시장, 한복 시장, 신발 시장 등 테마별 시장들이 모여 있다. 그 외에 포장지와 상자, 종이류를 파는 방산시장, 말린 생선들을 파는 중부시장, 한약 재료들을 파는 경동시장, 먹거리가 다양한 광장시장이 있다.

1 동대문은 서울 어디에 있습니까?
Where in Seoul is Dongdaemun Gate located?

2 한약 재료를 파는 시장 이름이 무엇입니까?
What is the name of the market that sells the ingredients for oriental medicine?

Like Namdaemun Gate, Dongdaemun Gate used to be one of the big gates to enter the old capital, and it is located in the east among the four main gates. Dongdaemun Gate has the old name of Heunginjimun Gate, symbolizing benevolence among benevolence, righteousness, propriety and wisdom. Since there were many people coming and going in the capital, markets were formed around Dongdaemun Gate. Today, Dongdaemun markets are open 24 hours, as wholesale markets for merchants by night and as retail markets by day. In front of the market buildings, there is a stage so that people can see dance and singing performances on weekend nights. In the vicinity of Cheonggyecheon Stream and Dongdaemun Gate, markets are clustered by themes such as clothing market, *hanbok* market and shoes market. In addition, Bangsan Market sells wrapping papers, boxes and papers, Jungbu Market sells dried fish, Gyeongdong Market sells the ingredients for oriental medicine, and Gwangjang Market has diverse foods.

동대문 Dongdaemun Gate	물건 goods	한복 *hanbok*
근처 nearby	도매 시장 wholesale market	신발 shoe
시장 market	낮 day	그 외에 in addition
N처럼 like N	소매시장 retail market	포장지 wrapping paper
옛날 old, old times, old days	열다 to open	상자 box
수도 capital	건물 building, structure	종이류 paper
들어가다 enter	무대 stage	팔다 to sell
중 among	V$_R$아서/어서/여서 because/since V	방산시장 Bangsan Market
사대문 four main gates	춤 dance	말린 dried
동쪽 east	공연 performance	중부시장 Jungbu Market
인 benevolence	V$_R$을/ㄹ 수 있다 can V	한약 재료 ingredients for oriental medicine
상징하다 to symbolize	청계천 Cheonggyecheon Stream	
흥인지문 Heunginjimun Gate	주변에 in the vicinity of	경동시장 Gyeongdong Market
가지고 있다 to have	만들어지다 to be formed	먹거리 food
오가다 to come and go	모이다 to be clustered	다양한 various, diverse
상인 merchant	의복 clothing	광장시장 Gwangjang Market

009

인사동 ★★
Insadong

인사동은 북촌과 종로 사이에 있는 서울의 대표적인 문화 거리이다. 전통문화와 현대 문화가 공존하는 곳으로 주말뿐만 아니라 주중에도 많은 관광객들이 모인다. 지하철 3호선 안국역에서 내려서 인사동 큰길을 걸으면 골동품 가게, 화랑, 전통찻집 등을 볼 수 있다. 작은 골목에는 한식집과 고미술품 가게들이 모여 있고, 사찰 음식을 파는 유명한 맛집과 팥빙수 가게, 100년 전통의 오래된 떡집도 있다. 또한 실타래 엿, 붕어빵, 떡꼬치, 호떡, 계란빵 등 여러 종류의 길거리 음식도 맛볼 수 있다. 특이한 모양으로 지어진 상가인 쌈지길에는 다양한 디자인의 공예품점, 기념품 가게, 식당이 있어서 다양한 볼거리와 먹거리를 즐길 수 있다. 인사동은 차 없는 거리이고 길에서 사주와 점을 봐 주는 곳도 있다. 판소리, 사물놀이와 같은 전통 공연이나 태권도, 택견과 같은 무술 시범도 볼 수 있다.

1 북촌과 종로 사이에 있는 서울의 대표적 문화 거리는 무엇입니까?
What is Seoul's representative cultural district between Bukchon and Jongno?

2 인사동에서 맛볼 수 있는 길거리 음식은 무엇입니까?
What street foods can you try in Insadong?

Insadong, located between Bukchon and Jongno, is one of Seoul's representative cultural districts. It is a place where traditional and modern cultures exist together, and many tourists gather here not only on weekends but also during the weekdays. If you get off at An-guk Station of subway line No. 3 and walk down the Insadong main street, you can see antique shops, art galleries and traditional teahouses. In small alleys, Korean restaurants and antique art galleries are clustered, and there are good restaurants that sell Korean temple food, stores that sell shaved ice with red beans and a rice cake store with a 100-year tradition. You can also taste many kinds of street food such as honey string taffy, crucian carp cake, rice cake skewer, Korean sweet pancake, and egg bread. At Ssamjigil, which is a shopping mall built in a unique shape, you can enjoy diverse attractions and foods as there are arts and crafts shops of diverse designs, souvenir shops and restaurants. Insadong is a pedestrian-only street, and there are places on the street for *saju* fate reading and fortunetelling. You can also see traditional performances like *pansori* and *samulnori*, and the demonstration of martial arts such as *taekwondo* and *taekkyon*.

어휘와 표현 — Words & Expressions

인사동 Insadong
북촌 Bukchon
종로 Jongno
대표적인 representative
문화 culture
거리 district, streets
전통 traditional
현대 modern
공존하다 exist together, coexist
곳 place, spot
뿐만 아니라 not only
주중 weekdays
관광객 tourist
모이다 to gather
N호선 line No.
안국역 An-guk Station
V_R(으)면 if/when V
골동품 antique
화랑 art gallery
찻집 teahouse
등 such as, including
골목 alley

한식집 Korean restaurant
고미술품 antique art
모여 있다 to be clustered/gathered
사찰 음식 Korean temple food, Buddhist cuisine
맛집 good restaurant
팥빙수 shaved ice with red beans
또한 in addition
실타래 엿 honey string taffy, Korean court cake
붕어빵 crucian carp cake, fish-shaped bread with sweet red bean filling
떡꼬치 rice cake skewer
호떡 Korean sweet pancake
계란빵 egg bread
여러 종류 many kinds
길거리 음식 street food
특이하다 to be unique
모양 shape, form
지어지다 to be built

상가 shopping mall
쌈지길 *Ssamjigil*
다양하다 to be diverse
디자인 design
공예품점 arts and crafts shop
기념품 souvenir
볼거리 attraction
먹거리 food
사주 *saju* fate (four pillars of destiny)
점 fortunetelling
판소리 *pansori*, traditional Korean narrative song
사물놀이 *samulnori*, traditional Korean percussion performance
N와/과 같은 like/such as N
공연 performance
태권도 *taekwondo*
택견 *taekkyon*
무술 martial art
시범 demonstration

010

북촌 한옥 마을*
Bukchon Hanok Village

북촌 한옥 마을은 서울의 경복궁과 창덕궁 사이 언덕에 위치해 있다. 조선 시대에 왕족이나 관리들이 모여 살던 곳으로 골목길과 집들이 잘 보존되어 있다. 그리고 민화, 인형, 칠기, 자수, 한지 공방들이 모여 있어서 장인들과 함께 전통 공예품을 직접 만들어 볼 수도 있다. 또한 화랑도 많고 불교 미술 박물관, 동양 문화 박물관, 세계 장신구 박물관에서 고전과 현대 미술을 감상할 수 있다. 삼청동까지 이어지는 한옥마을에는 아기자기한 꽃집, 옷가게, 장신구 가게가 있고, 그 사이사이에 여러 종류의 전문 식당들이 있어서 산책하는 사람들의 눈과 입을 즐겁게 해 준다. 이곳에는 민박할 수 있는 한옥들도 있다. 근처에는 북악산 동남쪽 입구에 있는 삼청 공원도 있어서 산책객들이 쉬면서 조용한 산의 정취를 느낄 수 있다.

1 서울의 한옥마을은 어디에 있습니까?
Where is Seoul's hanok village?

2 북촌 한옥 마을에는 어떤 박물관이 있습니까?
What kind of museums are there at Bukchon Hanok Village?

Bukchon Hanok Village is located on the hill between Seoul's Gyeongbokgung Palace and Changdeokgung Palace. This is where the royal family or officials used to live in the Joseon period, and the alleys and houses of the times are well preserved. And since workshops to create folk paintings, dolls, wooden lacquer wares, embroidery, and *hanji* papers are clustered here, you can try making traditional craftwork products firsthand with artisans. In addition, there are many art galleries, and you can enjoy classic and contemporary arts at the Buddhist Arts Museum, Asian Cultural Art Museum, and the World Jewelry Museum. Bukchon Hanok Village continues to Samcheong-dong, and there are charming flower shops, clothing and accessory stores, together with many kinds of specialty restaurants here and there, pleasing the eyes and palates of strollers. There are also *hanok* buildings available for lodging. In the vicinity, there is the Samcheong Park at the southeast entrance of Bugaksan Mountain, so strollers can take a break and feel the calm atmosphere of the mountain.

북촌 Bukchon
한옥마을 *hanok* village
경복궁 Gyeongbokgung Palace
창덕궁 Changdeokgung Palace
언덕 hill
위치하다 to be located
조선 시대 the Joseon Dynasty
왕족 royal family
관리 official
모이다 to gather
살다 to live
곳 place, spot
골목길 alley
보존되다 to be preserved
민화 folk painting
인형 doll
칠기 wooden lacquer ware
자수 embroidery
한지 *hanji* paper, traditional Korean paper

공방 workshop
모여 있다 to be clustered
장인 artisan, craftsman
함께 together
전통 traditional
공예품 craftwork
직접 firsthand, directly
V_R을/ㄹ 수 있다 can V
또한 in addition
화랑 art gallery
불교 미술 Buddhist arts
동양 문화 박물관 Asian Cultural Art Museum
세계 장신구 world jewellery
고전 classic
현대 미술 modern art, contemporary art
감상하다 to appreciate
삼청동 Samcheongdong
이어지다 to continue

아기자기한 charming
장신구 accessory
사이사이에 here and there
여러 종류 many kinds
전문 식당 specialty restaurant
산책하다 to take a walk
즐겁게 하다 to please
민박 tourist lodging
근처 vicinity
북악산 Bugaksan Mountain
동남쪽 southeast
입구 entrance
삼청 공원 Samcheong Park
산책객 stroller
쉬다 to rest
V_R(으)면서 V-ing
조용한 quiet, calm
정취 atmosphere, mood
느끼다 to feel

011

홍대 앞 거리 ★★

Hongdae (Hongik University) Streets

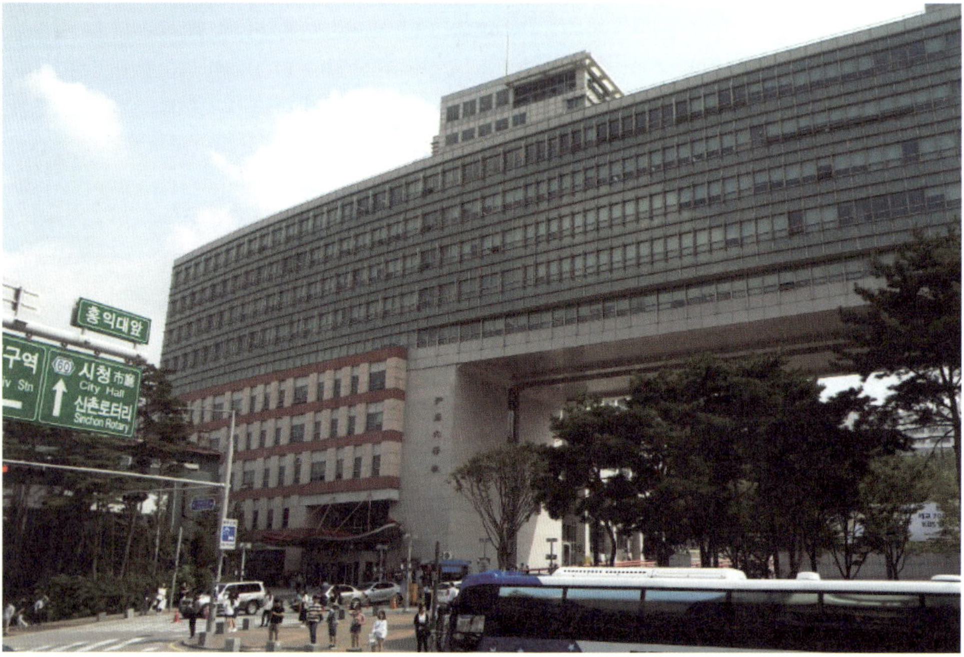

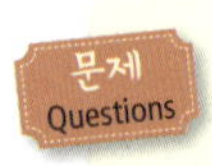

홍대 앞(홍익대학교 앞)은 활기와 재치가 넘치는 전형적인 젊은이들의 거리이다. 특색 있는 라이브 카페가 많아서 한국의 '언더그라운드' 문화가 시작된 곳도 바로 여기이다. 주말 밤이면 젊은 음악인들이 개성 있는 음악을 연주한다. 그래서 클럽이나 라이브 카페는 젊은이들로 북적거린다. 매주 토요일 오후에는 수공예품 프리마켓이 열려서 재능 있는 예술인들이 만든 독특하고 재미있는 물건들을 판다. 이처럼 홍대는 한국 젊은이들의 예술과 패션 문화를 대표하는 곳이다. 홍대 주변에는 먹거리도 퓨전 스타일이 많다. 외국 관광객들을 위한 크고 작은 게스트하우스가 많이 있다.

문제 Questions

1 한국의 언더그라운드 문화가 시작된 곳은 어디입니까?
Where did Korean underground culture begin?

2 프리마켓은 언제 열립니까?
When does the free market open?

Hongdae-ap (area in front of Hongik University) is a typical street of youth where energy and wit overflow. This is where Korean 'underground' culture began as there are many distinctive live cafés. On weekend nights, young musicians play their own unique music. Naturally clubs and live cafés are crowded with young people. Every week on Saturday afternoon, the handcraft free market opens, selling unique and interesting goods made by talented artists. Thus Hongdae is a place that represents the arts and fashion culture of Korean youth. In the vicinity of Hongdae, foods are often offered in a fusion style, and you can find small and large guesthouses for foreign tourists.

홍대 Hongdae, Hongik University
활기 energy, vigor
재치 wit
넘치다 to explode, to overflow
전형적인 typical
젊은이 youth, young people
특색 있다 to be distinctive
라이브 카페 live café
언더그라운드 underground
곳 place

바로 none other than
젊다 to be young
음악인 musician
개성 있다 to be unique, to be of one's own
연주하다 to play
북적거리다 to be crowded
매주 every week
프리마켓 free market
재능 있다 to be talented

예술인 artist
독특하다 to be unique
패션 fashion
대표하다 to represent
주변 vicinity, surroundings
먹거리 food
퓨전 스타일 fusion style
관광객 tourist
N을/를 위한 for N
게스트하우스 guesthouse

012

강남 *
Gangnam

강남은 서울의 한강 남쪽 지역을 가리킨다. 강남은 1970년대부터 새롭게 도시화가 진행된 곳으로 강남만의 이미지가 만들어졌다. 고궁이나 재래시장, 작은 골목들이 많은 강북에 비해 상대적으로 강남은 큰 빌딩과 대로, 백화점 등이 많아서 현대적인 분위기를 느낄 수 있다. 테헤란로에는 고층 건물들이 모여 있고 압구정동과 청담동에는 세계적인 명품 가게들이 있다. 압구정 로데오거리는 젊은이들이 즐겨 찾는 패션 거리이다. 그리고 신사동 가로수길에는 예쁜 옷가게, 독특한 레스토랑이나 찻집 등이 있다. 강남에는 연예인 기획사뿐만 아니라 젊은이들을 위한 클럽, 연예인들이 하는 식당도 많아서 외국인 팬들도 많이 찾아온다. 특히 가수 싸이의 〈강남 스타일〉로 세계적으로 유명해져서 강남을 찾는 관광객들이 해마다 늘고 있다.

문제
Questions

1 강남은 어디에 있습니까?
Where is Gangnam?

2 강남에서 젊은이들이 즐겨 찾는 패션 거리 이름은 무엇입니까?
What is the name of the fashion street where young people often visit in Gangnam?

Gangnam refers to area south of Hangang River in Seoul. Gangnam is the place where new urbanization has occurred since the 1970s, and it has a distinctive image of its own. Compared to Gangbuk (area north of the river), where there are many old palaces and small, traditional alleys, you will feel a modern atmosphere in Gangnam because there are many tall buildings, large streets and department stores. At Teheran-ro Street, high-rise buildings are clustered; in Apgujeong-dong and Cheongdam-dong, there are global luxury brand stores. Rodeo Street in Apgujeong-dong is a fashion street where young people visit often. And at Garosugil in Sinsa-dong, there are pretty clothing stores, unique restaurants and teahouses. Because there are not only entertainment management agencies but also clubs for the youth and restaurants run by celebrities in Gangnam, many foreign fans visit this area. Especially since singer Psy's "Gangnam Style" has gained worldwide fame, tourists visiting Gangnam are increasing every year.

강남 Gangnam	상대적으로 respectively	젊은이 youth, young people
한강 Hangang River	큰 big, large	즐겨 찾다 to visit often
남쪽 south, southern	빌딩 building	패션 fashion
지역 region	대로 main street/road	신사동 Sinsa-dong
가리키다 to refer to, to indicate	백화점 department store	가로수길 Garosugil
70년대 in the 1970s	V_R아서/어서/여서 because/since V	독특하다 to be unique
새롭게 newly	현대적인 modern, contemporary	연예인 기획사 entertainment management agency
도시화 urbanization	분위기 atmosphere	
진행되다 to occur	느끼다 to feel	N뿐만 아니라 not only N but also
곳 place	테헤란로 Teheran-ro Street	클럽 club
이미지 image	고층 건물 high-rise building	팬 fan
만들어지다 to be created	모여 있다 to be clustered	싸이 Psy
고궁 old palace	압구정동 Apgujeongdong	〈강남 스타일〉 "Gangnam Style"
재래시장 traditional market	청담동 Cheongdamdong	관광객 tourist
작은 small	세계적인 global, worldwide	해마다 every year
골목 alley	명품 luxury brand	늘다 to increase
강북 Gangbuk	로데오거리 Rodeo Street	

013

서울 지하철 *
Seoul Metropolitan Subway

서울의 지하철은 1974년에 처음 개통되었다. 현재 1호선에서 9호선까지 있고, 경의중앙선, 공항철도 등이 있다. 지하철 기본요금은 1,500원(2023)이고, 65세 이상의 노인은 무료이다. 지하철은 대부분 상가와 연결되어 있는데, 특히 고속버스 터미널역, 명동역 지하상가는 아주 커서 쇼핑하기가 편리하다. 공항철도가 생기면서 지하철로 인천국제공항에서 서울 시내까지 한 시간 안에 갈 수 있게 되었다. 한국의 지하철은 깨끗하고 쾌적한 편으로 곳곳에 휴식 공간이 있고 시와 그림들이 전시되어 있다. 지하철 안에는 교통약자석과 임산부석이 있어 교통 약자들이 보다 편하게 지하철을 이용할 수 있다. 무선 인터넷 와이파이가 연결되어 있어서 지하철 안에서 TV 방송도 쉽게 볼 수 있고, 외국인을 위한 다국어 안내 방송도 있다. 어떤 지하철역은 주변 환경과 역사를 잘 반영하고 있다. 충무로역에서는 영화 거리를, 경복궁역에서는 조선 왕실 분위기를 느낄 수 있다.

1 서울 지하철은 언제 개통이 되었습니까?
When did the Seoul Metropolitan Subway start service?

2 서울 지하철은 현재 몇 호선까지 있습니까?
How many numbered lines does the Seoul Metropolitan Subway have?

The Seoul Metropolitan Subway first started service in 1974. Currently it consists of lines 1 to 9, as well as the Gyeongui Line and the Airport Railroad Express. The basic fare is 1,500 won (as of 2023), and senior citizens who are 65 years or older can ride for free. Most of the subway stations are connected to shopping malls; in particular, the underground shopping malls at Express Bus Terminal and Myeongdong Station are convenient for shopping because they are very large. With the opening of the Airport Railroad Express, it is now possible to get to downtown Seoul from Incheon International Airport within one hour. Korea's subway is quite clean and pleasant, having resting spaces all over and displaying poems and paintings. In the subway trains, there are seats designated for the elderly, the disabled and the weak, as well as seats designated for pregnant women so that the more vulnerable users of public transportation may use the subway with greater ease. Since Wi-Fi is offered, you can easily watch TV on the subway. Multilingual announcements for foreigners are offered, too. Some subway stations have well incorporated its surroundings and history; you can feel the film street in the Chungmuro Station, you can feel the atmosphere of the royal family in the Gyeongbokgung Palace Station.

지하철 subway
처음 first
개통되다 to start service, to open
N호선 line (number) N
경의중앙선 Gyeongui Line
공항철도 Airport Railroad Express
기본요금 basic fare
세 age, year(s) old
N 이상 N or over/more
노인 senior citizen, the elderly
무료 free of charge
대부분 most of
상가 shopping mall
N와/과 연결되다 to be connected to N
특히 in particular
고속버스 터미널 Express Bus Terminal
역 station
명동 Myeongdong
지하 underground
크다 to be big/large

V_R아서/어서/여서 because/since V
쇼핑하기 to shop, shopping
편리하다 to be convenient
생기다 to open
인천국제공항 Incheon International Airport
V_R을/ㄹ 수 있다 can V
깨끗하다 to be clean
쾌적하다 to be pleasant
편 fairly, quite
곳곳에 all over, everywhere
휴식 rest
공간 space
시 poem, poetry
그림 painting
전시되다 to be exhibited/displayed
교통약자석 seat designated for the elderly, the disabled, the weak
임산부석 seat designated for pregnant women

무선 wireless
와이파이 Wi-Fi
연결되다 to be connected
방송 broadcasting
쉽게 easily
외국인 foreigner
N을/를 위한 for N
다국어 multilingual
안내 방송 announcement
어떤 some, certain
주변 surrounding
환경 environment
역사 history
반영하다 to reflect
충무로 Chungmuro
거리 street
경복궁 Gyeongbokgung Palace
조선 Joseon
왕실 royal family
분위기 atmosphere
느끼다 to feel

014

제주도와 한라산 *
Jejudo Island and Hallasan Mountain

제주도는 한반도 남서쪽에 있는 한국에서 가장 큰 섬으로 기후가 온화하고 해변이 아름다워 신혼여행지로도 유명하다. 화산섬인 제주도에는 남한에서 가장 높은 한라산(1,950m)이 있다. 한라산은 해돋이로 유명한 성산일출봉, 용암 동굴과 함께 세계유산에 등록되었다. 제주도는 아름다운 자연 환경으로 유명한데 온난한 기후로 희귀 식물이 많고, 해안 쪽에는 폭포와 기둥처럼 쭉쭉 뻗은 바위들이 있어서 남국적 정서를 느낄 수 있다. 해변 산책로인 올레길을 걸으면 제주도의 아름다움을 곳곳에서 감상할 수 있다. 제주도는 화산암으로 만든 수호신 돌하르방과 해산물을 따는 해녀로도 유명하다. 제주해녀문화는 2016년 유네스코 무형 문화유산으로 등록되었다. 이 섬에 가면 감귤, 전복, 옥돔이나 흑돼지고기 같은 향토 음식을 맛볼 수 있다.

1 남한에서 가장 높은 산은 무엇입니까?
What is the highest mountain in South Korea?

2 제주도에서 세계 자연 유산에 기록된 것은 무엇입니까?
What are enlisted as the World Heritage site in Jejudo Island?

Jejudo Island is the biggest island in Korea, in the southwest part of the Korean peninsula; it is famous as a honeymoon destination for its mild climate and beautiful beaches. Jejudo Island is a volcanic island, and it has the highest mountain in South Korea, Hallasan Mountain (1,950m). It has been enlisted as a World Heritage site together with Seongsan Ilchulbong famous for which is watching the sunrise and visiting the lava tubes. Jejudo Island is well known for beautiful natural environment; there are many rare species of plant life due to its mild climate; on the beaches, you can feel the southern sentiment as there are waterfalls and rocks rising straight like pillars. If you walk along Ollegil, a series of walking trails along the beach, you can enjoy the beauty of Jejudo Island everywhere. Jejudo Island is also well known for the guardian spirit of *dolhareubang* (Stone Grandpa), and for *hanyeo* who harvest seafood. Culture of Jeju Haenyeo was registered as a UNESCO intangible cultural heritage in 2016. When you visit this island, you can also taste local foods like tangerine, abalone, sea bream and black pork.

제주도 Jejudo Island, Jeju-do/Province

한라산 Hallasan Mountain

한반도 Korean Peninsula

남서쪽 southwest

가장 the most

큰 big

섬 island

기후 climate

온화하다 to be mild

해변 beach

아름답다 beautiful

신혼여행지 honeymoon destination

유명하다 to be famous/well known

화산섬 volcanic island

가장 the most

높은 high

해돋이 sunrise

성산일출봉 Seongsan Ilchulbong

용암 lava

동굴 cave

세계유산 World Heritage

등록되다 to be enlisted, to be registered

자연환경 natural environment

온난한 mild

희귀 식물 rare plant life

해안 coast

쪽 side, part

폭포 waterfall

기둥 pillar

N처럼 like N

쭉쭉 뻗다 to stretch, to be straight

바위 rock

남국적 정서 southern sentiment

느끼다 to feel

V_R을/ㄹ 수 있다 can V

산책로 walking trail

올레길 Ollegil, Olle Trail

아름다움 beauty

곳곳에서 all over, everywhere

감상하다 to enjoy, to appreciate

화산암 volcanic rock

수호신 guardian spirit

돌하르방 *dolhareubang*, Stone Grandpa

해산물 seafood

따다 to pick, to collect

해녀 *haenyeo*, female divers who harvest seafood

감귤 tangerine

전복 abalone

옥돔 sea bream

흑돼지고기 black pork

N 같은 like N

향토 local, folk

맛보다 to taste

015

경주와 경주 남산 ★★
Gyeongju and Gyeongju Namsan Mountain

경주는 천년 동안 신라(기원전 57~935)의 수도였다. 그래서 경주 시내에는 신라 시대의 별궁과 커다란 왕릉이 곳곳에 남아 있다. 신라의 천문 관측대인 첨성대는 동아시아에서 가장 오래된 석조 건물(633)이다. 이것은 당시의 건축 기술과 천문학에 대한 관심을 짐작하게 한다. 신라는 불교가 국교였기 때문에 곳곳에 불교 유적이 많이 남아 있다. 불교 예술의 아름다움을 보여 주는 대표적인 유적으로 불국사와 석굴암, 그리고 경주 남산이 있다. 경주 남산은 40여 개의 계곡과 산줄기로 이루어진 산으로, 신라 시대의 절터, 불상, 불탑, 석등 등이 산의 여기저기에 많이 남아 있어서 '지붕 없는 박물관'이라고 불린다. 특히 거대한 바위에 새겨진 불상들은 신라인들의 깊은 신앙심을 보여 준다. 남산에는 신라의 궁궐 터나 고분 등 역사 유적도 많다. 이처럼 오랜 역사가 잘 보존되어 있는 경주와 경주 남산은 유네스코 세계유산에 등록되어 있다.

문제
Questions

1 신라의 수도는 어디입니까?
Where was the capital of Silla?

2 경주 남산을 왜 '지붕 없는 박물관'이라고 부릅니까?
Why do we call Namsan Mountain in Gyeongju 'the roofless museum'?

Gyeongju was the capital of the Silla Kingdom (BCE 75–CE 935) for one thousand years. That is why royal villas and huge royal tombs remain all over the mountain. Cheomseongdae Observatory, the astronomical observatory of Silla, is the oldest stone structure in East Asia (633). This allows us to estimate the building technology and the interest in astronomy at the time. Since Buddhism was Silla's state religion, many Buddhist relics remain all over the place. As for representative remains showing the beauty of Buddhist arts, there are Bulguksa Temple, Seokguram Grotto and Gyeongju Namsan Mountain. Gyeongju Namsan Mountain is a mountain consisting of about 40 valleys and mountain ranges; it is called 'the roofless museum' because Buddhist temple sites, images of Buddha, pagodas and stone lamps remain all over the mountain. In particular, Buddha's images, engraved in the enormous rocks, show us the deep religious faith of the Silla people. At Namsan Mountain, there are many historic sites such as the site of Silla's royal palace and tombs. Thus well preserving a long history, Gyeongju and Gyeongju Namsan Mountain are registered as a UNESCO World Heritage site.

경주 Gyeongju	건축 architecture	등 such as, and the like
남산 Namsan Mountain	기술 technology, skills	여기저기 all over, here and there
천년 a thousand years	천문학 astronomy	남다 to remain
신라 Silla (Kingdom)	N에 대한 regarding N, about N	V_R아서/어서/여서 because/since V
기원전 BCE	관심 interest	지붕없는 박물관 roofless museum
수도 capital	짐작하다 to estimate, to guess	불리다 to be called
시대 era, age	불교 Buddhism	특히 in particular
별궁 royal villa	국교 state religion	거대하다 to be huge/enormous
커다란 large, huge	유적 remains, historic sites	바위 rock
왕릉 royal tomb	예술 art	새겨지다 to be engraved
곳곳에 all over, everywhere	아름다움 beauty	신라인들 Silla people
남아 있다 to remain	대표적인 representative	깊다 to be deep
천문 관측대 astronomical observatory	불국사 Bulguksa Temple	신앙심 religious faith
첨성대 Cheomseongdae Observatory	석굴암 Seokguram Grotto	보여 주다 to show
동아시아 East Asia	계곡 valley	궁궐터 site of royal palace
가장 the most	산줄기 mountain range	고분 tomb
오래되다 to be old	이루어지다 to be made, consist of	역사 history
석조 건물 stone structure	절터 Buddhist temple site	보존되다 to preserve
당시 at the time, then	불상 statue of Buddha	세계유산 World Heritage
	불탑 pagoda	등록되다 to be registered/enlisted
	석등 stone lamp	

016

하회마을 ★★
Hahoe Folk Village

하회마을은 풍산 류씨 가문이 600년 동안 모여 사는 씨족 마을이다. 이곳은 산과 강이 조화를 이루어서 풍수지리적으로 살기 좋은 전통 마을이다. 현재 이 마을에는 기와집과 초가집 150여 호가 남아 있는데 가문의 유명한 인물들이 살았던 고택들과 16세기에 세워진 병산 서원도 잘 보존돼 있다. 하회마을은 한옥 체험 마을로 지정돼 있어서 옛 풍습을 직접 체험해 볼 수 있고 하회 별신굿 탈춤도 구경할 수 있다. 탈박물관에서는 여러 지방의 전통 탈과 탈춤 그리고 세계 탈춤의 역사를 발견할 수 있다. 하회마을은 2010년에 '한국의 역사 마을'로 병산 서원은 2019년에 유네스코 세계유산에 등록되었다.

1 하회마을은 어떤 마을입니까?
What kind of village is Hahoe Folk Village?

2 하회마을에서 유명한 춤은 무엇입니까?
What is the famous dance in Hahoe Folk Village?

Hahoe Folk Village is a clan village where the Ryu clan of Pungsan has gathered and lived together for 600 years. This is a traditional village that is good to live in from a feng shui perspective, as the mountains and rivers are in harmony. At present, there remain about 150 tile-roof and straw-roof houses; old houses in which famous persons of this family used to live and Byeongsanseowon (Confucian academy) built in the 16th century are well preserved. Hahoe Folk Village is designated as a *hanok* experience village, so you can have a firsthand experience of old customs and watch the Hahoe *Byeolsingut* (special ritual drama to the gods) mask dance. At the Hahoe Mask Museum, you can find traditional masks and mask dances of many regions and the global history of mask dance. Hahoe Folk Village was registered as the Historic Villages in Korea in 2010, and Byeongsanseowon was registered as a UNESCO World Heritage Site in 2019.

하회 Hahoe	호 *ho*, unit to count buildings	직접 firsthand
마을 village	남다 to remain	별신굿 *Byeolsingut*, special ritual drama to the gods
풍산 류씨 Ryu clan of Pungsan	인물 person	탈춤 mask dance
가문 family	고택 old house	탈박물관 Mask Museum
모이다 to gather	세기 century	여러 many
씨족 마을 clan village	세워지다 to be built	지방 local
조화를 이루다 to be in harmony	병산 서원 Byeongsanseowon (Confucian Academy)	탈 mask
풍수지리적으로 from feng shui perspective	보존되다 to be preserved	세계 world
살기 좋다 to be livable, to be good to live in	체험 experience	역사 historic
현재 at present	지정되다 to be designated	발견하다 to find
기와집 tile-roof house	옛 old	세계유산 World Heritage
초가집 straw-roof house	풍습 customs	등록되다 to be registered

017

부여와 백제 유적 ★★★
Buyeo and Baekje Historic Sites

충청남도 부여는 1,300년 전 백제(기원전 18~660)의 수도였다. 이곳에는 왕궁터와 왕릉, 그리고 부소산성과 가장 오래된 인공 연못 "궁남지" 등 건축, 예술 면에서 발전했던 백제 문화 유적들이 모여 있다. 또한 부여에는 백제 궁녀들이 외침에 절개를 지키려고 절벽에서 강물로 몸을 던진 낙화암이 있다. 낙화암은 '꽃이 떨어진 바위'라는 뜻으로 많은 예술가들에게 영감을 준 곳이다. 부여에는 천 년 전의 시간을 살펴볼 수 있는 곳이 많다. 부여를 감싸고 도는 백마강에서 황포 돛배를 타고 유적들을 돌아보면 백제의 화려했던 시간과 함께 나라가 패망한 슬픔을 동시에 느낄 수 있다. 만수산의 무량사는 '시간도 지혜도 세지 않는다'는 뜻으로 천년 고찰의 고풍스러움을 그대로 간직하고 있는 절이다. 한국 불교문화의 보고인 공주 갑사도 멀지 않은 곳에 있으니 함께 둘러보면 좋다.

1 백제의 수도는 어디였습니까?
Where was Baekje's capital?

2 부여에는 어떤 유적지들이 있습니까?
What historic sites are there in Buyeo?

Buyeo in Chungcheongnam-do was the capital of the Baekje Kingdom (BCE 18–CE660) 1,300 years ago. Baekje culture was advanced from the aspects of arts and architecture, and historic sites of that culture are gathered here, including the site of the royal palace, royal tombs, Busosanseong Fortress, and the oldest artificial pond of Gungnamji. In addition, there is Nakhwaam Rock in Buyeo, where Baekje court ladies threw themselves into the river to protect their chastity. Nakhwaam means "the cliff of falling flowers," and it is a place that has inspired many artists. In Buyeo, there are many places you can look back a thousand years. If you look around the historic sites in a Hwangpo sailboat along the Baekmagang River that wraps and flows around Buyeo, you can feel at the same time the glorious times of Baekje and the sorrow from the defeat and collapse of the country. Mansusan Mountain's Muryangsa Temple has the meaning of 'reckoning neither time nor wisdom,' and it retains the antiquity of a thousand-year-old temple intact. Gongju Gapsa Temple, a repository of Korean Buddhist culture, is not far away from here, so it would be good to look around both temples.

부여 Buyeo
백제 Baekje (Kingdom)
유적 historic site, remains
충청남도 Chungcheongnam-do, South Chungcheong Province
기원전 BCE
수도 capital
왕궁터 the site of royal palace
왕릉 royal tomb
부소산성 Busosanseong Fortress
오래되다 to be old
인공 연못 artificial pond
궁남지 Gungnamji pond
건축 architecture
예술 art
면 aspect
발전하다 to develop, to be advanced
모여 있다 to gather
궁녀 court lady

외침 foreign invasion
절개를 지키다 to protect one's integrity/chastity
절벽 cliff
강물 river
몸 body
던지다 to throw
낙화암 Nakhwaam Rock
떨어지다 to fall, to drop
바위 rock
뜻 meaning
예술가 artist
영감을 주다 to inspire
살펴보다 to look backward
감싸고 돌다 to wrap and move/flow around
백마강 Baekmagang River
황포 돛배 Hwangpo sailboat
돌아보다 to look around
화려하다 to be glorious, to be splendid

패망하다 to defeat/collapse
슬픔 sorrow, sadness
동시에 at the same time, simultaneously
만수산 Mansusan Mountain
무량사 Muryangsa Temple
지혜 wisdom
세다 to reckon, to count
천년 a thousand years
고찰 old temple
고풍스러움 antiquity, antique atmosphere
그대로 intact, as it is
간직하다 to retain
절 temple
불교문화 Buddhist culture
보고 repository
갑사 Gapsa Temple
둘러보다 to look around

018

부산과 자갈치시장 ★★
Busan and Jagalchi Market

부산은 항구 도시로 한국에서 두 번째로 큰 도시이다. 부산에는 가 볼만한 관광지가 많다. 여름에는 백만 명의 사람들이 모이는 해운대 해수욕장이 있고, 광안리 해수욕장에서 보이는 야경으로 유명한 광안대교, 바닷가의 해동용궁사, 해변 산책길 태종대, 감천문화마을 등이 있다. 부산 앞바다에는 오륙도, 동백섬과 같은 아름다운 섬들이 있고, 제주도나 일본과도 가까워서 배로 갈 수 있다. 또한 한국에서 가장 큰 수산 시장인 남포동 자갈치시장에서 신기한 모양과 색의 생선과 해물들을 살 수 있다. 손님이 어항 속에 살아 있는 생선을 고르면 식당에서 바로 먹을 수 있게 준비해 준다. 부산에는 유명한 먹거리도 많은데 대표적으로 밀면, 곰장어, 부산 어묵 등이 있다.

1 한국에서 가장 큰 수산 시장은 어디입니까?
What is the largest fish market in Korea?

2 부산의 먹거리 명물은 무엇입니까?
What are the famous food items of Busan?

Busan is a port city, and it is the second largest city in Korea. There are many tourist attractions worth visiting in Busan. There is Heaundae Beach where a million people would gather in summer; there is Gwang-andaegyo Bridge famous for its nightscape seen from Gwangalli Beach; there is Haedong Yonggungsa Temple at the seaside; and there is the coastal trail of Taejongdae; there is Gamcheon Culture Village. In the coastal waters of Busan, there are beautiful islands like Oryukdo Island and Dongbaekseom Island. It is also possible to go to Jejudo Island or Japan by ship since Busan is within a short distance from them. You can also buy fish and seafood of unusual shapes and colors at Nampo-dong's Jagalchi Market, the largest fish market in Korea. When a customer picks live fish from the fish tank, the fish is prepared so that the customer can eat it at the restaurant right away. There are many famous food items in Busan, of which *milmyeon* (wheat noodles), *gomjang-eo* (sea eel) and *Busan eomuk* (fish cake) are the most representative.

부산 Busan	바닷가 seaside	손님 guest, customer
자갈치시장 Jagalchi Market	해동용궁사 Haedong Yonggungsa Temple	어항 fish tank
항구 port	해변 산책길 coastal trail	속 in, inside
도시 city	태종대 Taejongdae	살아 있다 to be alive, to be live
두 번째 second	오륙도 Oryukdo Island	고르다 to choose, to pick
V_R을/ㄹ 만하다 to be worth V-ing	동백섬 Dongbaekseom Island	바로 right away, immediately
관광지 tourist attraction	섬 island	V_R을/ㄹ 수 있다 so that can V
백만 million	또한 also	준비하다 to prepare to make/cook
모이다 to gather	가장 the most	먹거리 food items
해운대 Haeundae	수산 시장 fish market	대표적으로 representatively
해수욕장 beach	남포동 Nampodong	밀면 wheat noodle
광안리 Gwangalli	신기하다 to be unusual	곰장어 sea eel
보이다 to be seen	모양 shape	어묵 fish cake
야경 nightview	해물 seafood	
광안대교 Gwangandaegyo Bridge		

019

동해안과 설악산 국립 공원 *
Donghae Coast and Seoraksan National Park

동해안은 산과 바다가 만나는 아름다운 해안이다. 육지로는 태백산맥을 타고 오대산, 속리산, 태백산 등이 솟아 있고, 바다로는 긴 해안을 따라서 경포대와 속초 등에 해수욕장들이 끝없이 펼쳐져 있다. 그래서 바다와 산을 즐기려는 사람들이 항상 끊이지 않는다. 특히 강원도에 있는 설악산에는 '흔들바위'와 같이 특이한 모양의 바위들이 많다. 그리고 사계절 모두 각기 다른 아름다움을 가지고 있다. 봄에는 철쭉 등 수많은 꽃들이 산을 뒤덮고, 여름에는 맑고 깨끗한 계곡과 폭포가 시원하다. 특히 백담계곡은 절벽, 맑은 물, 조약돌, 울창한 숲이 있어 등산객들에게 잊을 수 없는 추억을 남긴다. 가을에는 단풍잎이 화려하고, 겨울에는 눈 풍경도 볼만하다. 설악산에는 다양한 등산 코스가 있으며, 백담사와 신흥사 같은 오래된 절들도 있어서 등산객이 자신의 취향에 맞게 선택할 수 있다.

1 동해안의 유명한 해수욕장은 무엇입니까?
What are the famous beaches on the Donghae Coast?

2 설악산은 어디에 있습니까?
Where is Seoraksan Mountain?

The Donghae coast is a beautiful coast where mountains and sea meet. On land, mountains like Odaesan Mountain, Songnisan Mountain and Taebaeksan Mountain are rising on the Taebaeksanmaek Mountains; at sea, beaches are spread endlessly along a long coast at Gyeongpodae Pavilion, Sokcho and other places. That is why the stream of people who want to enjoy the sea and the mountains never stops. In particular, at Seoraksan Mountain in Gangwon-do, there are many rocks in unique shapes, such as the Rocking Stone. And all four seasons have different beauty. In the spring, numerous flowers, including royal azalea, cover the mountains; in the summer, it is cool in the clean and clear valleys and waterfalls. Baekdam Valley especially has cliffs, clear water, pebbles and thick forest, leaving memories that hikers can never forget. In the fall, maple leaves are gorgeous and in the winter, the landscape of snow is worth watching. There are various hiking routes at Seoraksan Mountain: there are also old temples like Baekdamsa Temple and Sinheungsa Temple, so hikers can make a choice following their tastes.

어휘와 표현 \ Words & Expressions

동해안 Donghae coast
설악산 Seoraksan Mountain
국립 공원 national park
바다 sea, ocean
아름다운 beautiful
해안 coast
육지 land
태백산맥 Taebaeksanmaek Mountains
타다 to be on
오대산 Odaesan Mountain
속리산 Songnisan Mountain
태백산 Taebaeksan Mountain
솟아 있다 to rise
긴 long
N을/를 따라서 along N
경포대 Gyeongpodae Pavilion
속초 Sokcho
해수욕장 beach
끝없이 endlessly
펼쳐져 있다 to spread
즐기나 to enjoy
항상 always
끊이다 to run out, to stop

V_R지 않다 do not V
특히 in particular, especially
강원도 Gangwon-do/Province
흔들바위 rocking stone
특이한 unique
모양 shape
바위 rock
사계절 four seasons
모두 all, every
각기 each
가지다 to have
철쭉 royal azalea, rhododendron
수많은 numerous
뒤덮다 to cover
맑다 to be clear
깨끗하다 to be clean
계곡 valley
폭포 waterfall
시원하다 to be cool
백담계곡 Baekdam Valley
절벽 cliff
조약돌 pebble
울창한 thick

숲 forest
등산객들 hikers
잊다 to forget
V_R을/ㄹ 수 없다 cannot V
추억 memory
남기다 to leave
단풍잎 maple leaf
화려하다 to be gorgeous, to be splendid
눈 snow
풍경 landscape, scenery
V_R을/ㄹ 만하다 to be worth V-ing
등산 hiking, mountain climbing
코스 course, route
백담사 Baekdamsa Temple
신흥사 Sinheungsa Temple
오래된 old
절 Buddhist temple
등산객 hiker
자신 one's own
취향 taste
N에 맞게 following N
선택하다 to make a choice

다도해와 해상 국립 공원 ★★

Dadohae and Haesang (Marine Archipelago) National Park

다도해는 '섬이 많은 바다'라는 뜻으로 전라남도 홍도에서 남해 여수 앞바다까지를 가리킨다. 한국에 있는 3천여 개의 섬 중 1,700여 개의 섬이 이곳에 모여 있다. 홍도, 거제도, 진도, 한산도, 보길도가 그중에서 큰 섬들이다. 이곳에는 특이한 해안 지형과 온화한 기후로 난대성 식물이 경관을 이루어 한국에서 가장 큰 해상 국립 공원이 만들어졌다. 새들의 서식지, 염전, 해송이 가득 찬 소나무 숲과 모래 해변, 조용한 어촌 등이 어우러져 아름답다. 다도해에서 통통배를 타고 아기자기한 섬들을 지나며 볼 수 있는 일몰 또한 인상적이다. 이 지역 특산물로는 장어, 홍어, 돌김, 매생이가 있고, 남해의 대표적인 도시 통영은 동피랑 벽화 마을, 구항구의 충무 김밥, 그리고 나전 칠기가 유명하다. 여수에서는 돌산공원에서 해상 케이블카를 타고 오동도 자산공원까지 갈 수 있다. 바다를 가로지르며 거북선대교 등 아름다운 풍경을 감상할 수 있다.

<table>
<tr><td>문제
Questions</td><td>

1 다도해는 무슨 뜻입니까?
What does Dadohae mean?

</td><td>

2 통영은 무엇으로 유명합니까?
What is Tongyeong famous for?

</td></tr>
</table>

Dadohae means 'sea with many islands,' and it refers to the area from Hongdo Island, Jeollanam-do to the waters of Yeosu, Namhae. Of some 3,000 islands in Korea, about 1,700 are gathered here. Hongdo Island, Geojedo Island, Jindo Island, Hansando Island and Bogildo Island are the bigger islands among them. The biggest marine national park in Korea was formed here since the unique coastal landforms and warm temperate plants from the mild climate created a superb landscape. It is beautiful since birds' habitations, salt farms, pine tree forest, filled with sea pines, sand beaches and fishing villages exist in harmony. The sunset is also impressive, which you can see as you board a chug boat and pass by charming little islands. The local specialties of this region include eel, skate, *dolgim* laver and *maesaengi* (seaweed fulvescens); Tongyeong, a city that represents Namhae is famous for Dongpirang Mural Village, Chungmu *gimbap* of the old port, and *najeon chilgi* lacquer ware. In Yeosu, you can take the marine cable car from Dolsan Park to Odongdo Jasan Park. You can enjoy beautiful scenery such as Geobukseon Bridge as you cross the sea.

다도해 Dadohae

해상 국립 공원 Haesang (Marine Archipelago) National Park

섬 island

전라남도 Jeollanam-do, South Jeolla Province

홍도 Hongdo Island

남해 Namhae

여수 Yeosu

가리키다 to indicate, to refer to

N여 about N

모여 있다 to be gathered

거제도 Geojedo Island

진도 Jindo Island

한산도 Hansando Island

보길도 Bogildo Island

특이하다 to be unique

해안 지형 coastal landform

온화하다 to be mild

기후 climate

난대성 식물 warm temperate plant

경관 landscape, scenery

이루다 to create

서식지 habitation

염전 salt farm

해송 sea pine

가득 to be full

차다 to be filled

소나무 pine tree

숲 forest

모래 sand

해변 beach

어촌 fishing village

어우러지다 to be in harmony, to be mingled

통통배 chug boat

이기지기하다 to be charming and cute/little

일몰 sunset

또한 also

인상적이다 to be impressive

지역 특산물 local/regional specialty

장어 eel

홍어 skate

돌김 *dolgim* laver

매생이 *maesaengi*, seaweed fulvescens

대표적 representative

도시 city

통영 Tongyeong

동피랑 Dongpirang

벽화 마을 mural village

구항구 old port

충무 Chungmu

나전칠기 *najeon chilgi*, lacquer ware

보성 차밭 ★★
Boseong Tea Plantation

보성 차밭은 전라남도 보성에 있다. 넓고 아름다운 녹차 밭은 남해와 만나서 절경을 이룬다. 차밭을 따라 내려가면 가까운 곳에 해수욕장도 있다. 그래서 영화, 드라마, 광고의 촬영 장소로 많이 이용된다. 보성은 한국에서 가장 오래된 차밭이며 그 규모는 제주도 다음으로 크다. 해마다 보성에는 다양한 축제가 열리는데 녹차를 주제로 한 여러 가지 행사를 경험할 수 있다. 5월에 '보성 다향제'라는 녹차 축제가 열리고, 차의 풍년을 기원하는 〈다신제〉, 〈찻잎 따기〉, 〈차 아가씨 선발 대회〉도 있다. 또한 12월에서 2월까지 녹차밭에서 화려한 〈보성 차밭 빛 축제〉도 열린다. 먹거리도 다양하고 녹차밭 주변에는 가 볼 만한 전통 찻집들이 많다. 그리고 녹차 국수, 녹차 비빔밥, 녹차 아이스크림 등을 맛볼 수 있는 식당들도 있으니 잊지 말고 꼭 한번 먹어 보자.

1 보성에서 5월에 열리는 축제는 무엇입니까?
What is the festival that is held in Boseong in May?

2 녹차로 만들 수 있는 음식은 무엇입니까?
What are the foods that can be made from green tea?

Boseong Tea Plantation is located in Boseong, Jeollanam-do. The spacious and beautiful green tea plantation meets the South Sea and forms a magnificent view. If you go down following the green tea plantation, you will also find a beach close at hand. That is why this place is frequently used as the filming location for movies, TV dramas and commercials. Boseong is the oldest tea plantation in Korea and the size is the second largest, next to that of Jejudo Island. Every year, various festivals are held in Boseong and you can experience many events that have the theme of green tea. In May, Boseong Dahyangje or Green Tea Festival is held; there are also Dasinje, or tea ritual to gods praying for good harvest, as well as Picking Tea Leaves and Miss Tea Pageant. There are diverse foods and many traditional teahouses worth visiting in the vicinity of the green tea plantation. And there are restaurants where you can taste green tea noodles, green tea *bibimbap* and green tea ice cream; do not miss the opportunity to taste these foods.

보성 Boseong
차밭 tea plantation
전라남도 Jeollanam-do, South Jeolla Province
넓다 to be spacious
녹차 밭 green tea plantation
남해 Namhae
절경 magnificent view, superb scenery
이루다 to make
N을/를 따라(서) along N, following N
내려가다 to go down
가깝다 to be close, to be near
곳 place, spot
해수욕장 beach
광고 advertisement, commercial

촬영 shooting, filming
장소 place
가장 the most
오래되다 to be old
규모 size
해마다 every year
주제 theme
행사 event
경험하다 to experience
〈보성 다향제〉 Boseong Dahyangje, Boseong Green Tea Festival
축제 festival
열리다 to be held
풍년 good harvest, rich year
기원하다 to pray

〈다신제〉 Dasinje Tea Ritual to the Gods
〈찻잎 따기〉 Picking Tea Leaves
〈차 아가씨 선발 대회〉 Miss Tea Pageant
화려하다 to be splendid
빛 축제 festival of lights
먹거리 food
주변 vicinity, surroundings
V_R을/ㄹ 만하다 to be worth V
국수 noodles
맛보다 to taste
V_R으니 V and
잊다 to miss
〜지 말고 do not V
꼭 to be sure to (do something)

Korean Culture in 100 Keywords

외국인 학습자를 위한 한국 문화 100선

IV. 사회와 일상생활
Society and Daily Life

한국어 *
The Korean Language

한국어는 한국 사람들, 북한 사람들과 해외 교포들이 모국어로 사용한다. 세계 언어 중에서 열세 번째로 많이 사용되는 언어이며 약 8,000만 명이 사용하는데 한류의 영향으로 한국어를 배우는 외국인들이 많이 늘어나고 있다. 한국어는 교착어에 속하기 때문에 조사가 있고 동사의 어미가 활용한다. 문장에서 주어와 목적어의 순서는 자유롭지만, 동사는 항상 끝부분에 있어야 한다. 주어는 생략되기도 한다. 한국어는 소리와 모양을 흉내 내는 말이 매우 풍부하고 나이, 사회적 지위, 가족 관계에 따라 높임말과 자신을 낮추는 말 등이 발달해 있다.

1 왜 한국어를 배우는 외국인들이 늘고 있습니까?
Why is the number of foreigners learning Korean increasing?

2 한국어 문장에서 동사는 어디에 있습니까?
Where is the verb located in a Korean sentence?

The Korean language is used as the mother tongue by South Koreans, North Koreans and ethnic Koreans overseas. It is the 13th most widely used language in the world and is used by about 80 million people. Due to the influence of *hallyu* (the Korean Wave), an increasing number of foreigners are learning Korean. Since Korean is an agglutinative language, it has postpositions and conjugated verbs. Although the ordering of subject and object is quite free within a sentence, the verb must remain at the end at all times. The subject of the sentence is sometimes omitted. Korean is rich in words that mimic sounds and forms; it is highly developed in honorific forms both to respect the other party and to lower oneself, according to age, social status, and family relations.

한국어 Korean (language)
북한 North Korea
해외 교포 ethnic Korean living overseas
모국어 mother tongue
사용하다 to use
세계 world
언어 language
중에서 of
한류 *hallyu* (Korean Wave)
영향 influence
늘다 to increase
교착어 agglutinative language

조사 postposition
동사 verb
어미 ending
활용하다 to use/conjugate
문장 sentence
주어 subject
목적어 object
순서 order
자유롭다 to be free
항상 at all times, always
끝 end
생략하다 to omit
V$_R$기도 하다 sometimes V

소리 sound
모양 form, shape
흉내 내다 to mimic
말 word
매우 very
풍부하다 to be rich
사회적 지위 social status
가족 family
관계 relationship, relations
N에 따라 according to N
높임말 honorific language
자신을 낮추다 to lower oneself
발달하다 to be developed

인구 ★
Population

대한민국의 인구는 약 오천만 명이다(2023). 삼천이백만 명이었던 1970년에 비해 인구는 약 1.6배 늘었지만, 인구 성장률은 2023년 마이너스를 기록하고 있다. 전체 인구의 50%가 서울과 수도권 지역에 거주하고 있어 수도권에 집중되어 있다. 이외에도 한국 동포들은 세계 곳곳에서 살고 있다. 북한 주민은 이천오백만 명이며, 중국과 미국, 일본에도 많은 동포들이 있다. 한국에서 살고 있는 외국인들도 많은데 현재(2023) 약 이백만 명의 외국인이 한국에 거주 중이다. 중국인, 동남아시아인, 미국인이 많은 수를 차지하고 있다. 최근에는 취업 외국인, 결혼이민자, 외국인 유학생이 늘어서 이제 한국에도 다문화 시대가 열렸다.

1 대한민국 인구는 몇 명입니까?
How big is the population of South Korea?

2 한국에는 어느 나라 외국인들이 제일 많이 삽니까?
Which countries have the largest number of foreigners living in South Korea?

The Republic of Korea has a population of around 50 million (as of 2023). The population has increased by 1.6 times since 1970 when it was 32 million, but the population growth rate is negative in 2023. 50 percent of the total population is concentrated in metropolitan areas, living in Seoul and other cities. In addition, there are ethnic Koreans all around the world. The North Korean population is 25 million, and there are many ethnic Koreans in China, the United States and Japan. There are many foreigners living in South Korea, and at present (2023), there are around two million foreign residents. By nationality, China, Vietnam, the United States account for the largest numbers. The increase in long-term stay by foreigners resulted from the increase in Chinese visitors, employed foreigners, immigrants by marriage, and foreign students studying in Korea. The era of multiculture has begun in Korea.

인구 population
대한민국 the Republic of Korea, South Korea
약 N around N
N에 비해 compared to N, against N
배 times
늘다 to increase
성장률 growth rate
이후 after, since
줄다 to reduce
전체 total, whole

수도권 지역 metropolitan area
거주하다 to live in, to reside
집중되다 to be concentrated
동포 ethnic
곳곳에서 all around the world
북한 North Korea
주민 resident
살다 to live
외국인 foreigner
현재 at present, now
중국인 Chinese

동남아시아인 South-East Asian
미국인 American
취업 employment
결혼이민자 immigrant by marriage
유학생 foreign student
이제 now
다문화 multiculture
시대 era, age
열리다 to open, to begin

성과 이름 *
Family Name and First Name

한국 사람들의 이름은 대부분 세 글자로 되어 있다. 첫 글자는 성이고 나머지 두 글자는 이름이다. 성을 먼저 쓰고 그다음에 이름을 쓴다. 이름을 지을 때에는 좋은 의미의 글자를 고른다. 최근에는 이름을 자유롭게 짓는 부모들도 많지만 보통은 집안 어른에게 부탁하거나 작명소를 찾는다. 이름, 생일, 태어난 시간이 아이의 삶에 좋은 영향을 끼친다고 생각한다. 한국인의 성으로는 김이 21%로 제일 많고, 그다음은 이 14%, 그다음은 박, 최, 정, 강 순으로 많다. 한국 여자들은 결혼 후에도 남편 성을 쓰지 않는다. 하지만 아이들은 주로 아버지 성을 쓰고 요즘은 아버지 어머니 성을 함께 쓰는 경우도 있다.

1 한국 사람들의 이름은 보통 몇 글자로 되어 있습니까?
How many characters are there usually in Korean names?

2 한국에서 제일 많은 성은 무엇입니까?
What is the most common family name in Korea?

A Korean name usually consists of three characters. The first character is the family name, and the latter two characters make the given name. The family name is written first, followed by the first name. When Koreans give a name, they select characters with good meanings. Nowadays many parents give a name without constraint, but people normally ask the elder of the family or visit a naming agency. They believe the child's name as well as the date and time of birth, has a positive influence on the child's life. Of all the Korean family names, Kim is the most common, accounting for 21 percent of the total, followed by Lee (14%), Park, Choi, Jeong and Kang. A Korean woman does not use their husband's family name even after marriage. Although children mainly use their father's family name, some people use the family names of both parents these days.

성 family name, surname
이름 first name, given name
대부분 mainly, largely
글자 character
N(으)로 되어 있다 consist of N
첫 first
나머지 rest
먼저 first
그다음에 then, later
이름을 짓다 to give a name
V_R을/ㄹ 때 when V
좋은 good

의미 meaning
고르다 to select, to pick
최근에 recently
자유롭게 without constraint, freely
부모 parents
집안 어른 an elder (member) of the family
부탁하다 to ask
V_R거나 V or
작명소 naming agency
찾다 to visit/find

태어나다 to be born
V_R는다고 생각하다 to think/believe that V
제일 the most, first
결혼 marriage
후 after
남편 husband
V_R지 않다 do not V
하지만 but, yet, however
함께 together
경우 case

호칭 *
Titles Addressing People

한국 사람들은 같은 나이의 친구가 아니면 서로를 이름으로 부르는 경우가 적다. 대부분 상대방과의 관계에 따른 호칭으로 부른다. 형제 사이에서 동생은 이름으로 부르지만, 자기보다 나이가 많은 형제는 형, 언니, 누나, 오빠라는 호칭을 사용한다. 또한 한국 사회에서는 가족 호칭인 어머니, 아버지, 아저씨, 아줌마, 이모 등은 가족이 아닌 사람에게도 사용한다. 길에서도 모르는 노인을 할아버지 또는 할머니라고 부른다. 직장에서는 상대방의 성 뒤에 직급을 붙여 "김 과장", "박 부장님" 등으로 부른다. 호칭은 한국인들에게도 아주 복잡하지만 인간관계에서 중요한 역할을 한다.

1 자기보다 나이가 많은 여자 형제를 뭐라고 부릅니까?
What do Koreans call an older female sibling in Korean?

2 길에서 모르는 노인을 어떻게 부릅니까?
What do Koreans call an old person they don't know on the street?

Koreans seldom call each other by name unless they are friends of the same age. They address each other by a title according to the relationship with the other party. For an older sibling, titles such as *hyeong* (older brother for a man), *eonni* (older sister for a woman), *nuna* (older sister for a man), and *oppa* (older brother for a woman) are used. In Korean society, the family titles of mother, father, uncle, aunt and *imo* (aunt who is mother's sister) are used for people who are not real family members. When Koreans meet an old person they don't know on the street, they address the person as Grandfather or Grandmother. At work, they use a job title after the other party's family name, calling them 'Kim *Gwajang*' or 'Park *Bujang-nim*.' Titles are quite complicated even for Koreans, but they play an important role in interpersonal relationships.

호칭 title, name
같은 like
V_R(으)면 If V
서로 each other
부르다 to call
경우 case
적다 few
상대방 the other party
관계 relationship, relations
N에 따른 according to N
형제 sibling
사이 relationship, relations
동생 younger sibling
자기 self
N보다 than N
나이가 많은 older, elder

형 *hyeong* (older brother for a man)
언니 *eonni* (older sister for a woman)
누나 *nuna* (older sister for a man)
오빠 *oppa* (older brother for a woman)
사회 society
아저씨 uncle
아줌마 aunt
이모 aunt (mother's sister)
등 and the like
길 street
모르는 unknown
노인 old person
할아버지 grandfather

또는 or
할머니 grandmother
직장 office, work
성 family name
직급 job title
붙이다 to add
과장 *gwajang* (manager)
부장 *bujang* (senior manager)
N님 N-*nim* (-*nim* after a name or a title indicates the highest form of honorifics)
복잡하다 to be complicated
인간 관계 interpersonal relationship
중요한 important
역할을 하다 to play a role

005

숫자 *
Numbers

한국의 숫자는 고유어와 한자어가 있다. 고유어는 '하나, 둘, 셋…'이고, 한자어는 '일, 이, 삼…'이다. 보통 양은 고유어를 사용하고 순서는 한자어를 사용한다. 나이를 말할 때 보통 고유어로 '한 살, 두 살, 세 살…'을 사용하지만 서류에는 한자어로 '일 세, 이 세, 삼 세…'를 사용한다. 날짜, 가격, 전화번호는 한자어를 쓴다. 2016년 6월 6일은 '이천십육 년 유 월 육 일'이라고 하고, 38,400원은 '삼만 팔천사백 원'이라고 한다. 또 전화번호 010-9703-4863은 '공일공에 구칠공삼에 사팔육삼'이라고 한다. 그러나 시간을 말할 때는 시는 고유어로, 분은 한자어로 말한다. 8시 36분은 '여덟 시 삼십육 분'이라고 한다. 건물의 층을 말할 때는 '일 층, 이 층, 삼 층'이라고 한다.

문제
Questions

1 다음 시간을 말해 보세요. 11시 30분입니다.
Please say the following time in Korean: It is 11:30.

2 다음 전화번호를 말해 보세요. 010-2290-3368입니다.
Please say the following phone number in Korean: 010-2290-3368

There are native and Sino-Korean words for Korean numbers. 1, 2, 3 are '*hana*, *dul*, *set*' in native words and '*il*, *i*, *sam*' in Sino-Korean words. In general, native words are used for quantity and Sino-Korean words are used for an order. When Koreans mention age, they commonly use native words like '*han-sal*, *du-sal*, *se-sal*,' but on formal documents, they use Sino-Korean words like '*il-se*, *i-se*, *sam-se*.' For dates, prices, and telephone numbers, Sino-Korean words are used. That is why you read 2016-06-06 as '*icheonsibyuk-nyeon yu-wol yuk-il*,' and KRW 38,400 as '*samman palcheon sabaek won*.' If the phone number is 010-9703-4863, you read *it as* '*gong-il-gong-eh gu-chil-gong-sam-eh sa-pal-yuk-sam*.' But for time, you use native words for the hour and Sino-Korean words for minutes. Therefore, 08:36 reads as '*yeodeolb-si samsibyuk-bun*.' When you refer to the floor of a building, you say '*il-cheung, i-cheung, sam-cheung*.'

숫자 number	세 age	원 won
고유어 native word	날짜 date	그러나 but
한자어 Sino-Korean word	가격 price	시/시간 hour/time
양 quantity	쓰다 to use	분 minute
사용하다 to use	N(이)라고 하다 to say N	건물 building
순서 order	만 ten thousand	층 floor
나이 age	천 one thousand	
서류 document	백 one hundred	

006

나이 *
Age

한국 사람들은 처음 만나면 보통 나이를 묻는다. 나이는 한국 사회에서 말투와 위아래 관계를 정하는 데 중요하기 때문이다. 보통 나이를 물을 때는 "몇 살이에요?"라고 묻고 어른들에게는 "연세가 어떻게 되세요?"라는 존댓말을 사용한다. "무슨 띠예요?"라고 간접적으로 물을 때도 있다. 한국에는 한국 나이와 만 나이가 있다. 2023년 6월 28일부터 '만 나이 통일법'이 시행되었다. 한국 나이는 일상생활에서 주로 사용하지만 공식적인 문서에서는 만 나이를 사용한다. 지금까지 한국 나이는 태어난 날에 한 살이고 다음 해 부터는 1월 1일에 한 살을 더 먹었다. 이제는 다른 나라들처럼 만 나이로 계산하여 각자의 생일에 한 살을 더 먹는다. 새 법이 시행되어 한국 나이 사용 풍습이 변화될 전망이다.

문제
Questions

1 한국에는 어떤 나이가 있습니까?
What kinds of age are there in Korea?

2 간접적으로 나이를 물을 때 어떻게 말합니까?
What do Koreans say when they indirectly ask the other person's age?

When Koreans meet someone for the first time, they generally ask how old the other person is. It is because age is very important to determine the manner of speech and superior-subordinate relationship. When asking how old the person is, they generally say, "*Myeotsal-ieyo?*", and they respectfully say "*Yeonsega eoteokke doeseyo?*" to seniors. Sometimes, Koreans indirectly ask how old someone is by saying, "In what animal year were you born?" There are the Korean age and the age after the day you are born (*man-nai*) in Korea. The 'Man-nai Unification Act' came into effect on June 28, 2023. The Korean age is mainly used in everyday life, but in official documents the age after the day you were born is used. Until now, Koreans were one year old on the day they were born, and from the following year, they turned one older on January 1st. Now, like in other countries, people age one year more on their birthdays. With the new law coming into effect, Korean age customs are expected to change.

어휘와 표현 Words & Expression

나이 age
처음 first
V_R(으)면 if V
묻다 to ask
사회 society
말투 the manner/way of speech
위아래 관계 superior-subordinate relationship
정하다 to determine
V_R는 데 to V

중요하다 to be important
때문이다 It is because
V_R을/ㄹ 때 when/if V
어른들 seniors, elders
N에게 to N
연세 age (honorific)
존댓말 honorific
띠 animal year
긴접적으로 indirectly

만 나이 age after the day you are born
일상생활 everyday life
사용하다 to use
공식적 official
문서 document
태어나다 to be born
날 day
그다음 해 the following year
더 more

007

결혼식 ★★
Wedding Ceremony

한국에서는 두 사람이 결혼 약속을 하면 양가 부모와 가족들이 만나서 첫인사를 하는데 이를 상견례라 한다. 상견례 이후에 결혼식 날짜를 정한 뒤 청첩장을 보내고 결혼식을 준비하는데 주로 예식장, 호텔 또는 교회나 성당에서 한다. 봄, 가을은 결혼식을 많이 하는 시즌이라서 미리 예식장을 예약해야 한다. 결혼식 전에 신부 집에서 신랑 집으로 혼수와 예단을 보내고, 신랑 집은 신부 집으로 함을 전달한다. 신랑 친구들은 함을 전달할 때 흥겹게 큰소리로 "함 사세요."라고 외치며 동네에 결혼식을 알린다. 결혼식 날에는 일반적으로 신랑신부가 정장 턱시도와 웨딩드레스를 입고 결혼식을 하고, 식이 끝나면 한복으로 갈아입고 '폐백'을 드린다. '폐백'은 가족들에게 큰절을 드리며 인사하는 의식이다. 그리고 피로연을 마친 후 신혼여행을 떠난다. 신혼여행에서 돌아오면 먼저 신부 집에 들르고 친정어머니가 준비한 '이바지 음식'을 가지고 신랑 집으로 간다.

1 한국은 언제가 결혼 시즌입니까?
When is the wedding season in Korea?

2 식이 끝난 후 신랑 신부가 가족들에게 큰절하는 의식을 뭐라고 부릅니까?
What do you call the traditional ritual after a wedding ceremony in which the bride and the groom make a deep bow to their families?

In Korea, when two people have decided to get married, parents and members of both families meet for the first time, which is called *sanggyeonnye* (meeting between families of the bride and the groom). After this meeting, they determine the date of the wedding, send out invitations and prepare for the wedding. The venue is usually a wedding hall, a hotel, or a Christian or a Catholic church. Koreans need to make a reservation for the wedding venue well in advance during spring and fall, as these are the busy wedding seasons. Before the wedding, the bride's family sends gifts to the groom's family and the groom's family sends a wedding gift chest to the bride's home. When the friends of the groom deliver this wedding gift chest, they yell cheerfully and loudly, "*Ham-saseyo!* (Buy the wedding gift chest!)," telling the neighborhood that there is a wedding. On the wedding day, the bride and the groom are generally dressed in Western clothes like a tuxedo and a wedding gown for the ceremony. After the ceremony, they change into traditional *hanbok* for *pyebaek*. *Pyebaek* is the ritual of paying respects to both families by making a deep bow. After the wedding banquet, the bride and groom leave for their honeymoon. When they come back from the honeymoon, the couple visits the bride's home first, takes the *ibaji* food prepared by the bride's mother, and goes to the groom's home.

결혼식 wedding ceremony
양가 both families
상견례 *sanggyeonnye*, meeting between families of the bride and the groom
청첩장 wedding invitation
예식장 wedding hall
또는 or
교회 Christian church
성당 Catholic church
시즌 season
미리 in advance
신부 bride
신랑 groom

혼수 예단 wedding gifts
함 wedding gift chest
전달하다 to deliver
흥겹게 cheerfully
외치다 to yell
동네 neighborhood, village
알리다 to tell, to inform
정장 formal suit
턱시도 tuxedo
웨딩드레스 wedding gown
갈아입다 to change
폐백 *pyebaek*, a ritual of paying respects to both families by making a deep bow

드리다 to give
큰절 deep bow
의식 ritual
피로연 wedding banquet
마치다 to finish
신혼여행 honeymoon
먼저 first
N에 들르다 to visit N
친정어머니 (married woman's) mother
이바지 음식 *ibaji* food, food carefully prepared by the bride's mother for the groom's family

교육 제도 ★★
Educational System

한국의 교육은 초등학교 6년, 중학교 3년, 고등학교 3년, 대학교 4년 제도이다. 의무 교육은 초등학교 7세부터 중학교 15세까지이다. 공립 학교와 사립 학교로 나눠지고, 일반 학교와 특수 목적 고등학교, 자율 고등학교로 나눠진다. 일반 학교는 보통 거주 지역에 따라 추첨을 통해서 학교 배정을 받지만 시험을 통해 특수 목적 고등학교에 입학할 수 있다. 특수 목적 고등학교의 종류에는 예술 고등학교, 과학 고등학교, 외국어 고등학교가 있고 직업 교육 특성화 고등학교 등이 있다. 일반 고등학교를 지원하는 학생들은 명문 학교에 가기 위해 학군이 좋은 곳으로 이사를 하는 경우가 종종 있다. 특히 서울의 강남구와 서초구는 명문 사립 학교가 많아서 강남 8학군이라고 부른다. 한국에서 가장 중요한 시험은 대학 입학 시험이다. 기본적으로 대학 학사는 4년 과정이고 석사는 대학원에서 2~3년, 박사는 3년 과정이다.

문제
Questions

1 한국의 의무 교육은 몇 살까지입니까?
To what age does the mandatory education apply in Korea?

2 한국 대학 학사는 몇 년입니까?
How long is the undergraduate university degree in Korea?

Korea's educational system consists of six years of elementary school, three years of middle school, three years of high school, and four years of university. Its mandatory education is between age 7 in elementary school and age 15 in middle school. Schools are divided into public and private. High schools are classified into general, special purpose and autonomous high schools. While general high schools are assigned by a lucky draw system according to the area of residence, it is possible to go to a special purpose or autonomous private high school by taking a test. The types of special purpose high schools include arts, science, foreign languages, and vocational and technical. Students applying to a general high school often move to a neighborhood in a good school district. In particular, Gangnam-gu and Seocho-gu of Seoul, with many prestigious private schools, are called the 8th School District. The most important test in Korea is the university entrance exam. An undergraduate degree is basically a 4-year program; a master's is a 2-to-3 year program and doctoral degree is a 3-year program in graduate school.

교육 education (al)
제도 system
초등학교 elementary school
중학교 middle school
고등학교 high school
대학교 university
의무 mandatory
공립 public
사립 private
일반 학교 general school
특수 special
목적 purpose
자율 autonomous

거주 residential, residence
지역 region, area
N에 따라 according to N
추첨 lottery, lucky draw
N을/를 통해서 through N
배정을 받다 to be assigned
입학하다 to enter
예술 arts
과학 science
직업 vocation(al)
특성화 고등학교 vocational and technical high school
지원하다 to apply

명문 prestigious
학군 school district
경우 case
종종 often
특히 in particular
강남 Gangnam
구 gu (Korean administrative district)
학사 undergraduate degree
과정 program, course
석사 master's degree
대학원 graduate school
박사 doctoral degree, ph.D.

009

대학 입학 시험 ★★★
University Entrance Exam

한국의 교육열은 세계적으로 유명하다. 학생들은 어려서부터 학교 교육뿐만 아니라 성적을 높이기 위해서 과외 수업을 받는 것이 일반적이다. 이렇게 치열하게 경쟁하는 이유는 명문 대학에 들어가기 위해서이다. 고등학교 내신 성적과 대학에서 보는 논술 시험 등도 중요하지만 대학 입학을 위해 가장 중요한 것은 '수능'이라고 불리는 대학 수학 능력 시험이다. 수능 시험은 3학년이 끝나는 11월 중순에 보는데 시험 보는 날 분위기는 매우 독특하다. 가족들이 수험생의 합격을 바라며 대학교 교문에 엿을 붙이기도 하고 선후배들이 수험생들을 격려하고 응원한다. 또한 듣기 평가에 방해가 되지 않도록 그 시간에 비행기나 헬리콥터 운항을 제한하고, 수험생의 등교 시간에 방해되지 않도록 회사에서는 출근 시간을 늦추기도 한다. 수험생 가족들은 백일 전부터 교회나 성당, 절을 찾아가서 기도를 하기도 한다.

1 한국의 대학 입학 시험을 무엇이라고 부릅니까?

What is the university entrance exam in Korea called?

2 합격을 바라는 마음으로 교문 앞에 붙이는 '이것'의 이름은 무엇입니까?

What do people stick to the front gates of universities wishing students good luck to pass the test?

Korea's education fever has worldwide fame. It is customary that from a young age, students have not only regular school education but also private lessons to get better grades. The reason for such heated competition is to enter a prestigious university. While high school academic reports and essay tests given by universities are important, the so-called CSAT, or College Scholastic Ability Test called *suneung* is the most important to enter a university. The CSAT is done at the end of the high school senior year in mid-November, and the atmosphere on this day of the test is quite unique. Families stick *yeot* (sticky taffy) to the front gates of university buildings, hoping for the admission of test takers. Also, seniors and juniors from the same high school cheer and support the test takers. In order not to disturb the listening test, airplanes and helicopters are restricted to fly during the test time. Companies delay work hours so as not to hinder test takers as they go to school for their test. Some families of test takers visit Christian or Catholic churches or Buddhist temples from 100 days prior to the test and offer prayers.

대학 입학 시험 university entrance exam
교육열 education fever
세계적으로 worldwide
어려서부터 from young age
교육 education
성적 grade
높이다 to increase
과외 수업 private lesson
일반적이다 to be customary
치열하게 heatedly
경쟁하다 to compete
이유 reason
명문 대학 prestigious university
내신 성적 academic reports

논술 시험 essay test
수능 CSAT
대학 수학 능력 시험 College Scholastic Ability Test
학년 school year
중순 mid
분위기 atmosphere
독특하다 to be unique
수험생 test takers
합격 admission
바라다 to wish
교문 front gate of school
엿 *yeot*, Korean taffy
선후배 seniors and juniors
격려하다 to cheer

응원을 하다 to support
평가 evaluation
방해가 되다 to disturb
V_R지 않도록 in order not to V
헬리콥터 helicopter
운항 to fly
제한하다 to restrict
등교 to go to school
출근 to go to work
늦추다 to delay, to postpone
교회 Christian church
성당 Catholic church
절 Buddhist temple
기도 prayer

010

병역 의무 ★
Duty of Military Service

대한민국 국적의 남자들은 만 18세부터 병역 의무가 있다. 학생들은 공부를 마칠 때까지 입대를 연기할 수 있다. 병역 기간은 육군과 해병대는 18개월, 해군은 20개월, 공군은 21개월인데 5주 동안 기본 군사 훈련을 받은 후에 부대에 배치된다. 계급에 따라서 다르지만 60만 원부터 100만 원정도까지의 월급도 받는다. 입대 날에는 부모님, 친구들, 또는 여자 친구가 훈련소까지 같이 갈 수 있다.

1 대한민국 남자는 몇 살부터 병역 의무가 있습니까?

At what age does a Korean man become required to fulfill his duty of military service?

2 병역 기간은 얼마 동안입니까?

How long is the period of military service?

Men of Korean nationality have a duty of military service starting from the age of 18, but students can postpone enlistment until they finish their study. The period of military service is 18 months for the Army and the Marine Corps, 20 months for the Navy, and 21 months for the Air Force. After basic military training for five weeks, the men are deployed to a camp. They get a monthly pay of about from 600 thousand won to 1million won, although the amount differs according to rank. On the day of enlistment, parents, friends or girlfriends can accompany the men to the training camp.

Words & Expression

병역 military service
의무 duty
대한민국 Republic of Korea
국적 nationality
만 age after the day of you are born
마치다 to finish
V_R을/ㄹ 때 when V
입대 enlistment

연기하다 to postpone
V_R을/ㄹ 수 있다 can V
기간 period
개월 month
주 week
동안 for, during
기본 군사 훈련 basic military training
부대 camp

배치되다 to be stationed
계급 rank
N에 따라서 according to N
다르다 to differ
N 정도 about N
월급 monthly pay
날 day
또는 or
훈련소 training camp

011

설날 *
Seollal (New Year's Day)

새해의 첫날을 설날이라고 한다. 설날은 추석과 함께 한국에서 가장 중요한 명절이다. 양력 설날과 음력 설날이 있다. 전통적으로 음력 설날이 양력 설날보다 더 중요해서 삼 일을 쉰다. 이날은 가족들이 모두 모여 새해를 맞이하기 때문에 오랫동안 만나지 못한 친척, 친지들을 만날 수 있다. 설날 아침에는 보통 한복을 입고 조상님께 차례를 지낸다. 그리고 나서 집안 어른들과 존경하는 어른들께 세배를 한다. 어른에게 세배를 드릴 때는 "새해 복 많이 받으세요."라고 말한다. 세배를 하면 어른들은 아이들에게 세뱃돈을 준다. 그리고 가족과 함께 떡국을 먹는다.

1 설날 아침 어른들께 하는 인사를 무엇이라고 합니까?
On the morning of New Year's Day, Koreans pay respect to elders. What is it called?

2 설날에 무엇을 먹습니까?
What do Koreans eat on Seollal?

The first day of a new year is called *Seollal*. This New Year's Day is the most important traditional holiday in Korea, together with *Chuseok*. There is the Solar New Year's Day on January 1 and the Lunar New Year's Day. Traditionally, the Lunar New Year's Day has been considered more important, so people take a break for three days. Since all family members gather together to welcome the new year on this day, people can meet relatives and close friends they have not seen for a long while. On the morning of *Seollal*, Koreans normally wear *hanbok* and perform an ancestral rite. Then they perform *sebae*, making a deep new year's bow to the elder members of the family and other seniors whom they respect. When Koreans bow to seniors, they say, "*Sahae bok mani badeuseyo* (All the best for the New Year)!" After the new year's bow is done, elders give children money gifts. Then they eat *tteokguk* (sliced rice cake soup) with the family.

설날 *Seollal* (New Year's Day)

새해 new year

첫날 first day

가장 the most

명절 traditional holiday

양력 solar calendar

음력 lunar calendar

보다 더 more

중요하다 to be important

쉬다 to rest

가족 family

모이다 to gather together

오랫동안 for a long time

V$_R$지 못하다 could not V

친척 relatives

친지 close friend

한복 *hanbok*

입다 to wear

조상 ancestor

–께 to (honorific)

차례를 지내다 to perform an ancestral rite

집안 어른 elder members of the family

존경하다 to respect

세배를 하다/드리다 to make a deep bow

복 good luck

V$_R$ (으)면 if V

–에게 to

세뱃돈 money gift for new year's bow

N와/과 함께 with N

떡국 *tteokguk* (sliced rice cake soup)

012

추석 *
Chuseok

음력 8월 15일은 추석이다. 추석은 온 가족이 모여서 조상님께 한 해의 추수를 감사드리는 전통 명절이다. 전통적으로 추석과 설날에는 한복을 입는다. 그리고 햇곡식과 햇과일로 음식을 만들어 조상님께 차례도 지낸다. 대표적인 추석 음식으로 송편이 있다. 송편은 그 해에 추수한 밤, 깨, 콩, 팥 등을 넣어서 만드는 떡이다. 밤에는 보름달을 보고 소원을 빌기도 한다. 이처럼 추석은 한국인에게 중요한 명절이기 때문에 3일의 휴일 동안 고향에 가는 사람들이 많다. 그래서 고속 도로의 교통이 복잡하고, 미리 예약하지 않으면 대중교통 표를 구하기 어렵다. 그렇지만 선물을 준비해서 고향으로 가는 사람들의 마음은 즐겁고 행복하다.

1 추석은 언제입니까?
When is *Chuseok*?

2 추석에 먹는 떡 이름이 무엇입니까?
What is the name of the rice cake Koreans eat on *Chuseok*?

August 15 by the lunar calendar is *Chuseok. Chuseok* is a traditional holiday when all family members gather together and thank ancestors for the year's harvest. Traditionally, people have worn *hanbok* on *Chuseok* and *Seollal.* On *Chuseok*, people make food with newly-harvested grains and fruits, performing ancestral rites and expressing gratitude. The signature food of *Chuseok* is *songpyeon. Songpyeon* is a type of rice cake made with fillings of that year's crops such as chestnut, sesame, bean and red bean. People also watch the full moon at night and make a wish. Thus, *Chuseok* is an important traditional holiday for Koreans, and many people return to their hometown during the three-day holidays. Naturally, there is heavy traffic on the highways, and it is difficult to get a public transportation ticket without making a reservation for in advance. But people still feel pleased and happy as they return to their hometown with gifts they have prepared.

추석 *Chuseok*
음력 lunar calendar
온 all
모이다 to gather together
조상님 ancestor
–께 to (honorific)
한 해 one year
추수 harvest
감사드리다 to thank
전통 tradition
명절 traditional holiday
한복 *hanbok*
햇곡식 a new crop of grain
햇과일 newly-harvested fruit

차례를 지내다 to perform ancestral rite
송편 *songpyeon*, rice cake made with various fillings
추수하다 to harvest
밤 chestnut
깨 sesame
콩 soy bean
팥 red bean
등 and the like
넣다 to put
떡 rice cake
보름달 full moon
소원을 빌다 to make a wish
휴일 holiday

고향 hometown
고속 도로 highway
교통 traffic
대중교통 public transportation
표 ticket
미리 in advance
예약하다 to book, to make a reservation
그렇지만 but
선물 gift
준비하다 to prepare
N(으)로 to N
마음 heart
즐겁다 to be pleased
행복하다 to be happy

013

한의학 ★★★
Traditional Korean Medicine

한의학은 한국의 전통 의학이다. 사람의 몸은 작은 우주로 기관들 사이에 흐름이 있다고 보고 병을 치료한다. 한국 사람들은 보통 서양 의학과 한의학을 함께 이용한다. 한의원에서는 침, 뜸, 부항 등을 이용한 치료를 하고 한약을 처방한다. 서울 경동시장, 경상도 영천 한약재 시장에 가면 약 400여 종의 한약재를 살 수 있다. 한의학에서 가장 잘 알려진 책은 《동의보감》이다. 이 책은 한의학의 백과사전이라고 할 수 있다. 조선 시대 한의사 허준(1537~1615)이 썼는데 그에 관한 드라마가 만들어질 정도로 유명하다. 이 책은 조선 한의학에 큰 영향을 미쳤을 뿐만 아니라, 18세기에 일본과 중국에도 소개됐고, 다른 여러 나라에서도 번역이 됐다. 《동의보감》은 2009년에 유네스코 기록 유산에 등재됐다.

1 한의학의 치료 방법은 무엇입니까?
What are the treatment methods of traditional Korean medicine?

2 유네스코 기록 유산에 등재된 한의학 책은 무엇입니까? 그리고 저자는 누구입니까?
What is the book on traditional Korean medicine listed on UNESCO's Memory of the World Register? Who is the author?

Traditional Korean medicine is the country's traditional study of medicine. It considers that the human body is a small universe where there are flows among organs in treating diseases. Koreans generally use both Western and Korean medicine. Traditional Korean medical clinics perform treatments using acupuncture, cautery and cupping, and prescribe herbal medicine. If you visit Seoul Gyeongdong Market or Yeongcheon Medicinal Herb Market in Gyeongsang-do, you can buy around 400 types of medicinal herbs. The most famous book on traditional Korean medicine is *Donguibogam: Principles and Practice of Eastern Medicine* by Heo Jun. Heo Jun (1537~1615) was a doctor of Joseon era, whose fame led to the creation of a contemporary TV drama series. His book *Donguibogam* can be called an encyclopedia of traditional Korean medicine. The book not only exerted a huge influence on the study of medicine in Joseon, but also was introduced to Japan and China in the 18th century. It has been translated in many other countries. *Donguibogam* was listed on UNESCO's Memory of the World Register in 2009.

한의학 traditional Korean medicine

전통 tradition

의학 medicine

몸 body

우주 universe

기관 organ

흐름 flow

치료하다 to treat

서양 의학 Western medicine

한의원 traditional Korean medical clinic

침 acupuncture

뜸 cautery

부항 cupping

한약 herbal medicine

처방하다 to prescribe

경동시장 Gyeongdong Market

경상도 Gyengsang-do, Gyeongsang Province

영천 Yeongcheon

한약재 medicinal herb

알려지다 to become well-known

《동의보감》 *Donguibogam: Principles and Practice of Eastern Medicine*

백과사전 encyclopedia

조선시대 Joseon era

허준 Heo Jun

한의사 traditional Korean medical doctor

V$_R$을/ㄹ 정도로 as to V

영향을 미치다 to exert influence

세기 century

소개되다 to be introduced

번역이 되다 to be translated

기록 유산 Memory of the World Register

등재되다 to list

014

노래방 *
Noraebang (Singing Room)

노래방은 돈을 내고 노래를 부를 수 있는 오락 시설이다. 노래방 가격은 보통 시간당 지불하는데 코인 노래방처럼 곡 당 지불하는 경우도 있다. 한국 사람들은 보통 노래하기를 좋아한다. 그래서 노래방이 아주 많고 한 건물 전체가 노래방인 경우도 있다. 코인 노래방과 헤드셋 노래방처럼 종류도 다양하다. 직장인들이 회식 후에 노래방에 가기도 하고 친구들과 생일 파티를 노래방에서 하기도 한다. 음료수도 주문할 수 있다. 이렇게 한국인들은 직장 동료들끼리, 친구들끼리, 가족들끼리 노래를 부르러 노래방에 간다.

1 돈을 내고 노래하는 오락 시설을 뭐라고 부릅니까?
What do you call an entertainment facility where you pay to sing a song?

2 노래방 가격은 보통 어떻게 지불합니까?
How is the singing room generally paid for?

Noraebang is an entertainment facility where you can pay to sing a song. The price of the singing room is generally on a pay-per-hour system, but there is also a pay-per-song system as applied by *Coin Noraebang*. Koreans generally like to sing, that is why there are so many singing rooms. In certain cases, a whole building is filled with singing rooms. The types vary, such as *Coin Noraebang* and *Headset Noraebang*. Office workers go to the singing room after a work and dinner and friends go to the singing room to have a birthday party. You can also order drinks there. Thus, Koreans go to a singing room with colleagues at work, with friends and with family.

노래방 *noraebang*, singing room   건물 building   음료수 drinks
돈을 내다 to pay (money)   전체 whole   주문하다 to order
오락 entertainment   경우 case   V$_R$을/ㄹ 수 있다 can V
시설 facility   헤드셋 headset   이렇게 thus
가격 price   종류 type   직장 동료 colleagues at work
시간당 per hour   다양하다 to be various, to vary   끼리 among, with
지불하다 to pay   직장인 office worker   V$_R$(으)러 가다 to go to V
코인 coin   회식 team dinner, company dinner
V$_R$기를 좋아하다 to like to V   V$_R$기도 하다 may V

015

찜질방 ★★
Jjimjilbang (Korean Dry Sauna)

찜질방은 피로를 풀기 위해 가는 한국식 사우나이다. 찜질방에는 다양한 사우나 시설이 있다. 쑥 사우나, 황토 사우나, 참숯 사우나, 소금 사우나처럼 뜨거운 사우나도 있지만, 얼음 사우나처럼 차가운 사우나도 있다. 목욕탕도 다양해서 찻물, 쑥물, 수압을 이용한 마사지 시설 등이 골고루 갖추어진 경우가 많다. 찜질방은 남녀가 같이 이용하는데 목욕탕은 따로 이용한다. 보통 찜질방에서는 티셔츠와 반바지와 수건을 빌려준다. 또한 PC방, 오락실, 영화방, 노래방, 헬스클럽, 식당 등이 있어서 편리하게 이용할 수 있다. 사우나의 열기를 이용해서 구운 계란과 식혜를 먹는 것도 찜질방의 별미이다. 대부분 24시간 영업을 하기 때문에 이곳에서 잠을 잘 수도 있다. 그래서 여행자들도 많이 이용한다.

문제
Questions

1 한국식 사우나는 무엇입니까?
What is a Korean-style sauna called?

2 찜질방을 왜 여행자들이 많이 이용합니까?
Why do travelers often use *jjimjilbang*?

Jjimjilbang is a Korean dry sauna where people visit to recover from fatigue. It has various sauna facilities: there are hot ones like mugwort sauna, red clay sauna, charcoal sauna and salt sauna, and there are also cold ones like ice sauna. The bath tubs are also diverse, often offering a well assorted set-up including water infused with tea or mugwort, or a massage facility using water pressure. The dry sauna facilities are used both by men and women, but the baths are separately used between men and women. In general, *jjimjilbang* lends customers a t-shirt, a pair of shorts and a towel. The *jjimjilbang* is convenient to use as it also has an Internet café, game room, movie room, singing room, gym, restaurants and other facilities inside. The delicacy of Korean dry sauna includes baked egg using the heat of sauna and *sikhye* (sweet rice drink). Most of the *jjimjilbang* are open 24 hours, so you can sleep there. That is why travelers often use this place.

찜질방 *jjimjilbang*, Korean Dry Sauna

피로를 풀다 to recover from fatigue

V_R기 위해 to V

한국식 Korean, Korean-style

사우나 sauna

쑥 mugwort

황토 red clay

참숯 charcoal

소금 salt

N처럼 like N

뜨겁다 to be hot

얼음 ice

차갑다 to be cold

목욕탕 bath tub

찻물 tea infused water

수압 water pressure

마사지 massage

시설 facility

골고루 well-assorted

갖추다 to be equipped with

남녀 men and women

따로 separately

티셔츠 t-shirt

반바지 shorts

수건 towel

빌려주다 to lend

PC방 PC room, internet café

오락실 game room

영화방 movie room

헬스클럽 gym

열기 heat

굽다 to bake

계란 egg

식혜 *sikhye*, sweet rice drink

별미 delicacy

영업을 하다 to open

때문에 because of, that is why

여행자 traveler

단풍놀이 ★★
Fall Foliage Picnic

한국의 가을 산은 빨간색, 주황색, 노란색 등으로 물드는 단풍으로 유명하다. 많은 한국인들이 단풍을 구경하러 산에 가는데 이것을 '단풍놀이'라고 한다. 단풍놀이는 가족이나 친구들과 가거나, '단풍 관광버스'나 '단풍 열차'를 타고 단체로 떠나기도 한다. 단풍으로 가장 유명한 산은 계곡, 바위, 절벽이 아름다운 설악산이고, 그다음이 '가을 산'으로 불리는 내장산이다. 서울에서도 단풍놀이를 즐길 수 있는 곳이 많다. 가을이면 거리가 온통 노란 은행잎으로 뒤덮이는 경복궁, 단풍잎으로 유명한 창덕궁 후원, 덕수궁 돌담길, 남산 산책로, 북한산 등도 볼 만하다.

1 단풍을 보러 가는 것을 뭐라고 부릅니까?
What do you call the activity to go and see fall foliage?

2 단풍으로 유명한 산을 써 보십시오.
Please write down the names of the mountains famous for autumn foliage.

Korean mountains in fall are famous for their foliage colored red, orange, yellow, etc. Many Koreans go to the mountains to view fall foliage, which is called fall foliage picnic. People may go on this picnic with family and friends, or in a group riding fall foliage tourist bus or fall foliage train. The most famous mountain for fall foliage is Seoraksan Mountain with beautiful valleys, rocks and cliffs, followed by Naejangsan Mountain which is known as the Autumn Mountain. There are many other places in Seoul where you can enjoy a fall foliage picnic. It is worth seeing Gyeongbokgung Palace whose nearby streets are covered with yellow gingko leaves, Huwon Garden of Changdeokgung Palace famous for maple leaves, the stonewall walkway of Deoksugung Palace, Namsan Mountain trails and Bukhansan Mountain.

어휘와 표현 Words & Expression

단풍놀이 fall foliage picnic
빨간색 red (color)
주황색 orange (color)
노란색 yellow (color)
물들다 to be colored
V_R거나 V or
관광버스 tourist bus
열차 train
단체 group

계곡 valley
바위 rock
절벽 cliff
설악산 Seoraksan Mountain
불리다 to be called
내장산 Naejangsan Mountain
즐기다 to enjoy
온통 entirely
은행잎 gingko leaf

뒤덮이다 to be covered
경복궁 Gyeongbokgung Palace
창덕궁 후원 Huwon Garden of Changdeokgung Palace
덕수궁 Deoksugung Palace
돌담길 stonewall walkway
산책로 trail
북한산 Bukhansan Mountain
V_R을/ㄹ 만하다 to be worth V ing

017

등산 *
Hiking

한국에는 산이 많은데 도시 가운데에도 산이 있다. 그래서 가장 쉽게 할 수 있는 한국인들의 여가 활동은 등산이다. 산에 갈 때는 보통 등산복을 입고 배낭을 메는데 등산로가 있어서 등산하기에 편리하다. 특히 북한산 성벽길이나 둘레길을 걸으면 서울의 다양한 경치를 볼 수 있다. 한국의 산은 경사가 가파르고 바위들 사이로 계곡물이 흘러서 경치가 아주 좋다. 정상에 올라 "야호!"하고 소리를 지르면 시원한 기분을 느낄 수 있다. 등산 후에는 산 입구에 있는 식당에 가서 식사를 하거나 음료수를 마신다. 평소에 여가 시간이 많지 않은 한국 사람들에게 등산은 좋은 여가 활동이다.

1 한국에서 도시인들이 쉽게 할 수 있는 여가 활동이 무엇입니까?
What is the leisure activity that Korean city people can do the most easily?

2 서울의 유명한 등산로가 무엇입니까?
What are the famous hiking trails in Seoul?

There are many mountains in Korea, and some of them are right in the middle of the city. That is why the leisure activity that Koreans can do the most easily is hiking. When they go hiking, they usually wear climbing clothes and carry a backpack. Hiking is easy as there are many hiking trails. It is possible to view Seoul's diverse scenery by walking along the Fortress Wall Trail or Dullegil Trail at Bukhansan Mountain. The scenery in Korean mountains is great as slopes are steep and water runs among valleys. When people climb to the top and cry out, "*Yaho* (I made it)!," they can feel refreshed. After hiking, Koreans usually eat or drink at restaurants at the mountain entrance. To Koreans who usually do not have enough free time, hiking is a good leisure activity.

등산 hiking, mountain climbing
도시 city
가운데 in the middle
가장 the most
쉽게 easily
V_R을/ㄹ 수 있다 can V
여가 활동 leisure activity
등산복 climbing clothes
배낭을 메다 to carry a backpack
등산로 hiking trail
V_R아서/어서/여서 as/because V
편리하다 to be convenient

북한산 Bukhansan Mountain
성벽길 Fortress Wall Trail
N(이)나 N or
둘레길 Dullegil Trail
걷다 to walk
다양한 various
경치 landscape, scenery
경사 slope
가파르다 steep
바위 rock
사이 among, between
계곡물 water in the valley

흐르다 to run/flow
정상 top
오르다 to climb
야호 *Yaho!*, Viva, I made it
소리를 지르다 to cry out
V_R(으)면 if V
입구 entrance
V_R거나 V or
음료수 drink, beverage
평소 usually
V_R지 않다 to not V

018

집들이 *
Housewarming

한국에서는 이사를 하면 새집에 들어오는 액운을 막고 행운을 비는 고사를 지낸다. 그리고 가까운 사람들을 새 집에 초대하여 음식을 대접하는데 이를 집들이라고 한다. 집들이 선물은 다양하다. 세제나 비누 선물은 그 집의 행운이 거품처럼 잘 일어나고, 두루마리 휴지는 일들이 술술 잘 풀리라는 뜻이다. 가게에서는 이런 집들이 선물용 상품을 판다. 그리고 이사를 하면 팥 시루떡을 이웃에 돌려서 인사를 한다.

1 한국에서는 어떤 집들이 선물을 합니까?
What kinds of housewarming gifts are given in Korea?

2 이사를 하면 어떤 음식을 이웃에 돌립니까?
What kind of food do Koreans deliver to neighbors when they move to a new house?

In Korea, when people move into a new house, they perform a *gosa* ritual to prevent misfortune and pray for good luck. They invite close friends to the new house and serve food, which is called *Jipdeuli*. Gifts for housewarming are diverse. A gift of detergent or soap is meant to bring a lot of luck to the house, as soap makes a lot of bubbles rise, and a gift of toilet paper is meant for everything to go as smoothly as unrolling toilet paper does. Stores sell such housewarming gift items. When Koreans move to a new house, they deliver steamed rice cake topped with red beans to neighbors to greet them and say hello.

어휘와 표현   Words & Expression

집들이 housewarming

이사를 하다 to move into a new house

V_R(으)면 if V

새집 new house

액운 misfortune

막다 to prevent

행운 good luck

빌다 to wish, to pray

고사를 지내다 to perform a *gosa* ritual

선물 gift

다양하다 to be diverse

세제 detergent

N(이)나 N N or N

비누 soap

거품 lather, bubble

일어나다 to

두루마리 roll of paper

휴지 tissue, toilet paper

술술 easily, smoothly

풀리다 to unroll

V_R(으)라는 뜻이다 to be meant to V

선물용 상품 gift item

팔다 to sell

팥 시루떡 steamed rice cake topped with red beans

이웃 neighbor

돌리다 to give out, to deliver

인사하다 to greet

019

비상 시 긴급 전화 ★★
Emergency Phone Numbers

비상 전화번호는 나라마다 다르다. 한국에서는 다음과 같은 전화번호를 알아두면 편리하다. 화재, 재난, 응급 구조는 119, 도둑이나 소매치기와 같은 범죄 신고는 112, 미아 찾기나 가출 신고는 182, 테러 신고는 111로 전화하면 된다. 여성과 아동 보호를 위한 전화는 1366, 아동 학대의 경우는 129이다. 이주 여성 상담이나 통역 지원은 1577-1366에 전화하면 된다. 일기 예보는 131, 교통 정보는 1331에 전화하면 정보를 얻을 수 있다. 한국에서 여행할 때 1330으로 전화하면 관광 정보를 받을 수 있다.

1 한국에서 응급 구조는 몇 번입니까?
What is the emergency rescue number in Korea?

2 범죄 신고는 몇 번입니까?
What is the number to report a crime?

Each country has different emergency numbers. In Korea, it would be handy to remember the following phone numbers. You can call 119 for fire, disaster and emergency rescue; 112 to report a crime like theft or pickpocketing; 182 to find missing children or to report runaway persons; 111 to report terrorism; 1366 to protect women and children; 129 to report child abuse; 1577-1366 for counseling or translation support for migrant women; 131 for weather forecast information; and 1331 for traffic information. When you travel in Korea, you can call 1330 to get tourism information.

비상 시 emergency	소매치기 pickpocketing	학대 abuse
긴급 전화 emergency phone numbers	범죄 crime	경우 case
다르다 to be different	신고 report	이주 여성 migrant woman
N와/과 같은 like N	미아 missing children	상담 counseling
알아 두다 to remember	찾기 to find	통역 translation
편리하다 to be handy	가출 runaway	지원 support
화재 fire	테러 terrorism	일기 예보 weather forecast
재난 disaster	여성 woman	교통 traffic
응급 구조 emergency rescue	아동 child	정보 information
도둑 theft	보호 protection	관광 tourism, sightseeing

Korean Culture in 100 Keywords

외국인 학습자를 위한 한국 문화 100선

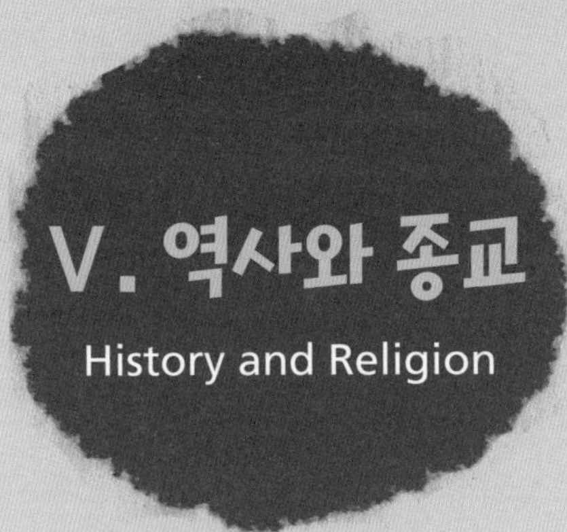

V. 역사와 종교
History and Religion

001

단군 신화 ★★
The Dangun Myth

건국 신화에 의하면, 하늘 신 환인은 환웅이라는 아들이 있었다. 환웅은 인간 세상에서 살기를 바랐다. 그래서 3,000명의 신하와 태백산으로 내려왔다. 그 산에는 호랑이와 곰이 살았는데 환웅을 찾아와서 "사람이 되고 싶습니다."라고 말했다. 환웅은 호랑이와 곰에게 사람이 되고 싶으면, 100일 동안 굴 속에서 마늘과 쑥을 먹으면서 지내라고 했다. 호랑이는 참지 못하고 굴에서 나왔지만, 곰은 어려움을 이겨내고 여자가 됐다. 이 여자와 환웅 사이에서 단군이 태어났다. 단군은 기원전 2333년에 고조선(기원전 2333~기원전 108)을 세우고 한민족의 시조가 됐다. 건국 기념일인 개천절은 10월 3일이다. 이날은 공휴일이다.

1 한민족의 시조는 누구입니까?
Who is the progenitor of the Korean people?

2 한국 건국 기념일을 뭐라고 부릅니까?
What is the national foundation day of Korea called?

According to the national foundation myth, Hwanin the Lord of Heaven had a son named Hwanwung. Hwanwung yearned to live in the human world, so he descended on Taebaeksan Mountain with 3,000 vassals. On the mountain lived a tiger and a bear; they came to Hwanwung and said, "We want to become humans." Hwanwung told the tiger and the bear that they had to spend 100 days in a cave eating only garlic and mugwort. While the tiger could not persevere and left the cave, the bear overcame the challenge and became a woman. Dangun was born to this woman and Hwanwung. Dangun founded Gojoseon (2333-108 BCE) in 2333 BCE and became the progenitor of the Korean people. *Gaecheonjeol*, National Foundation Day is on October 3, which is a national holiday.

단군 Dangun	V_R기를 바라다 to yearn to V	어려움 challenge, difficulty
신화 myth	신하 vassal, follower	이겨내다 to overcome
한반도 Korean peninsula	태백산 Taebaeksan Mountain	태어나다 to be born
역사 history	호랑이 tiger	기원전 BCE
건국 national foundation, to found a nation	곰 bear	고조선 Gojoseon, Ancient Joseon
	되다 to become	세우다 to found/establish
N에 의하면 according to N	굴 cave	한민족 the Korean people
하늘 신 Lord of Heaven	마늘 garlic	시조 progenitor
환인 Hwanin	쑥 mugwort	기념일 anniversary
환웅 Hwanwung	V_R(으)면서 V-ing	개천절 *Gaecheonjeol*, National Foundation Day
인간 human	참다 to persevere	
세상 world	V_R지 못하다 cannot V	공휴일 national holiday

002

원효대사 ★★★
Great Master Wonhyo

원효대사(617~686)는 신라 시대 스님으로 한국 불교계에서 가장 존경받는 스님이다. 그는 〈해골물 일화〉로 유명하다. 원효대사는 당나라로 유학 가다가 하룻밤을 동굴에서 지내게 되는데 자다가 목이 말라서 바가지에 담긴 물을 마시고 잠이 들었다. 그런데 그다음 날 아침에 그는 자신이 마신 물이 해골에 있었던 것을 보고 큰 깨달음을 얻었다. '모든 것이 내 마음에 달려 있다.'라는 진리를 깨달은 것이다. 그래서 당나라 유학을 포기하고 신라로 돌아온 후 불교 대중화에 힘썼다. 왕족과 권력층에 제한되어 있던 불교를 일반 백성들에게 가르친 것이다. 그는 백성들에게 어려운 교리를 몰라도 '나무아미타불' 부처님의 이름을 부르는 것만으로도 극락세계에 갈 수 있다는 희망을 주었다. 뿐만 아니라 원효대사는 중요한 불교 서적을 많이 남겨서 중국과 일본 불교에도 영향을 끼쳤다. 그 결과 지금까지도 원효 사상은 해외 유명 대학에서 연구되고 있다.

1 신라 시대의 스님으로 한국에서 가장 존경받는 스님은 누구입니까?
Who is the Buddhist monk of the Silla Dynasty that is most admired in Korea?

2 원효대사에 대한 유명한 일화는 무엇입니까?
What is the famous story involving Great Master Wonhyo?

Great Master Wonhyo (617-686 CE) was a Buddhist monk of the Silla Dynasty, and he was of the most respected monks in the Buddhist circle of Korea. He is famous for the 'Story of Water in a Skull.' When Wonhyo was on his way to Tang to study, he spent one night in a cave. He woke up from sleep because of thirst, found water in a large bowl, drank it and went back to sleep. But the next morning, he saw that the water he drank was inside a human skull and attained the great enlightenment. Wonhyo realized the truth that "Everything depends on the mind." He then gave up his plan to study in Tang and came back to Silla and worked to popularize Buddhism. Up until then, Buddhism had been limited to royalty and the powerful elite, but Wonhyo started to teach it to the general public. He gave hope to the people that they could go to paradise by simply chanting the name of Buddha *Namu Amitabul*,' without having to know difficult doctrines. In addition, Great Master Wonhyo authored many important Buddhist writings and exerted influence on Buddhism in China and in Japan. As a result, Wonhyo's ideology has been studied in prestigious universities overseas even now.

어휘와 표현 \ Words & Expression

원효대사 Great Master Wonhyo
신라 시대 Silla Dynasty
스님 Buddhist Monk, *seunim*
불교계 Buddhist circle
존경받다 to be admired, to be respected
〈해골물 일화〉 'Story of Water in a Skull'
당나라 Tang (dynasty)
유학 overseas study
동굴 cave
목이 마르다 to be thirsty
바가지 bowl
담기다 to be in, to be contained
해골 (human) skull

깨달음을 얻다 to attain/reach enlightenment
N에 달려 있다 to depend on N
진리 truth
깨닫다 to realize
포기하다 to give up
불교 Buddhism
대중화 popularization, to popularize
힘쓰다 to pursue, to work to
왕족 royalty
권력층 the powerful elite
제한되다 to be limited
일반 general
백성 people

교리 doctrine
부처 Buddha
나무아미타불 *Namu Amitabul* (Buddhist mantra)
극락 heaven, paradise
희망 hope
뿐만 아니라 in addition to
서적 writing, book
영향을 끼치다 to exert influence on
사상 ideology, idea
해외 overseas
연구되다 to be studied

003

세종대왕 ★★★
King Sejong the Great

세종대왕(1397~1450)은 조선 시대 네 번째 왕으로 한국인들이 가장 존경하는 역사적 인물이다. 셋째 아들로 태어나서 22세에 왕이 되었다. 어려서부터 독서와 공부를 좋아하고 형제들과 사이가 좋았고 부모에게도 효자였다. 세종대왕은 왕이 된 후, 신분을 가리지 않고 유능한 사람들을 많이 뽑았다. 그리고 과학, 경제, 국방, 예술, 문화 등 모든 분야에도 업적을 남겼다. 또한 여러 제도를 정비하였고 국방에도 힘쓴 결과 현재 한반도 국경선이 이때 완성되었다. 음악에도 뛰어나서 악보를 체계화하고 새로운 악기도 만들었다. 또한 과학에도 관심이 많아서 백성들을 위해 측우기, 해시계를 발명하게 했다. 한글을 만든 것도 세종대왕이다. 만 원짜리 지폐에 세종대왕의 초상화가 있고 광화문에 동상이 있다. 새로 생긴 행정 도시 이름도 세종대왕의 이름을 따서 지은 세종시이다.

1 누가 한글을 만들었습니까?
Who created hangeul?

2 얼마짜리 지폐에 세종대왕 초상화가 있습니까?
Which Korean won bill has the portrait of King Sejong the Great?

King Sejong the Great (1397-1450) was the fourth king of the Joseon Dynasty and he is one of the historical figures most admired by the Korean people. He was born as the third son and became a king at the age of 22. From a young age, he liked reading and studying. He was on good terms with his siblings, and he was filial son to his parents. After having risen to the throne, King Sejong the Great selected many competent people undeterred by status. He made achievements in all fields including science, economy, national defense, arts and culture. In addition, he organized several institutions and worked hard for national defense. As a result, the current national borders of the Korean peninsula were completed during this period. He also excelled in music, making musical score systematic and having new musical instruments created. He was also very much interested in science, and had rain gauge and sun dial invented for the people. It is also King Sejong the Great who created *hangeul*. The 10,000 Korean won bill has the portrait of King Sejong the Great, and his statue is in Gwanghwamun. The newly-made administrative city of Korea is named Sejong-si, after King Sejong the Great.

세종대왕 King Sejong the Great	유능하다 to be competent	체계화하다 to make systematic
조선 시대 Joseon Dynasty	뽑다 to select, to choose	악기 musical instrument
왕 king	과학 science	관심 interest
존경하다 to respect	경제 economy	백성 people, general public
역사적 historical	국방 national defense	측우기 rain gauge
인물 figure	분야 area, field	해시계 sun dial
태어나다 to be born	업적 achievement	발명하다 to invent
어려서부터 from a young age	제도 institution	지폐 bill, note
독서 reading	정비하다 to maintain, to organize	초상화 portrait
사이가 좋다 to be on good terms with	한반도 Korean peninsula	광화문 Gwanghwamun
	국경선 national borders	동상 statue
효자 filial son	완성되다 to be completed	행정 administrative, administration
신분 status	뛰어나다 to excel	세종시 Sejong-si
가리다 to be selective/deterred by	악보 music, score	

004

이순신 장군과 거북선 ★★
Admiral Yi Sun-sin and the *Geobukseon*

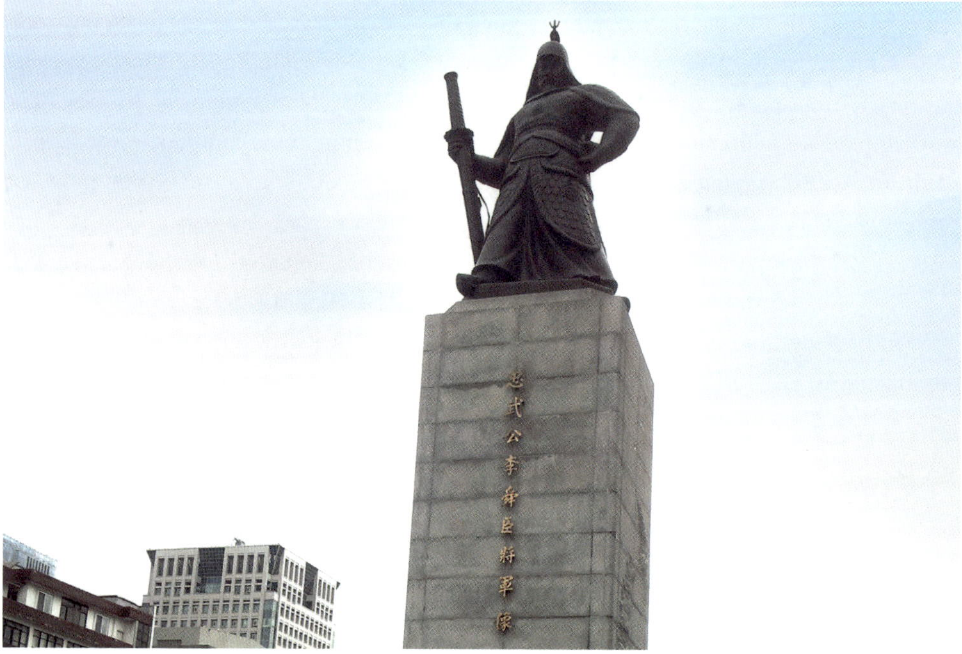

세종대왕과 함께 이순신(1545~1598) 장군은 한국인들에게 역사적으로 가장 존경받는 인물이다. 그는 거북선을 개발해서 임진왜란(1592~1598) 때 일본과의 해전에서 나라를 구한 영웅으로 추앙받고 있다. 세계 최초의 철갑선으로 알려진 이 거북선은 용의 머리를 달고 입과 꼬리에서 총을 쏘게 만들었다. 그리고 배 위에는 칼과 창을 꽂아서 적이 올라올 수 없게 했다. 부하들을 통솔하는 지도력, 탁월한 전략과 능수능란한 전술로 이순신 장군은 일본군과 전투마다 이겼다. 무인이면서도 《난중일기》와 시조 등 많은 글을 남긴 그는 오늘날에도 드라마, 소설, 뮤지컬, 영화, 만화 등을 통해 칭송되고 있다. 서울 광화문에는 이순신 장군과 거북선 동상이 있다. 백 원짜리 동전에도 이순신 장군의 초상이 새겨져 있다.

1 일본과의 해전에서 승리한 조선 시대 장군의 이름은 무엇입니까?
What is the name of the admiral who won naval battles against Japan in the Joseon era?

2 이순신 장군이 개발한 배의 이름은 무엇입니까?
What is the name of the ship developed by Admiral Yi Sun-sin?

Together with King Sejong the Great, Admiral Yi Sun-sin (1545-1598) is one of the historical figures most admired by the Korean people. He is revered as the hero who developed the *Geobukseon* (the turtle ship) and saved the country at the maritime battles against Japan during the Japanese Invasion of Korea (1592-1598). Known as the world's first armored battleship, the turtle ship was made to have a dragon's head, and its mouth and tail could fire a cannon. The ship's deck was studded with spears and blades to deter the enemy from boarding. Admiral Yi won every battle against the Japanese navy with his leadership to command his subordinates, outstanding strategies and masterful tactics. Although he was a military officer, he authored many writings including *A War Diary* and 'sijo' poems. Today, he is praised through various media such as TV drama, fiction, musical, film and cartoon. At Gwanghwamun in Seoul, there is a statue of Admiral Yi and the *Geobukseon*. His portrait is engraved on the 100 Korean won coin.

Words & Expression

이순신 Yi Sun-sin
장군 general
거북선 *Geobukseon* (the turtle ship)
역사적으로 historically
존경받다 to be admired, to be respected
인물 figure
개발하다 to develop
임진왜란 Japanese Invasion of Korea in 1592
해전 naval/maritime battle
구하다 to save
영웅 hero
추앙받다 to be revered
세계 world

최초 first
철갑선 armored ship
용 dragon
달다 to attach, to put
꼬리 tail
총을 쏘다 to shoot a gun
칼 blade, knife, sword
창을 꽂다 to put a spear into
적 enemy
부하 follower, subordinate
통솔하다 to lead
지도력 leadership
탁월하다 to be outstanding
전략 strategy
능수능란하다 to be masterful, to be an expert

전술 tactic
전투 battle, combat
이기다 to win
무인 military officer
《난중일기》 *A War Diary*
시조 *sijo*, traditional Korean poetry
소설 fiction, novel
칭송되다 to be praised
광화문 Gwanghwamun
동상 statue
동전 coin
초상 portrait
새겨지다 to be engraved/inscribed

신사임당 ★★
Shin Saimdang

신사임당(1504~1551)은 16세기 화가, 작가, 시인이다. 또한 한국의 대학자이고 정치가인 율곡 이이(1537~1584)의 어머니이다. 그녀는 자수 솜씨가 뛰어났고 시와 그림에도 재주가 많았다. 특히 산수화와 포도, 풀, 벌레 그림을 잘 그렸다. 또한 훌륭한 문장가였고 고전과 역사 지식에도 해박했다. 유교의 영향으로 조선 시대의 여자들은 마음껏 자신의 재능을 펼칠 수 없었다. 그러나 신사임당은 현모양처라는 전통 여성상에만 묶여 있지 않고 진보적이고 강한 자의식을 가진 여성이었다. 그녀의 작품은 신사임당의 생가인 강원도 강릉 오죽헌에서도 볼 수 있다. 신사임당은 5만 원짜리 지폐의 인물이다.

문제
Questions

1 신사임당은 누구입니까?
Who was Shin Saimdang?

2 신사임당의 생가는 어디입니까?
Where can you find her birthplace?

Shin Saimdang (1504-1551) was a painter, writer and poet from the 16th century. She was also a mother of Yulgok Yi I (1537~1584), a great Joseon scholar and politician. Saimdang had outstanding embroidery skills and great talents for poetry and painting. She was particularly good at landscape and paintings of grapes, grass and insects. She was also an excellent writer and very knowledgeable in classics and history. Due to the influence of Confucianism, women in the Joseon era could not let their talent run as free as they liked. However, Shin Saimdang was not bound to the traditional image of woman that is a wise mother and good wife; she was a woman with a liberal and strong sense of self. Her works can be seen at her birthplace Ojukheon House in Gangneung, Gangwon-do. Shin Saimdang is a figure we can now see on the 50,000 Korean won bill.

신사임당 Shin Saimdang	풀 grass	전통 tradition(al)
세기 century	벌레 insect	여성상 image of woman
화가 painter	훌륭하다 to be outstanding	묶여 있다 to be bound
작가 writer	문장가 writer	진보적 liberal, progressive
시인 poet	고전 classic	강하다 to be strong
대학자 great scholar	역사 history	자의식 sense of self
정치가 politician	지식 knowledge	작품 work (of art)
율곡 이이 Yulgok Yi I	해박하다 to be knowledgeable, to be learned	생가 birthplace
자수 embroidery	영향 influence	강원도 Gangwon-do/Province
솜씨 skill	마음껏 as much as one likes	강릉시 Gangneung-si
뛰어나다 to be outstanding, to excel	재능 talent	오죽헌 Ojukheon House
시 poetry	펼치다 to let run free, to show	지폐 bill, note
재주 talent	현모양처 a wise mother and good wife	인물 figure
산수화 landscape		

이황 ★★★
Yi Hwang

이황(1501~1570)은 조선 시대 성리학을 대표하는 학자이다. 관직에 욕심이 없던 그는 왕의 부름에도 불구하고 고향인 안동에 서당을 짓고 학문을 하면서 책을 쓰고 제자들을 가르쳤다. 조선 시대에는 나이와 서열이 중요했는데 유교의 대가였던 58세의 이황은 자신보다 25세나 젊은 학자의 비판을 받아들이고, 8년 동안 편지로 토론했다. 이 일화는 그의 겸허한 학자적 자세와 지혜로운 성품을 보여 준다. 지식과 행동의 일치를 주장하고, 인간과 자연을 존중한 이황의 '경' 사상은 한국 정신 문화의 귀중한 유산이다. 조선 시대부터 지금까지 그의 도덕 철학은 한국인들에게 큰 가르침을 준다. 이황이 세운 도산 서당과 그를 모신 도산 서원은 지금도 한국 성리학의 중요한 곳이다. 도산 서원은 2019년 세계 문화 유산으로 등재되었다. 천 원짜리 지폐에 이황의 초상이 그려져 있다.

1 조선 시대 성리학을 대표하는 학자는 누구입니까?
Who is the scholar that represents Neo-Confucianism of the Joseon era?

2 이황을 모신 서원 이름은 무엇입니까?
What is the name of the Confucian academy that enshrines Yi Hwang?

Yi Hwang (1501-1570) was a scholar that represents Neo-Confucianism of the Joseon era. Without any ambition for public office, Yi built a private academy 'seodang' in his hometown Andong, pursued study, wrote books and taught pupils. During the Joseon period, age and rank were important; yet, 58-year-old Yi Hwang, the great master of Confucianism accepted criticism from a scholar who was younger than him by 25 years and debated with him for eight years. This episode shows his humble scholastic attitude and wise character. Yi's 'gyeong (reverence, single-mindedness)' ideology is a valuable heritage of Korean moral culture, maintaining the agreement of knowledge and action, respecting both humans and nature. From the Joseon era up to now, his moral philosophy has given a great lesson to Koreans. The Dosan Seodang which Yi built, and the Dosanseowon Confucian Academy which enshrines Yi, remain to be important spots for Korean neo-Confucianism today. Dosanseowon was listed as a World Cultural Heritage in 2019. Yi Hwang's portrait appears on 1,000 Korean won bill.

이황 Yi Hwang

조선 시대 Joseon era/period

성리학 Neo-Confucianism

학자 scholar

관직 public office

욕심 ambition, greed

왕 king

부름 summon

불구하고 despite

안동 Andong

서당 *seodang*, schoolhouse, lecture hall

짓다 to build

학문 learning, study

제자 pupil

서열 rank

유교 Confucianism

대가 great master

비판 criticism

토론하다 to debate

일화 episode

겸허하다 to be humble

자세 attitude

지혜롭다 to be wise

성품 character, disposition

지식 knowledge

행동 action

일치 agreement

주장하다 to maintain

인간 human

존중하다 to respect

경 *gyeong* (reverence, single-mindedness)

사상 idea, thought

정신문화 moral culture, spiritual culture

귀중하다 to be valuable

유산 heritage

도덕 moral

철학 philosophy

가르침 lesson

도산 Dosan

서원 *seowon*, private Confucian academy

지폐 bill

초상 portrait

007

한국의 종교 ★★
Religions of Korea

한국에는 종교의 자유가 있다. 토속 신앙은 무속 신앙이고 그 후 불교와 성리학, 천주교, 개신교 등을 받아들였다. 현재 한국 사람들의 반 이상이 종교를 갖고 있는데, 개신교 신자가 가장 많고 그 다음이 불교 신자이고 그 다음이 천주교 신자이다. 불교는 삼국 시대(기원전 57~668)에 들어와 통일 신라 시대(668~892)와 고려 시대(918~1392)에 꽃을 피웠다. 한국의 절들은 이 시대에 많이 세워졌는데 특히 해인사의 팔만대장경은 한국인들의 깊은 불교 신앙을 보여 준다. 신유교인 성리학은 고려 말기에 들어와서 조선 시대(1392~1910)의 정치와 윤리의 기본이 되었다. 성리학으로 인한 유교적 가치관은 지금도 한국 사회에 영향을 주고 있다. 천주교는 18세기 말에 이승훈이 북경에서 영세를 받고 돌아와 전파하면서 알려지기 시작했다. 19세기 말에는 개신교가 들어와서 크게 발전했다.

문제
Questions

1 한국의 토속 신앙은 무엇입니까?
What is the folk belief of Korea?

2 불교는 언제 한국에 들어왔습니까?
When was Buddhism introduced to Korea?

There is freedom of religion in Korea. Korea's folk belief was shamanism, but the country later accepted Buddhism, neo-Confucianism, Roman Catholicism and Protestantism. Today, more than half of Koreans have a religion: Protestants account for the largest group, followed by Buddhists and then by Roman Catholics. Buddhism was introduced during the Three Kingdoms period (57 BCE–668 CE), and prospered in Unified Silla (668-892) and Goryeo (918-1392). Many Korean Buddhist temples were built during the period; in particular, the Tripitaka Koreana (*Palman Daejanggyeong*) at Haeinsa Temple shows the strong Buddhist faith of Koreans. *Seongnihak* or neo-Confucianism was introduced during the late Goryeo period and became the basis of politics and ethics in the Joseon period (1392-1910). The Confucian values from the neo-Confucianism still have an influence on Korean society. Catholicism started to spread as Yi Seung-hun came back from Beijing after having been baptized and propagated the religion. By the end of the 19th century, Protestantism was introduced and greatly advanced.

종교 religion

자유 freedom

토속 신앙 folk belief

무속 신앙 shamanism

불교 Buddhism

성리학 *Seongnihak*, neo-Confucianism

천주교 Catholicism, the Roman Catholic church

개신교 Protestantism, the Protestant church

갖다 to have

신자 believer

삼국 시대 the period of Three Kingdoms

통일신라 Unified Silla

고려 Goryeo

꽃을 피우다 to prosper, to bloom

절 Buddhist temple

세워지다 to be built

특히 in particular

해인사 Haeinsa Temple

팔만대장경 Tripitaka Koreana (*Palman Daejanggyeong*)

깊다 to be strong, to be deep

조선 Joseon

정치 politics

윤리 ethics

기본 basis

유교적 가치관 Confucian values

영향을 주다 to have an influence

세기 말 at the end of the century

알려지다 to be known, to spread

크게 greatly

발전하다 to advance

008

고인돌 ★★
Dolmen

'고인돌'은 주로 지배층의 무덤이나 제단으로 사용되었다. 아시아, 유럽, 북아프리카를 통해 총 6만 개 정도가 있다. 그중 절반 이상이 한국에 있다. 한반도에서는 고인돌이 기원전 10세기에서 기원전 2세기 사이에 만들어진 것으로 추정된다. 한국 고인돌은 형태가 다양해서 고인돌의 변천사를 연구하는 데 중요한 자료로 평가된다. 전라도 고창, 화순 지역과 강화도에 많으며, 고인돌은 2000년에 세계유산으로 등재되었다. 고인돌뿐만 아니라 경상도, 전라도에는 공룡 발자국도 발견되어서 한반도에서 다양한 선사 시대 유적을 감상할 수 있다.

1 한반도에서는 고인돌이 언제 만들어졌습니까?
When were dolmens made on the Korean peninsula?

2 한반도에서 고인돌이 많이 발견된 곳은 어디입니까?
In which place were many of the Korean dolmens discovered?

A 'dolmen' served mainly as a tomb or an altar for the ruling class. In total, there are around 60,000 dolmens in Asia, Europe and North Africa, of which more than half are in Korea. It is estimated that the dolmens on the Korean peninsula were made between the 10th and the 2nd century BCE. Korean dolmens have various shapes, and hence are seen as important materials in studying the history of change in dolmens. Many of them are located in Gochang and Hwasun areas in Jeolla-do and in Ganghwado Island, and they were listed as UNESCO World Heritage Sites in 2000. In addition to dolmens, dinosaur footprints were discovered in Gyeongsang-do and Jeolla-do, where it is possible to see and enjoy the remains from prehistoric ages on the Korean peninsula.

고인돌 dolmen	이상 or more	화순 Hwasun
지배층 the ruling class	한반도 the Korean peninsula	지역 area, region
무덤 tomb	기원전 BCE	강화도 Gangwhado Island
제단 altar	만들어지다 to be made	세계유산 World Heritage
사용되다 to be used, to serve	추정되다 to be estimated	등재되다 to be listed
아시아 Asia	형태 form, shape	공룡 dinosaur
유럽 Europe	변천사 history of change	발자국 footprint
북아프리카 North Africa	연구하다 to study	발견되다 to be discovered/found
총 total	중요하다 to be important	선사 시대 prehistoric ages/times
정도 about, around	자료 material, data	유적 relic, remains
그중 of which	전라도 Jeolla-do/Province	감상하다 to appreciate, to enjoy
절반 half	고창 Gochang	

009

무속 신앙 ★★★
Shamanism

무속 신앙은 한국의 토속 신앙이다. 무속 신앙에서 신령과 인간의 중재자를 무당이라고 부른다. 무당은 미래를 예언하거나 병자를 치유하는 능력이 있다고 알려져 있다. 무당은 두 종류가 있다. 강신무는 무병이 생긴 후에 내림굿을 통해서 무당이 되고, 세습무는 집안 대대로 무속 음악과 굿을 배워서 무당이 된다. 무당이 신들과 교섭하는 의식을 굿이라고 한다. 이때 나쁜 기운을 떨쳐 버리고 복을 비는데 옛날에는 굿이 마을의 큰 잔치이기도 했다. 요즘도 새로운 사업을 시작하거나 이사를 가면 재수굿을 하거나 행운을 비는 고사 풍습을 볼 수 있다. 굿에는 여러 가지 종류가 있다. 그중에서도 어부의 안전이나 풍어를 기원하는 서해안 대동굿, 풍년을 비는 강릉 단오제와 동해안 별신굿 등이 유명하다. 며칠 동안 계속되는 굿도 있다. 굿은 춤, 노래, 음악을 포함한 종합 예술로 인정받는다.

문제
Questions

1 무속신앙에서는 신과 인간의 중재자를 뭐라고 부릅니까?
In shamanism, what do you call the mediator between spirits and humans?

2 무당이 신들과 교섭하는 의식이 무엇입니까?
What is the ritual in which a shaman talks to spirits?

Shamanism is Korea's folk belief. In shamanism, the mediator between spirits and humans is called *mudang* (shaman). *Mudang* is known to have the ability to predict the future or heal the sick. There are two types of *mudang*: '*Gangsinmu*' becomes a shaman after first developing a spirit sickness and then having a '*naerimgut*' ceremony to cure it; '*seseummu*' becomes a shaman after learning the shamanism craft and music in the family for generations. The ritual in which a shaman talks to gods is called '*gut*.' On this occasion, people shake off bad spirits and pray for good fortune. In the old times, *gut* was a big festival of a village. Today, we can still see the custom of *jaesugut* or '*gosa*' (praying for good luck) when people start a new business or move to a new house. There are many types of *gut*. Among them: *Daedonggut* of the west coast is for wishing a big catch; Gangneung Danoje Festival is for praying for a rich year, and *Byeolsingut* of the east coast. Some types of *gut* continue for days. *Gut* is recognized as a composite art, as dance, song, and music are all mingled in it.

무속 shamanism
신앙 belief
토속 folk
신령 spirit
인간 human
중재자 mediator
무당 *mudang*, shaman
미래 future
예언하다 foretell, predict
병자 the sick
치유하다 to cure/heal
능력 ability
강신무 *Gangsinmu*, shaman through *naerimgut*
무병 spirit sickness
내림굿 *Naeriumgut*, a ceremony to receive spirit

세습무 *Seseummu*, shaman through inheritance
집안 family
대대로 for generations
신 god, spirit
교섭하다 to communicate/talk
의식 ceremony, ritual
굿 *gut*, Korean shamanistic ritual
나쁜 기운 bad energy/spirit
떨쳐 버리다 to cast/shake off
복 good fortune
빌다 to pray for
옛날 old times
마을 village
새롭다 to be new
사업 business, project
재수굿 *jaesugut*, shaman rite for good luck

고사 *gosa*, Korean ritual praying for good luck
풍습 custom
어부 fisherman
안전 safety
풍어 big catch
기원하다 to pray for, to wish
서해안 the west coast
대동굿 *Daedonggut*
풍년 good harvest, rich year
단오제 Danoje Festival
동해안 the east coast
별신굿 *Byeolsingut*
계속되다 to continue
종합 예술 composite art
인정받다 to be recognized

010

점과 사주 ★★
Fortunetelling and *Saju*

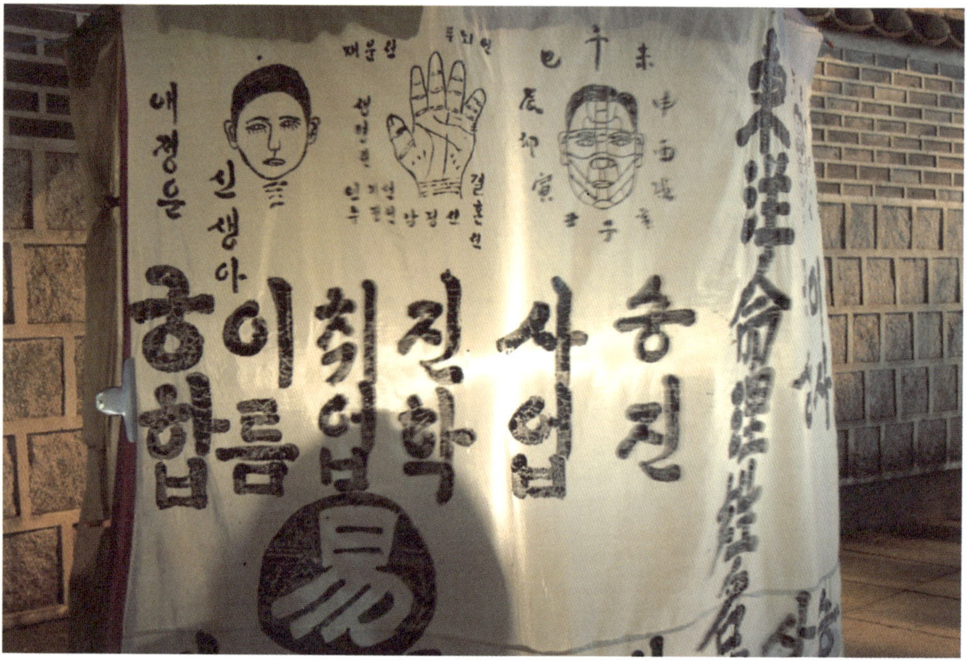

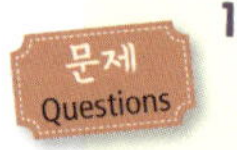

한국에서는 미래를 알기 위해서 점집에 가는 것을 자주 볼 수 있다. 특히 입시, 결혼, 취직, 사업, 이사를 결정할 때 점과 사주를 보기도 한다. 무속인이나 주역을 공부한 역술인에게 상담을 받기 위해서는 사주를 알아야 한다. 사주는 자신의 태어난 해, 달, 날, 시간을 말한다. 역술인들은 옛날부터 유명한 점성촌인 미아리에 모여 있었는데 요즘은 강남 패션의 중심지인 압구정 로데오거리 주변에도 있다. 또한 대학가 주변에도 사주 카페가 있어서 젊은이들이 결혼, 취업 등에 관해 상담하기도 한다. 연말연시에는 새해의 운수를 알기 위해서 점집을 찾기도 한다.

문제 Questions

1 사주는 무엇을 말합니까?
What does *saju* represent?

2 옛날부터 유명한 점성촌은 서울 어디에 있습니까?
Where in Seoul is the fortunetelling town located that is famous from old times?

In Korea, you can often see people go to fortunetellers to see the future. In particular, people may read their fortune and *saju* before their college entrance exams, marriage, employment, business and moving. In order to get consultation from a shaman or a fortuneteller who has studied *I-Ching*, you must know your *saju* (four pillars). *Saju* represents the year, month, day, and time of your birth. Fortunetellers used to gather in Miari, the famous fortunetelling town from old times; these days, they can be found in the Rodeo Street of Apgujeong, Gangnam's capital of fashion. There are also *saju* cafés in university areas, where young people may visit to seek counsel regarding marriage or employment. During the holiday season at the end and beginning of year, people sometimes visit the fortunetellers to read their new year's fortune.

점 fortunetelling
사주 *saju* (four pillars of destiny)
미래 future
위해서 to, for
점집 the fortunetellers
입시 college entrance exam
취직 employment
사업 business
이사 moving
부속인 shaman

주역 *I-Ching* (the Book of Changes)
역술인 fortuneteller
상담 consultation
태어나다 to be born
옛날부터 from old times
점성촌 fortunetelling town
미아리 Miari
강남 Gangnam
패션 fashion
중심지 capital, center

로데오거리 Rodeo Street
대학가 university area
사주 카페 *saju* café
젊은이 young people
N에 관해 regarding/about N
V_R기도 하다 sometimes V, may V
연말연시 holiday season at the end and beginning of year
새해 new year
운수 fortune

011

선 ★★★
Seon

한국 불교는 대부분이 '선' 불교이다. '선'은 명상으로 마음을 집중하는 수행 방법이다. 한국의 대표적 불교 종단인 조계종은 '선'을 수행의 기본으로 삼고 불경 공부를 한다. 서울 인사동 근처에 있는 조계사가 조계종의 본거지이다. 몸과 마음이 조용해야 '선'을 닦을 수 있다. 그래서 보통 마음이 흩어지지 않게 고요히 앉아서 명상을 한다. 스님들은 보통 여름과 겨울 각각 세 달 동안 명상만을 한다. 이런 명상 속에서 진리를 볼 수 있는 지혜로운 눈을 가질 수 있고 인간이 무엇인지를 깨닫고, 참다운 자기로 살 수 있게 된다. 이런 '선' 수행이 복잡한 사회 속에서 자기를 잃고 이기적이 되어 가는 현대인의 관심을 끌고 있다. 많은 절에 '선원'이 있는데 누구나 이곳에 머물면서 명상을 해 볼 수 있다.

1 명상으로 마음을 집중하는 불교 수행 방법은 무엇입니까?
What is the method of Buddhist asceticism that focuses your mind through meditation?

2 인사동 근처에 있는 절 이름은 무엇입니까?
What is the name of the temple near Insa-dong?

Korean Buddhism is largely *Seon* Buddhism. *Seon* is a way of asceticism that makes the mind be focused through meditation. Jogyejong (Jogye Order), the representative order of Korean Buddhism takes *seon* as the basis of asceticism in studying Buddhist scriptures. Jogyesa Temple near Insadong, Seoul, is the base of the Jogye Order. *Seon* can be cultivated only when the body and the mind are calm. That is why people generally meditate sitting quietly so that the mind may not be disturbed. Buddhist monks usually meditate for three months in summer and in winter, respectively. Amid such meditation, it is possible to have wise eyes, realize what human being is, and live as one's true self. Such *seon* asceticism is attracting modern people's attention as they are losing themselves and becoming selfish in this complex society. Many temples have *Seonwon* (*Seon* Center), and anyone can stay there to try meditation.

Words & Expression

선 *seon*
불교 Buddhism
대부분 mostly
명상 meditation
집중하다 to focus
수행 asceticism
방법 method, way
종단 (religious) order
조계종 Jogyejong, Jogye Order
기본 basis
삼다 to take
불경 Buddhist scriptures

인사동 Insadong
조계사 Jogyesa Temple
본거지 base, ground
몸 body
닦다 to cultivate, to develop
흩어지다 to be disturbed, to be scattered
고요히 calmly, quietly
스님 *seunim*, Buddhist monk
각각 respectively
진리 truth
지혜롭다 to be wise
가지다 to have

인간 human
깨닫다 to be enlightened, to realize
참다운 real, true
사회 society
잃다 to lose
이기적 selfish
현대인 modern people
관심을 끌다 to draw attention
선원 *Seonwon*, *Seon* Center
누구나 anyone, everyone
머물다 to stay

절 ★★
Buddhist Temple

절은 부처님을 모신 곳이다. 불교가 국교였던 삼국 시대(기원전 57~668)부터 고려 시대 (918~1392)까지 약 천 년 동안 수없이 많은 절이 있었다. 그러나 조선 시대(1392~1910)에는 불교가 탄압을 받아서 산에 있던 절들만 남게 됐다. 그래서 역사 깊은 절들은 보통 산에 있다. 한국 불교를 대표하는 절은 가야산의 해인사, 영취산의 통도사, 조계산의 송광사이다. 해인사에는 팔만대장경이 있고, 통도사에는 부처님 사리가 있다. 그리고 송광사에는 유명한 스님들의 유물이 보관되어 있는 박물관이 있다. 절에는 일반적으로 전통 건축 양식이 잘 보존되어 있어 주변의 자연 풍경과 어울려서 아름답다. 울창한 숲길과 시원한 계곡을 지나면 조용하고 평온한 절이 나온다. 그래서 불교 신자들뿐만 아니라 많은 여행자들도 도시 생활에서 벗어나 스트레스를 풀고 명상을 하기 위해 절을 자주 찾는다.

1 부처님을 모신 곳을 뭐라고 부릅니까?
What do you call the place where Buddha is enshrined?

2 한국 불교를 대표하는 절 세 곳을 써 보세요.
Please write the names of three Buddhist temples that represent Korean Buddhism.

A Buddhist temple is where Buddha is enshrined. For about a thousand years between the period of Three Kingdoms (57 BCE–668) and the Goryeo Dynasty (918-1392) when Buddhism was the state religion, there were countless Buddhist temples. Yet during the Joseon period (1392-1910), Buddhism was suppressed, and only the temples in the mountains remained. That is why temples with the longest history are usually in the mountains. The Buddhist temples that represent Korean Buddhism are: Haeinsa Temple at Gayasan Mountain; Tongdosa Temple at Yeongchuisan Mountain; and Songgwangsa Temple at Jogyesan Mountain. At Haeinsa, there is Tripitaka Koreana (*Palman Daejanggyeong*); at Tongdosa, there are Buddha's sarira, and at the Songgwangsa, there is a museum where the relics of famous Buddhist monks are kept. In a temple, traditional style of architecture is well preserved, which is beautiful and well in harmony with surrounding nature. When you pass densely wooded paths and cool valleys, you can run into a quiet and peaceful temple. That is why not only believers but also many travelers often visit Buddhist temples in order to get away from a city life, relieve stress and perform meditation.

013

불국사와 석굴암 ★★★
Bulguksa Temple and Seokguram Grotto

불국사는 신라 시대(기원전 57~935)의 수도인 경주에 지어진 사찰이다. 이 절에는 불교 문화를 대표하는 문화재가 7개나 있다. '불국'의 의미는 부처님의 나라라는 뜻으로 신라를 극락의 세계로 만들려고 했던 신라인들의 깊은 불교 신앙을 보여 준다. 이 절에는 단순하고 남성적인 석가탑과 화려하고 여성적인 다보탑이 마주 보고 있다. 불국사에서 4km쯤 떨어진 곳에 인조 동굴인 석굴암이 있다. 석굴암 내부에는 불교 세계를 대표하는 많은 불상들이 모셔져 있다. 그중에서도 석가여래 불상은 불교 예술의 극치라고 평가받는다. 불국사와 함께 석굴암은 불교의 사상을 잘 표현한 아름다운 건축물로 인정받아 세계유산으로 등재되었다.

1 불국사는 언제 지어졌습니까?
When was Bulguksa Temple built?

2 석가여래불상이 모셔진 인조 동굴의 이름은 무엇입니까?
What is the name of the artificial grotto where a statue of Sakyamuni Buddha is enshrined?

Bulguksa Temple is a Buddhist temple built in Gyeongju which was the capital of the Silla Dynasty (57 BCE-935). At this temple, there are as many as seven cultural properties that represent Buddhist culture. The meaning of *Bulguk* is 'a country of Buddha,' which shows the deep Buddhist faith of Silla people who pursued to make Silla a world of paradise. In this temple, there is a simple and masculine Seokgatap Pagoda and a glamorous and feminine Dabotap Pagoda. About 4km away from the Bulguksa is the artificial grotto of Seokguram. Inside eokguram, many Buddha statues are enshrined, which represent the Buddhist world. Among them, the statue of Sakyamuni Buddha is received as the culmination of Buddhist art. Bulguksa and Seokguram have been recognized as beautiful structures that express Buddhist ideas well, and hence have been listed on the UNESCO World Heritage.

불국사 Bulguksa Temple
석굴암 Seokguram Grotto
신라 시대 Silla Dynasty
수도 capital
경주 Gyeongju
지어지다 to be built
사찰 Buddhist temple
불교 Buddhism
문화재 cultural assets/properties
불국 *Bulguk*, country of Buddha
부처님 Buddha
뜻 meaning

극락 paradise
신라인들 the Silla people
신앙 faith
절 Buddhist temple
단순하다 to be simple
남성적 masculine
석가탑 Seokgatap
화려하다 to be glamorous
여성적 feminine
다보탑 Dabotap
마주 보다 to face each other
떨어지다 to be away from

인조 동굴 artificial grotto
내부 inside
불상 Buddhist statue
모셔지다 to be enshrined
석가여래 Sakyamuni
극치 culmination
평가받다 to be rated/received
사상 idea, thought
건축물 building, structure
인정받다 to be recognized
세계 유산 World Heritage
등재되다 to be listed

014

팔만대장경 ★★★
Tripitaka Koreana (*Palman Daejanggyeong*)

팔만대장경은 국보 제32호로 불교 경전이 81,258장의 목판에 새겨져 있다. 고려 시대 (918~1392) 몽골의 침입을 받았을 때 불교 신앙으로 나라를 구하기 위해 1237년부터 1248년까지 12년 동안 만들어졌다. 이 대장경은 어려운 상황 속에서 부처님에게 도움을 청한 고려인들의 깊은 신앙심을 보여 준다. 그 당시 동아시아에 알려진 불교의 경전, 계율, 논서, 불교 역사 등을 대장경에 모두 담았다. 이 팔만대장경은 세계에서 가장 오래된 인쇄 목판이다. 이 목판은 해인사의 가장 높은 곳에 위치한 장경각에 보존돼 있고 현재도 이 목판으로 인쇄를 할 수 있다. 목조 건물인 장경각은 800년 동안 이 대장경판을 그대로 보존할 수 있도록 지어진 신비로운 건물이다. 그래서 팔만대장경은 유네스코 세계 기록 유산으로, 장경각은 세계유산으로 기록됐다.

1 고려인들은 팔만대장경을 왜 만들었습니까?
Why did the Goryeo people created the Tripitaka Koreana (*Palman Daejanggyeong*)?

2 팔만대장경은 어디에 보존돼 있습니까?
Where is the Tripitaka Koreana (*Palman Daejanggyeong*) kept?

The Tripitaka Koreana *(Palman Daejanggyeong)* is Korea's National Treasure No. 32; Buddhist scriptures are engraved in these 81,258 wooden printing blocks. It was made for 12 years between 1237 and 1248 when Goryeo (918-1392) was invaded by Mongolia to save the country with Buddhist faith. The Tripitaka shows deep faith by the Goryeo people who sought help from Buddha amid difficult circumstances. Everything known in East Asia at the time, including Buddhist scriptures, precepts, treatises and Buddhist history, were contained in the Tripitaka. The Tripitaka Koreana is the oldest wooden printing block in the world, and they are stored in Janggyeonggak, located at the highest place in Haeinsa Temple. It is still possible to print scripts out of the wooden blocks. Janggyeonggak is a wooden building, a mystic one built so that the Tripitaka have been preserved intact for 800 years. That is why the Tripitaka Koreana was inscribed in the UNESCO Memory of the World Register and Janggyeonggak was listed as a World Heritage.

어휘와 표현   Words & Expression

팔만대장경 Tripitaka Koreana *(Palman Daejanggyeong)*
국보 national treasure
불교 경전 Buddhist scriptures
목판 wooden printing block
새겨지다 to be engraved, to be inscribed
고려 시대 Goryeo Dynasty
몽골 Mongolia
침입 invasion
구하다 to save
상황 situation, circumstances

도움을 청하다 to ask for/seek help
고려인들 the Goryeo people
신앙심 faith
그 당시 at the time, then
알려지다 to be known
계율 religious precepts
논서 treatise
역사 history
담다 to contain
인쇄 print
위치히다 to be located

장경각 Janggyeonggak
현재 at present, now
인쇄하다 to print
목조 건물 wooden building
그대로 intact
V_R을/ㄹ 수 있도록 so that may V
신비롭다 to be marvelous, to be mystic
세계 기록 유산 Memory of the World Register
기록되다 to be inscribed/listed

015

템플 스테이 ★★
Temple Stay

불교에 관심이 있거나 조용한 산사에서 쉬고 싶은 사람은 절에 머물면서 불교 문화를 체험할 수 있다. 이를 '템플 스테이' 혹은 산사 체험이라고 한다. 하루나 2박 3일 등 짧게 머물 수도 있고, 더 오랫동안 지낼 수도 있다. 외국인들을 위해서 영어가 가능한 절도 아주 많이 늘어났다. 그래서 한국어를 모르는 외국인들도 템플 스테이를 할 수 있다. 스님들은 보통 하루에 세 번 예불을 드린다. 새벽 4시쯤 해가 뜰 때와 점심 식사와 저녁 식사 전에 예불을 드리는데 절에서 머물면 이 예불에도 참여할 수 있다. 그리고 스님들과 함께 침묵 속에서 명상도 하고, 부처님께 드리는 108배와 한국 다례를 배울 수도 있다. 절에서는 육식을 안 하기 때문에 채식으로 된 사찰 음식도 맛볼 수 있다.

문제
Questions

1 템플 스테이는 무엇입니까?
What is a temple stay?

2 템플 스테이에서 체험할 수 있는 것은 무엇입니까?
What can you experience at a temple stay?

People who are interested in Buddhism or want to rest at a quiet temple in the mountains can stay at a temple and experience Buddhist culture. This is called a 'temple stay,' or a mountain temple experience. You can have a brief stay for a day, two nights and three days, or you can have a longer stay. For foreigners, the number of Buddhist temples where English is available has significantly increased, so those who do not speak Korean can also do a temple stay. Buddhist monks usually have three services per day. They have a Buddhist service at around 4 a.m. at sunrise, before lunch and before dinner. You can join these services when you stay at a temple. You can also meditate in silence with Buddhist monks and learn the 108 bows paid to Buddha and Korean tea ceremony. Since there is no meat diet at a Buddhist temple, you can try the Korean vegetarian temple food.

템플 스테이 temple stay	짧게 briefly	침묵 silence
불교 Buddhism	오랫동안 for a long time	명상 meditation
관심 interest	위해서 for	108배 108 bows
조용하다 to be quiet	가능하다 to be possible	다례 tea ceremony
산사 mountain temple	스님 *seunim*, Buddhist monk	육식 meat diet
절 Buddhist temple	예불을 드리다 to have a Buddhist service	때문에 because (of)
머물다 to stay	새벽 early morning, dawn	채식 vegetarian diet
체험하다 to experience	해가 뜨다 sunrise	사찰 음식 Korean temple food, Buddhist cuisine
2박 3일 2 nights and 3 days	참여하다 to join, to participate in	

016

서원 ★★★
Seowon (Confucian Academy)

서원은 조선 시대(1392~1910)의 유교 사립 학교이다. 신유교학파인 성리학자들은 인간의 본성을 연구하면서, 16세기부터 서원을 세우고 제자들을 가르쳤다. 그리고 옛 스승들의 제사도 서원에서 지냈다. 조선 시대에는 서원이 1,000여 곳이 넘었지만 현재는 47개만 남아 있다. 지금도 이곳에서 성리학자들을 기리는 제사를 지낸다. 경주의 옥산 서원은 조선 성리학의 선구자 이언적(1491~1553)을 모시고, 안동의 도산 서원은 성리학의 대가인 이황(1501~1570)을 모신다. 소박하고 자연과 잘 어울리는 서원의 건축 공간은 성리학의 가치관, 세계관, 자연관을 잘 보여 주고 있어서 문화와 교육 유산으로 보존되고 있다. 옥산 서원, 도산 서원 등 한국의 서원 9곳이 2019년 세계 문화 유산으로 등재되었다.

1 한국에서 유명한 서원은 어디입니까?
What are the famous *seowon* Confucian academies in Korea?

2 이황을 모신 서원은 어디에 있습니까?
Where is the *seowon* that enshrines Yi Hwang?

Seowon is a private Confucian academy under the Joseon Dynasty (1392-1910). Scholars of the neo-Confucian school *Seongnihak* studied the human nature, and they started to build Confucian academies from the 16th century to teach pupils. They also performed a memorial service for past masters at the *seowon*. The number of *seowon* was over 1,000 during the Joseon Dynasty, but only 47 remain at present. These places still perform memorial rites to pay tribute to neo-Confucian scholars today. Oksanseowon Confucian Academy at Gyeongju enshrines Yi Eon-jeok (1491-1553), the pioneer of Joseon's neo-Confucianism; Dosanseowon Confucian Academy at Andong enshrines Yi Hwang (1501-1570), the great master of neo-Confucianism. The architectural space of *seowon*, simple and in harmony with nature, well shows the values, worldview and view of nature of neo-Confucianism; hence, it is preserved as a cultural and educational heritage site. Nine Korean Confucian academies, including Oksanseowon and Dosanseowon, were listed as World Cultural Heritages in 2019.

서원 *seowon*, private Confucian academy

조선 시대 Joseon Dynasty/era

유교 Confucianism

사립 학교 private academy

신유교학파 school of neo-Confucianism

성리학자 scholar of neo-Confucianism

인간 human

본성 nature

연구하다 to study

세우다 to build

제자 pupil

스승 master

제사 memorial service, ancestral rite

기리다 to pay tribute

경주 Gyeongju

옥산 서원 Oksanseowon Confucian Academy

선구자 pioneer

이언적 Yi Eon-jeok

모시다 to enshrine

안동 Andong

도산 서원 Dosanseowon

Confucian Academy

대가 great master

이황 Yi Hwang

소박하다 to be simple

건축 architecture

공간 space

가치관 values

세계관 worldview

자연관 view of nature

문화와 교육 유산 cultural and educational heritage

보존되다 to be preserved

017

장례식, 제사, 차례 ★★
Funeral, *Jesa* and *Charye* Rituals

예전에는 사람이 죽으면 장례식을 집에서 했지만 요즘은 주로 병원에서 한다. 장례식장에 도착하면 영정 사진 앞에 향을 피우거나 흰색 꽃을 놓고 절을 한다. 그다음에 가족에게 "얼마나 슬프시겠습니까!"와 같은 위로의 말을 한다. 그리고 부조금을 내고 방문객들을 위해 준비한 음식을 먹는다. 이후에 각자의 종교에 따라 절이나 성당, 교회에서 추모식을 하기도 한다. 장례식이 끝나면 장사를 치르는데 전통적인 방식은 불교식 화장과 유교식 매장이다. 매장 방식을 따라 만든 무덤을 산소라고 부르는데 산소는 주로 산에 있다. 예전에는 묏자리가 좋으면 자손 대대로 복을 받는다고 해서, 풍수지리설에 따라 묏자리를 골랐다. 해마다 돌아가신 날에 가족들이 모여서 제사를 지낸다. 한식날과 추석에는 묘에 가서 차례를 지낸다.

1 한국의 대표적인 장례 방식은 무엇입니까?
What are the representative ways to do Korean funeral?

2 한국의 산소는 주로 어디에 있습니까?
Where are Korean graves mainly located?

In the past, when someone died, the funeral was held at home; now it is usually done at a hospital. When people arrive at the funeral hall, they either burn a stick of incense or place a white flower before the funeral portrait and make a bow. Then they deliver a word of condolences to the family such as "How sad you must be!" Then they pay condolence money and eat food prepared for visitors. Afterward, depending on each person's religion, a memorial service may be held at a Buddhist temple, a Roman Catholic Church or a Protestant church. After the funeral comes a burial or cremation; traditional methods are Buddhist-style cremation and Confucian style burial. A grave made following the burial method is called *sanso*, and this grave is usually in the mountains. In the past, people believed that a good resting place would bless descendents for generations, so they chose the grave site according to feng shui principles. Each year, family members gather together and perform a *jesa* memorial rite on the death anniversary. On *Hansik* Day and *Chuseok*, people visit the grave and perform a *charye* memorial rite.

장례식 funeral	각자 each, respective	산소 grave, tomb
제사 *jesa* memorial rite	종교 religion	묫자리 grave site, resting place
차례 *charye* memorial rite	절 Buddhist temple	자손 대대로 for generations
예전 in the past	성당 Roman Catholic church	복 blessing
영정 funeral portrait	교회 protestant church	V_R는/ㄴ다고 하다 it is believed to V
향 incense	추모식 memorial service	풍수지리설 feng shui principles
피우다 to burn	장사 burial, cremation	고르다 to pick, to select
V_R거나 V or	전통적 traditional	해마다 each year
놓다 to place	방식 method, way	돌아가시다 to die
절 bow	불교식 Buddhist style	모이다 to gather together
위로 condolences	화장 cremation	한식날 *Hansik* Day
부조금 condolence money	유교식 Confucian style	주석 *Chuseok*
방문객 visitor	매장 burial	묘 grave

018

천주교와 개신교 ★★
Roman Catholicism and Protestantism

한국은 아시아에서 두 번째로 기독교인이 많은 나라이다. 세계에서 가장 큰 10대 교회 중 6개가 한국에 있다. 외국인들은 한국에 있는 성당과 교회의 숫자와 크기에 놀란다. 한국 천주교는 외국인이 아닌 한국인들에 의해 선교가 이루어졌다. 18세기 말에 이승훈 (1756~1801)이 중국에서 세례를 받고 돌아온 후 한국인들에게 전파하기 시작했다. 당시에는 기독교가 금지되었기 때문에 여러 번 박해를 받았다. 하지만 천주교 신자들이 늘어나면서 한국에도 많은 성지가 생겼는데, 그 중에서도 19세기 말에 세워진 서울 명동 대성당은 순교자들을 모신 곳으로 한국 천주교의 상징이라 할 수 있다. 개신교는 천주교보다 조금 더 늦은 1879년에 시작되어 한국 인구의 20%가 개신교 신자가 될 정도로 빨리 발달했다. 기독교는 한국의 민주화 과정에서 중요한 역할을 했다.

1 한국은 언제 기독교가 들어왔습니까?
When did Christianity come to Korea?

2 19세기 말에 세워진 성당으로 한국 천주교의 상징은 어디입니까?
What is the cathedral built in the late 19th century that is the symbol of Korea's Roman Catholic Church?

Korea is the country that has the second largest Christian population in Asia. Among the 10 biggest churches of the world, six are in Korea. Foreigners are surprised at the number and the size of Roman Catholic and Protestant churches in Korea. The missionary work for Roman Catholicism in Korea was not done by foreigners but by Koreans. At the end of the 18th century, Yi Seung-hun (1756-1801) started to spread the religion, returning from China after having been baptized. At the time, Christianity was prohibited, so Christians were persecuted many times. Yet as the number of Roman Catholics increased, many sacred places appeared in Korea; among them, Seoul's Myeongdong Cathedral, built in the late 19th century, is rightly the symbol of Korea's Roman Catholic church, enshrining martyrs. The Protestant church started a little later than the Roman Catholic church in 1879, but it developed so quickly that 20% of the Korean population have become Protestants. Christianity has played an important role in the process of the pro-democracy movement in Korea.

천주교 Roman Catholicism

개신교 Protestantism

아시아 Asia

두 번째 second

기독교인 Christian

교회 Protestant church

성당 cathedral

숫자 number

크기 size

놀라다 to be surprised

N에 의해 by N

선교 missionary work

이루어지다 to be done

세기 말 at the end of century

이승훈 Yi Seung-hun

세례를 받다 to be baptized

전파하다 to spread

당시에 at the time

기독교 Christianity

금지되다 to be prohibited

때문에 because (of)

박해 persecution

성지 sacred place

명동 대성당 Myeongdong Cathedral

순교자 martyr

모시다 to enshrine

V_R을/ㄹ 정도로 so that V

민주화 pro-democracy movement

과정 process

역할를 하나 to play a role

019

판문점 ★★★
Panmunjeom

판문점은 서울에서 60km 떨어진 경기도 파주시에 있으며, 1953년 7월 27일 한국 전쟁의 휴전 협정이 체결된 곳이다. 한국 전쟁은 1950년 6월 25일에 일어나서 3년 동안 지속되었던 전쟁이다. 휴전 협정 이후에 판문점은 유엔군과 북한군의 공동경비구역(JSA)이 되었다. 판문점 비무장지대(DMZ)는 현재 남과 북이 대화할 수 있는 유일한 장소이다. 판문점 관광은 미리 신청을 해야 하는데, 공동경비구역에 있는 유엔 사령부 기지, '자유의 집', 본회담장, 군사 분계선, 제3초소 전망대, '돌아오지 않는 다리' 등을 방문할 수 있다. 도라 전망대에서는 북한이 아주 가깝게 보인다. 망원경으로 보면 개성시와 송악산 등을 볼 수 있다. 반세기 동안 일반인의 출입이 금지된 비무장지대에는 신라 시대 경순왕(897~978) 묘와 고려 시대 무덤 벽화 등 역사 유적들이 잘 보존되어 있다. 그리고 깨끗한 자연환경을 유지하고 있어서 생태적 가치도 크다.

1 한국 전쟁 휴전 협정이 체결된 곳은 어디입니까?
Where was the armistice agreement of the Korean War concluded?

2 판문점은 어디에 있습니까?
Where is Panmunjeom located?

Panmunjeom is located in Paju-si, Gyeonggi-do, 60km away from Seoul, and it is where the armistice agreement of the Korean War was concluded on July 27, 1953. The Korean War broke out on June 25, 1950 and continued for three years. After the armistice agreement, Panmunjeom became the Joint Security Area (JSA) of the United Nations forces and the North Korean army. The demilitarized zone (DMZ) of Panmunjeom is the only place where the North and South can hold talks. A Panmunjeom tour requires prior application, and it allows you to visit the United Nations Command camp at the JSA, 'Freedom House,' conference room, military demarcation line, the 3rd observatory post and 'Bridge of No Return.' At Dora Observatory, North Korea looks very close. Looking through a telescope, it is possible to see Gaeseong, Songaksan Mountain and many others. At the DMZ which has been off limits to the general public for half a century, there are well preserved historic remains, including the tomb of King Gyeongsun (897-978) of Silla Dynasty and tomb murals from the Goryeo Dynasty. Since it has maintained a natural clean environment, the DMZ also has a high ecological value.

판문점 Panmunjeom
떨어지다 to be away
경기도 Gyeonggi-do/Province
파주 Paju
전쟁 war
휴전 armistice, truce
협정 agreement
체결되다 to be concluded
일어나다 to break out, to take place
지속되다 to continue
유엔군 United Nations forces
북한군 North Korean army
공동경비구역(JSA) Joint Security Area (JSA)

비무장지대(DMZ) demilitarized zone (DMZ)
유일하다 only
미리 in advance
신청하다 apply for
사령부 command, headquarters
기지 base, camp
자유의 집 Freedom House
본 회담장 Conference Room
군사 분계선 military demarcation line
제3초소 전망대 the 3rd observatory post
돌아오지 않는 다리 Bridge of No Return
도라 전망대 Dora Observatory

망원경 telescope
개성시 Gaeseong (city)
송악산 Songaksan Mountain
일반인 general public
출입 entrance
금지되다 to be prohibited
경순왕 King Gyeongsun
묘 tomb
무덤 tomb
벽화 mural
유적 relics, remains
자연환경 natural environment
유지하다 to maintain
생태적 ecological
가치 value

020

이산가족 ★★
Dispersed Families

한국 전쟁(1950~1953)으로 많은 가족들이 남과 북으로 헤어지게 되었다. 남과 북으로 헤어져 사는 가족을 '이산가족'이라고 부른다. 대부분의 '이산가족'은 그 후 가족의 생사나 연락처도 모르고 있다. 지금까지도 서로 편지나 전화를 통해서 개인적으로 연락을 하는 것이 금지되어 있기 때문이다. 이러한 이산가족의 아픔을 덜어 주기 위해 1983년에 'KBS 특별 생방송 이산가족을 찾습니다'라는 방송을 했다. 그 결과 방송 2년 후인 1985년에 국가의 주선으로 소수의 이산가족들이 서울과 평양에서 처음 만났다. 이 방송의 기록물은 그 가치를 인정받아 2015년 유네스코 세계 기록 유산에 등재되었다. 그리고 2000년부터는 이산가족의 만남이 좀 더 규칙적으로 이루어졌다. 2005년부터 2007년까지는 헤어진 가족들이 화상으로 생사를 확인할 수 있었다. 그러나 이 행사는 남북 관계가 나빠지면 취소되는 경우도 있다. 이산가족의 반 이상이 80세가 넘은 노인들이라서 헤어진 가족을 다시 못 만날 수도 있다는 생각에 불안해한다. 명절 때 이산가족들은 휴전선 근처에서 북쪽을 바라보며 제사를 지내거나 통일을 기원한다.

1 '이산가족'이 한국 전쟁 이후에 처음으로 만난 때는 언제입니까?
When did the 'dispersed families' meet for the first time after the Korean War?

2 2015년에 유네스코 세계 기록 유산으로 등재된 한국 방송 이름은 무엇입니까?
What is the name of the Korean TV program that was inscribed in the UNESCO Memory of the World Register in 2015?

Due to the Korean War (1950-1953), many families were divided between the North and the South Korea. The families that have been separated between the North and the South are called 'dispersed families.' Most of the dispersed families have not known whether their family members are dead or alive, or how to contact them because it is still banned for them to make individual contact by mail or phone. In order to ease the pain of the dispersed families, the KBS Special Live Broadcast *Finding Dispersed Families* went on air in 1983. As a result, two years after the broadcast in 1985, a handful of dispersed families were reunited in Seoul and in Pyeongyang, through the arrangement of both states. The records of this broadcast were recognized for their values and were inscribed in the UNESCO Memory of the World Register in 2015. From 2000, the reunion of dispersed families has occurred more regularly. Between 2005 and 2007, it was possible for the families to confirm whether their family members were alive via video. However, this event sometimes has been canceled when the inter-Korean relations turn sour. Since a half or more of the dispersed families are in their 80s, the old people are agitated that they may not see their families again. On traditional holidays, dispersed families either perform a memorial service or wish for unification of Korea near the military demarcation line, facing north.

이산가족 dispersed families
한국 전쟁 the Korean War
남 the South (Korea)
북 the North (Korea)
헤어지다 to part with, to be separated
생사 life and death
연락처 contact
서로 each other
통해서 through, via
개인적으로 individually
금지되다 to be banned
생방송 live broadcast

국가 state
주선으로 by the arrangement of
소수 a few, a handful of
세계 기록 유산 Memory of the World Register
등재되다 to be inscribed/listed
규칙적으로 regularly
화상 video
확인하다 to check, to confirm
행사 event
관계 relations
나빠지다 to sour, to turn bad
취소되다 to be canceled

반 이상 half or more
넘다 to be over, to exceed
노인 old people
불안해하다 to be/feel agitated
명절 traditional holiday
휴전선 military demarcation line
바라보다 to look at
제사를 지내다 to perform a memorial/ancestral rite
통일 unification
기도하다 to pray for

Korean Culture in 100 Keywords

외국인 학습자를 위한 한국 문화 100선

VI. 예술과 문화
Arts and Culture

한지 ★★

Hanji (Korean Paper)

한지는 그 역사가 매우 오래되었다. 한국인들은 2세기에서 7세기 사이에 닥나무 껍질로 만든 종이를 사용하기 시작했다. 한지는 두껍고 질겨서 수명이 천 년 정도 된다. 그래서 옛날에는 문과 창문에 한지를 사용했다. 지금도 서예나 동양화를 그릴 때뿐만 아니라 필통, 장식장 등과 같은 생활용품을 만들 때도 사용한다. 자연 친화적인 한지로 만든 공예품은 전통 한지의 멋과 미를 보여 준다. 5월에는 전주에서, 9월에는 원주와 안동에서 한지 축제가 열리는데 특히 재미있는 것은 한지 옷 패션쇼다. 실크나 면을 섞어 만든 한지 옷은 아름답고 세탁도 가능해서 편리하다.

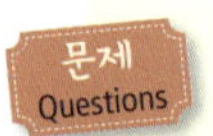

문제
Questions

1 한지는 어떤 나무로 만듭니까?
What kind of tree is used to make *hanji*?

2 한지로 유명한 도시는 어디입니까?
Which cities are famous for *hanji*?

Traditional Korean paper *hanji* has a very long history. The Korean people started using paper made from the inner bark of the paper mulberry (*dak*) tree between the 2nd and the 7th century. *Hanji* can last around a thousand years as it is thick and durable. That is why *hanji* was used for doors and windows in the old days. *Hanji* is still used not only for calligraphy and Korean oriental painting but also for making everyday items like pencil cases, armoires and lamps. Crafts made with eco-friendly *hanji* show the style and beauty of this traditional paper. *Hanji* festivals are held in May in Jeonju and in Wonju and Andong in September, and what is particularly interesting is the fashion show with *hanji* clothing. Clothing made from *hanji* blending silk or cotton is beautiful and easy-to-use because it is washable.

한지 *hanji* (Korean traditional paper made from paper mulberry tree)
역사 history
매우 very
오래되다 to be long
세기 century
닥나무 paper mulberry tree
껍질 bark
두껍다 to be thick
질기다 to be durable
수명 life
정도 about, around
옛날 old days

서예 calligraphy
동양화 oriental painting
그리다 to paint
뿐만 아니라 besides, not only
필통 pencil case
장식장 armoire
등 lamp
생활용품 daily/everyday item
자연 친화적 eco-friendly
공예품 craft, craftwork
전통 tradition
멋 style, charm
미 beauty

보여 주다 to display, to show
전주 Jeonju
원주 Wonju
안동 Andong
축제 festival
열리다 to be held
특히 particularly
패션쇼 fashion show
실크 silk
면 cotton
섞다 to blend, to mix
세탁 wash
가능하다 to be possible

002

택견 ★★
Taekkyon

택견은 한국에서 아주 오래된 전통 무예다. 곡선으로 움직이면서 마치 춤추듯이 공격과 방어를 하는 무예다. 이 무예는 마음을 닦고, 예를 지키고, 강인한 몸을 기르는 것이 목표다. 택견은 다른 운동들과 달리 부드럽고 자연스럽고 율동적인 동작을 바탕으로 하기 때문에 남녀노소 모두 즐길 수 있다. 2천 년 전 고구려 고분 벽화에서도 그 형태를 볼 수 있다. 고려와 조선 시대에는 무과의 필수였을 뿐만 아니라 어린이들까지도 택견을 할 정도로 보편화되었다. 택견은 세계적으로 그 가치를 인정받아 무술 중에서 최초로 2011년에 유네스코 인류 무형 문화유산으로 기록되었다.

1 왜 남녀노소 모두 택견을 할 수 있습니까?
Why is it that men and women of all ages can perform *taekkyon*?

2 유네스코 인류 무형 문화유산에 기록된 최초의 무술은 무엇입니까?
What was the first martial art that was inscribed to the UNESCO Representative List of Intangible Cultural Heritage of Humanity?

Taekkyon is a time-old traditional martial art in Korea. It is a martial art that makes movements in curves and employs offensive and defensive skills as if you are moving in a dance-like manner. The purpose of this martial art is to discipline the mind, observe proper decorum and train the body to be strong. Unlike other martial arts, *taekkyon* can be enjoyed by men and women of all ages because it is based on soft, natural and rhythmic movements. The form can be found in the 2,000 year-old-ancient tomb murals of Goguryeo. During the Goryeo Dynasty and the Joseon Dynasty, *taekkyon* was mandatory for the military examination, and furthermore, it was so generalized that even children performed this martial art. *Taekkyon*'s value was globally recognized, and it was inscribed on the UNESCO Representative List of the Intangible Cultural Heritage of Humanity in 2011 for the first time as a martial art.

택견 *taekkyon*
오래되다 to be long
전통 tradition
무예 martial art
곡선 curve
V_R듯이 as if V
공격 offense, offensive skills
방어 defense, defensive skills
마음을 닦다 to discipline the mind
예를 지키다 to observe proper decorum
강인하다 to be strong, to be tough
몸 body
기르다 to train
목표 goal, purpose
다르다 to be different

부드럽다 to be soft
자연스럽다 to be natural
율동적이다 to be rhythmic
동작 movement
바탕으로 based on
때문에 because
남녀노소 men and women of all ages
즐기다 to enjoy
고구려 Goguryeo
고분 ancient tomb
벽화 mural
형태 form
고려 Goryeo Dynasty
조선 시대 Joseon Dynasty, Joseon period
무과 military examination

필수 essential, mandatory
뿐만 아니라 furthermore, not only
어린이 child, children
V_R을/를 정도로 so as to V, so … that V
보편화되다 to be generalized
세계적으로 globally
가치 value
인정받다 to be recognized
중에서 among
최초로 first
인류 humanity
무형 문화유산 Intangible Cultural Heritage
기록되다 to be inscribed, to be recorded

003

인쇄술 ★★★
Printing Technology

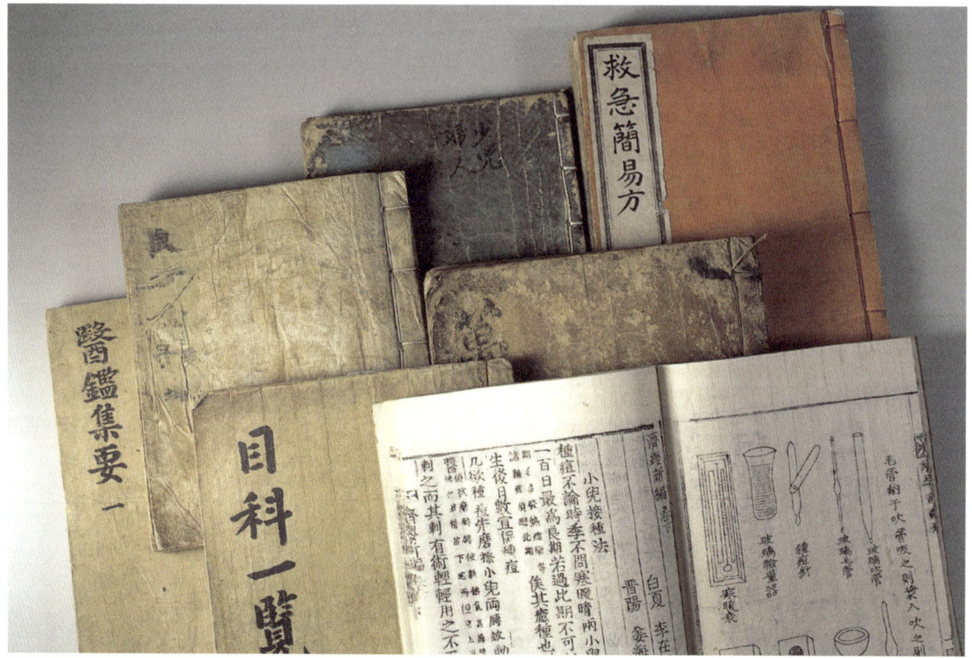

1966년 경주 불국사 석가탑에서 길이 약 620cm의 목판으로 찍은 두루마리를 발견했다. 이 것은 신라 시대 750년경에 인쇄된 《무구 정광 대다라니경》으로 세계에서 제일 오래된 목 판 인쇄물로 밝혀졌다. 751년 석가탑을 세울 때 탑 속에 넣어 보존한 것이다. 이렇게 인쇄 술의 선구자였던 한국은 고려 시대에 세계 최초로 금속 활자를 발명했다. 1234년에 금속 활자로 책을 인쇄했다고 기록에 적혀 있지만 이 책은 전해지지 않는다. 금속 활자로 인쇄 된 세계에서 가장 오래된 책은 《직지》이다. 《직지》는 백운 화상이 부처님의 가르침을 수 집한 책으로 1377년 청주 흥덕사에서 인쇄됐다. 19세기 말 한국에 온 프랑스 공사 콜랭 드 플랑시가 구입해서 현재는 프랑스 국립 도서관에 보관되어 있다. 구텐베르크의 성경보다 78년 먼저 인쇄된 《직지》는 2001년에 유네스코 세계 기록 유산에 등재됐다.

1 금속 활자로 인쇄된 세계에서 가장 오래된 책 은 무엇입니까?
What is the oldest existing book in the world that has been printed with metal type?

2 직지는 언제 인쇄됐습니까?
When was *Jikji* printed?

In 1966, a scroll of about 620cm long was discovered inside Seokgatap (Sakyamuni Pagoda). It turned out to be a copy of the oldest existing woodblock print *Mugujeonggwang Great Dharani Sutra* which was printed approximately in 750 in the Silla Kingdom. The copy was preserved inside the pagoda when Seokgatap was constructed in 751. Thus a pioneer in printing technology, Korea invented metal type for the first time in the world during the Goryeo Dynasty. According to records, metal type blocks were used to print a book in the year 1234; however, this book cannot be found. The oldest existing book printed with metal type is *Jikji*. It is a book of Buddha's teachings collected by Buddhist monk Baegun, and *Jikji* was printed at Heungdeoksa Temple in 1377. It was bought by Collin de Plancy, a French consul who came to Korea in the late 19th century. The book is currently preserved at the French National Library. *Jikji*, printed 78 years before the Bible was printed by Gutenberg, was enlisted on the UNESCO Memory of the World Register in 2001.

인쇄술 printing technology
경주 Gyeongju
불국사 Bulguksa Temple
석가탑 Seokgatap
길이 length
목판 woodblock
두루마리 scroll
발견하다 to discover, to find
신라 시대 Silla period, Silla Kingdom
경 about, around
인쇄되다 to be printed
《무구 정광 대다라니경》 *Mugujeonggwang Great Dharani Sutra*
세계 world
오래되다 to be long

인쇄물 print
밝혀지다 to turn out
세우다 to build, to construct
보존하다 to preserve
선구자 pioneer
고려 시대 Goryeo period, Goryeo Dynasty
최초 first
금속 활자 metal type
발명하다 to invent
기록 record
적히다 to be written
전해지다 to be found, to be passed down
《직지》 *Jikji*
백운 화상 Baegun Hwasang, Buddhist Monk Baekgun

부처 Buddha
가르침 teaching
수집하다 to collect
청주 Cheongju
흥덕사 Heungdeoksa Temple
말 end, late
공사 colsul
콜랭 드 플랭시 Collin de Plancy
구입하다 to buy/purchase
국립 national
보관되다 to be kept/preserved
구텐베르크 Gutenberg
성경 Bible
먼저 before, prior to
세계 기록 유산 Memory of the World Register
등재되다 to be enlisted

004

종묘 제례 ★★

Jongmyo Jerye (Royal Ancestral Memorial Rite of Joseon)

종묘 제례는 조선 왕실의 제사다. 왕과 왕비의 위패가 모셔져 있는 종묘에서 이 의식이 열린다. 이때 엄격한 유교 형식에 따라서 장엄하고 웅대한 궁중 음악이 연주된다. 여러 가지 전통 악기 연주와 더불어 노래와 춤이 어우러져 종묘 제례악을 이룬다. 600년이 넘는 시간 동안 연주되고 있기 때문에 역사적으로 매우 중요하다. 조선 시대에는 한 해에 여러 번의 제사를 지냈지만 1945년 광복 이후부터는 매년 5월, 10월의 첫 번째 일요일에 제례를 지낸다. 2001년 인류 무형 문화유산으로 등재되었고 지난 2015년 한·불 수교 130주년 기념행사로 해외 무대에서는 처음으로 파리 샤이오 궁에서 연주가 되었다.

문제 Questions

1 조선 왕실의 제사를 뭐라고 부릅니까?
What is the royal ancestral rite of the royal family during the Joseon Dynasty called?

2 종묘 제례 행사를 언제 종묘에서 볼 수 있습니까?
When can you see the *Jongmyo Jerye* event at Jongmyo?

Jongmyo Jerye is the memorial service for the royal family of Joseon. The ritual is held at *Jongmyo* Shrine where the ancestral tables of former kings and queens are enshrined. On this occasion, majestic and grand court music is played in accordance with strict Confucian style. Together with the performance of various traditional musical instruments, songs and dances come in harmony to make *Jongmyo Jeryeak*, or royal ancestral music. Having been performed for over 600 years, the music is historically very important. During the Joseon period, the ancestral rites were performed several times. However, the Korean liberation in 1945, the rites have been performed only on the first Sunday of May and October. In 2001, it was enlisted as Intangible Cultural Heritage of Humanity. In 2016, the music was played on a stage overseas for the first time at the Theatre National de Chaillot in Paris, for an event celebrating the 130th anniversary of diplomatic relations between Korea and France.

종묘 *Jongmyo* Shrine
제례 *jerye*, ancestral rite
조선 Joseon
왕실 royal family
제사 ancestral rite, memorial service
왕 king
왕비 queen
위패 ancestral table
모셔져 있다 to be enshrined
의식 rite, ritual
열리다 to be held
이때 on this occasion
엄격하다 to be strict
유교 형식 Confucian style
N에 따라서 according to/in accordance with N

장엄하다 to be majestic, to be solemn
웅대하다 to be grand, to be magnificent
궁중 court
연주되다 to be performed, to be played
여러 가지 several, various
전통 tradition(al)
악기 musical instrument
N와/과 더불어 together with N
어우러지다 to be in harmony
이루다 to make
넘다 to be over
역사적 historical
매우 very
중요하다 to be important

광복 liberation
이후 after
매년 every year
첫 번째 first
인류 무형 문화유산 Intangible Cultural Heritage of Humanity
등재되다 to be enlisted, to be inscribed
지난 last, past
한·불 수교 (establishment of) diplomatic relations between Korea and France
130주년 130th anniversary
기념행사 commemorative event
해외 무대 overseas stage
처음으로 for the first time
샤이오 궁 Theatre National de Chaillot

005

춘향전 ★★
Chunhyangjeon (The Tale of Chunyhang)

《춘향전》은 한국의 대표적인 고전 연애 소설이다. 조선 시대(1392~ 1910)에 한글로 쓰였다. 전라도 남원 사또 아들 이몽룡은 광한루에서 기생의 딸 춘향을 보고 한눈에 반한다. 두 사람은 신분이 다르지만 사랑하는 사이가 된다. 그러나 이몽룡의 아버지가 임기를 마치고 서울로 떠나면서 이몽룡과 춘향은 이별을 하게 된다. 새로 온 변 사또는 매일 기생들을 불러 잔치를 하는데 춘향이는 사또의 요구를 거절하여 감옥에 갇힌다. 서울로 간 이몽룡은 암행어사가 돼서 다시 남원으로 내려온다. 그리고 변 사또를 벌하고, 춘향을 다시 만나 행복하게 산다. 《춘향전》에는 신분이 다른 두 사람의 사랑, 춘향의 변함없는 사랑, 이몽룡에게 벌 받는 변 사또의 결말 등이 잘 그려져 있다. 이 작품은 판소리, 오페라, 뮤지컬, 소설, 영화, 만화 등 다양한 형태로 소개되었다. 지금도 남원에서는 음력 5월 단옷날에 춘향제를 열고 미스 춘향을 뽑는다.

문제
Questions

1 조선 시대 대표적인 연애 소설은 무엇입니까?
What is the most representative romance fiction of the Joseon period?

2 춘향과 이몽룡이 만난 곳은 어디입니까?
Where did Chunhyang and Yi Mong-nyong meet?

Chunhyangjeon is Korea's best known classic love story. It is written in *hangeul* under the Joseon Dynasty (1392-1910). Yi Mong-nyong, son of Namwon magistrate (*satto*) in Jeolloa-do falls in love at first sight at the Gwanghallu Pavilion when he sees Chunhyang, who is the daught of an artist-courtesan *gisaeng*. Although they belong to different status groups, the two become lovers. But Yi Mong-nyong and Chunhyang are forced to part as Mong-nyong's father completes his term and leaves for Seoul. Then the magistrate newly appointed to Namwon, Magistrate Byeon throws a feast every day inviting artist-courtesans. Chunhyang is imprisoned for not complying with the magistrate's request. Meanwhile, Mong-nyong becomes a secret royal inspector in Seoul and returns to Namwon. He punishes Magistrate Byeon, gets reunited with Chunhyang and lives happily ever after. *Chunhyangjeon* well portrays love between two people of different social status, Chunhyang's unchanging love, and the end of Magistrate Byeon who gets punished by Yi Mong-nyong. This work has been introduced in diverse forms including *pansori*, opera, musical, fiction, film and cartoon. Namwon still holds the Chunhyang Festival on the day of *Dano* in May on the lunar calendar, and selects 'Miss Chunhyang' in a beauty pageant.

어휘와 표현 — Words & Expression

《춘향전》 *Chunhyangjeon*
대표적 representative
고전 classic
연애 소설 romance fiction
판소리계 *pansori*-based
조선 시대 Joseon period
쓰이다 to be written
전라도 Jeolla-do
남원 Namwon
사또 magistrate
아들 son
이몽룡 Yi Mong-nyong
광한루 Gwanghallu Pavilion
기생 *gisaeng*, artist-courtesan
딸 daughter
한눈에 반하다 to fall in love at first sight

신분 rank, status
다르다 to be different
사이 relation
임기 term (of office)
마치다 to complete, to finish
이별하다 to part, to be separated
새로 newly
변 사또 Magistrate Byeon
잔치 feast, party
요구 demand, request
거절하다 to refuse
감옥에 갇히다 to be imprisoned
암행어사 royal secret agent
벌하다 to punish
변함없다 to be unchanging
결말 end

그려지다 to be portrayed
작품 work (of art)
판소리 *pansori*
오페라 opera
뮤지컬 musical
소설 fiction, novel
영화 film
만화 cartoon
다양하다 to be diverse
형태 form
소개되다 to be introduced
음력 lunar calendar
단옷날 Dano
춘향제 Chunhyang Festival
뽑다 to pick/select

판소리 ★★
Pansori

판소리는 고수의 북에 맞춰서 한 사람이 긴 이야기를 노래로 하는 공연 예술이다. 시장처럼 사람들이 많이 모이는 열린 장소에서 소리를 했기 때문에 판소리라고 불렀다. 18세기쯤에 시작되어 지금까지 불리는 작품은 〈춘향가〉, 〈심청가〉, 〈흥보가〉, 〈적벽가〉, 〈수궁가〉 다섯 편이다. 공연 시간은 두 시간에서 여덟 시간으로 작품마다 다르다. 소리꾼은 작품 속의 여러 인물들을 혼자서 노래로 연기한다. 거기에 고수의 북소리와 청중의 추임새가 합쳐져서 판소리가 완성된다. 판소리는 구비 문학, 음악, 연극의 종합 공연 예술이다. 해외에서도 임권택 감독의 영화 〈서편제〉(1993)와 〈춘향전〉(2000)을 통하여 판소리가 관심을 받기 시작했다. 2003년에는 유네스코 인류 무형 문화유산으로 등록되었다. 다섯 편의 전통 판소리 외에도 새로운 이야기에 판소리 음악을 만들어 부르는 창작 판소리도 국내외에서 큰 인기를 얻고 있다.

문제
Questions

1 판소리는 무엇입니까?
What is *pansori*?

2 지금까지 불리는 판소리 다섯 작품을 써 보세요.
Please write the titles of 5 *pansori* stories still being performed today.

Pansori is a performing art in which one person tells a long story in music (*sorikkun*) to the rhythms made by one drummer (*gosu*). The music is called *pansori* because the *sori* (sound) was sung at a *pan* (a place where many people gather) such as a market. It emerged approximately in the 18th century but only five stories are still performed today. *Chunhyangga*, *Simcheongga*, *Heungboga*, *Sugungga*, and *Jeokbyeokga*. The running time differs by story, ranging from 2 to 8 hours. The vocalist *sorikkun* performs various characters in the story all alone, singing a song. When the drum rhythms made by *gosu* and the rejoinders from the audience (*chuimsae*) are combined, the art of *pansori* is completed. *Pansori* started to attract attention overseas through *Sopyonje* (1993) and *Chunhyangjeon* (2000), both films by director Im Kwon-taek. In 2003, *pansori* was enlisted as a UNESCO Intangible Cultural Heritage of Humanity. In addition to five traditional *pansori* pieces, creative *pansori*, which involved making *pansori* music to new stories, is also gaining great popularity at home and abroad.

어휘와 표현 | Words & Expression

판소리 *pansori*	〈춘향가〉 *Chunhyangga*	구비 문학 oral literature
고수 *gosu*, drummer	〈심청가〉 *Simcheongga*	연극 theater
북 barrel drum	〈흥보가〉 *Heungboga*	종합 composite, synthetic
N에 맞추다 to N	〈적벽가〉 *Jeokbyeokga*	해외 overseas
길다 to be long	〈수궁가〉 *Sugungga*	임권택 Im Kwon-taek
공연 performance	편 piece	감독 director
예술 art	다르다 to be different, to differ	〈서편제〉 *Sopyonje*
모이다 to gather	소리꾼 *sorikkun*, *pansori* vocalist	〈춘향전〉 *Chunhyangjeon*
장소 place	속 in	N을/를 통하여 through N
소리를 하다 to sing	여러 several, various	관심을 받다 to attract attention
V_R기 때문에 because V	인물 character	인류 무형 문화유산 Intangible Heritage of Humanity
세기 century	청중 audience	
시작되다 to begin, to emerge	추임새 rejoinder	등록되다 to be enlisted, to be registered
불리다 to be performed/sung	합쳐지다 to be combined	
작품 work	완성되다 to be completed	

시조 ★★★
Sijo Poetry

청산리 벽계수야 수이 감을 자랑 마라

일도창해하면 다시 오기 어려웨라

명월이 만공산하니 쉬어간들 엇더리

황진이 (1506-1544)

Clear blue water running through the ravine, do not boast of flowing away easily.

Once you reach the ocean, it will be difficult to return.

Since the bright moon is shining above the empty mountain, why not rest before you leave?

Sijo by Hwang Jin-i (1506-1544)

시조는 '당시의 노래 곡조'라는 뜻으로 조선 시대에 유행했다. 한글로 쓰인 시조는 어려운 한시에 비해서 한국인의 감정을 있는 그대로 잘 전달할 수 있었다. 시조는 정형시이기 때문에 정해진 리듬에 맞춰 노래를 불러야 한다. 기본형은 각 장의 음절 수가 초장은 3. 4. 3(4). 4 , 중장은 3. 4. 3(4). 4 , 종장은 3. 5. 4. 3으로 전체 약 45자이다. 형식이 짧고 비교적 간단해서 왕에서 기생까지 다양한 사람들이 시조를 짓고 불렀다. 주제는 시대에 따라 다르지만 보통 유교적인 윤리관, 자연에 대한 예찬, 남녀 간의 사랑 등을 다뤘다. 비, 바람, 산, 대나무 등의 자연을 통해서 인간이 지녀야 할 덕목을 보여 주었다. 지금도 정형시인 현대 시조가 자유시와 함께 공존한다.

1 시조는 무슨 뜻입니까? What does *sijo* literally mean?	**2** 시조는 어느 시대에 유행했습니까? In which period did *sijo* prevail?

Sijo literally means the 'tune (*jo*) of the times (*si*),' which was popular during the Joseon Dynasty. Written in *hangeul*, *sijo* poems could deliver undisguised emotions of the Korean people compared to the difficult Korean poetry written in classical Chinese (*hansi*). Since *sijo* is a fixed verse, it must be sung to fixed rhythms. In its basic form, the number of syllables in each line is: 3-4-3(4)-4 in line 1; 3-4-3(4)-4 in line 2; and 3-5-4-3 in line 3, for a total of about 45 characters. As the poetic form is short and relatively simple, *sijo* was written and chanted by people from diverse backgrounds, including kings and gisaengs. The themes differed by period, but in general they addressed Confucian ethics, admiration for nature, and love between man and woman (romantic love). In particular, *sijo* showed the virtues people were supposed to have through nature, such as rain, wind, mountains and bamboo. Today, the fixed verse of modern *sijo* exists together with the free verses.

어휘와 표현 — Words & Expression

시조 *sijo* poetry, traditional Korean poetry
당시 the times, then
곡조 melody, tune
쓰이다 to be written
한시 *hansi*, Korean poetry written in classical Chinese
N에 비해서 compared to N
감정 emotion, feeling
있는 그대로 as it is, undisguisedly
전달하다 to convey, to deliver
정형시 fixed verse, poetry with a fixed form
리듬 rhythm
N에 맞춰 to N

기본형 basic form
각 장 each line
음절 수 the number of syllables
초장 first line, line 1
중장 second line, line 2
종장 third line, line 3
전체 total, whole
자 character, letter
형식 form, format
비교적 relatively
왕 king
기생 *gisaeng*, artist-courtesan
짓다 to create, to write
부르다 to chant, to sing
주제 theme

시대 period, the times
유교적 Confucian
윤리관 ethical belief, ethics
자연 nature
예찬 admiration
남녀 간 between man and woman
다루다 to address
대나무 bamboo
지니다 to have
덕목 virtue
현대 contemporary, modern
자유시 free verse
공존하다 to co-exist, to exist together

008

탈춤 ★★★
Talchum (Korean Mask Dance)

탈춤은 공연자와 관객들이 함께 즐기는 전통 가면극으로 서민들이 즐기던 놀이였다. 광대들이 양반, 무당, 첩, 승려로 분장하고 그들의 허위와 가식을 해학적으로 비판했다. 관객들은 그것을 보고 즐기며 카타르시스를 느꼈다. 탈춤은 이와 같은 해학과 비판적 성격 때문에 1980년대 민주화 운동에도 자주 등장했다. 다른 나라의 가면극과는 달리, 탈춤은 탁 트인 마당에서 진행되기 때문에 무대와 관객의 경계가 없다. 요즘도 서울 놀이 마당에 가면 누구나 쉽게 탈춤을 즐길 수 있다. 지방마다 고유한 탈춤놀이가 있는데, 특히 5월에 열리는 안동 지방의 하회탈춤축제가 유명하다. 탈춤을 보면 어려움 속에서도 웃음을 잃지 않았던 서민들의 해학을 읽을 수 있다.

1 탈춤은 누가 즐기던 놀이입니까?
Who enjoyed the play of *talchum*, the traditional Korean mask dance?

2 안동 지방의 탈춤놀이 이름이 무엇입니까?
What is the name of the mask dance performed in the Andong region?

Talchum is a traditional mask drama in which both performers and the audience have fun together, and it is a play enjoyed by commoners. Entertainers (*gwangdae*) dress up as *yangban* elite, shaman, concubine and Buddhist monk, criticizing their hypocrisy and pretense with humor. The audience has fun watching the mask dance performance and feel cathartic. Due to such satiric nature, the mask dance often appeared during the pro-democracy movement in the 1980s. Unlike the mask dances of other countries, Korean mask dance happens on an open ground, hence there is no boundary between the stage and the audience. Anyone can enjoy *talchum* easily today if they visit Seoul Nori Madang. Each region has a unique mask dance, and the Hahoe Mask Dance Festival of Andong region held in May is particularly famous. Watching the Korean mask dance, you can see the humor of commoners who never stopped smiling even amid difficulties.

탈춤 *talchum* (Korean mask dance)
공연자 performer
관객 audience
전통 tradition
가면극 mask play
서민 commoner, ordinary people
놀이 game, play
광대 clown, entertainer
양반 *yangban* elite
무당 *mudang*, shaman
첩 concubine
승려 Buddhist monk
분장하다 to dress as, to put on makeup

허위 fallacy, hypocrisy
가식 pretense
해학적 humorous
비판하다 to criticize
카타르시스 catharsis
느끼다 to feel
민주화 운동 pro-democracy movement
등장하다 to appear, to emerge
N와/과 달리 unlike N
탁 트이다 to be open, to be unhampered
마당 ground, yard
진행되다 to happen, to proceed
무대 stage

경계 boundary
놀이 마당 playground
누구나 anyone, everyone
지방 region
고유하다 to be unique
열리다 to be held, to open
안동 지방 Andong region
하회탈춤 Hahoe Mask Dance
축제 festival
어려움 challenge, difficulty
웃음 laughter, smile
잃다 to lose

009

풍속화와 민화 ★★★
Genre Painting and Folk Painting

풍속화는 조선 시대 후반에 시작된 화풍으로 서민들의 일상생활 모습을 담은 그림이다. 고려 시대까지는 불화를 주로 그렸고 조선 시대 전기에는 이상향을 담은 산수화를 그렸다. 선비들이 즐겼던 산수화와는 달리 풍속화는 일상적인 소재 때문에 처음에는 크게 인정받지 못했다. 그러나 18세기 후반에 김홍도, 신윤복과 같은 화가들이 나오면서 풍속화의 절정기를 맞는다. 김홍도는 서민들의 일상생활을 표현한 〈씨름〉, 〈빨래터〉, 〈서당〉 등의 작품을 남겼다. 반면 신윤복은 한량과 기녀들의 연애를 소재로 한 〈미인도〉, 〈주막도〉, 〈연당의 여인〉 등의 작품을 남겼다. 조선 후기에는 풍속화뿐만 아니라 민화도 인기를 끌었다. 민화는 생활 공간을 장식하기 위한 실용적인 목적으로 병풍, 책거리, 문방구, 공예품에 그린 그림을 말한다. 부적이나 탱화에도 민화를 그려 넣었는데 이러한 그림에는 그 당시 사람들의 신앙이 담겨 있다. 소박하고 익살스러운 민화는 보는 사람들에게 웃음을 자아내는 한국의 문화 유산이다.

1 18세기 후반에 풍속화로 유명했던 화가는 누가 있습니까?

Who are the artists that were famous in genre painting in the late 18th century?

2 생활 공간을 장식하기 위한 실용적인 목적으로 그린 그림은 무엇입니까?

What is the form of painting drawn for a pragmatic purpose of decorating living spaces?

Genre painting is an art that started in the late Joseon period, portraying aspects of commoner's everyday life. Buddhist painting prevailed in the Goryeo period and landscape portraying utopia prevailed in the early Joseon period. Unlike landscape painting enjoyed by Confucian scholars, genre painting was not greatly appreciated at first due to its ordinary subject matters. However, with the appearance of artists such as Kim Hong-do and Shin Yun-bok in the late 18th century, genre painting finally had its heyday. Kim Hong-do left works expressing the daily lives of commoners, including *Washing Place*, *Ssireum*, and *Seodang*. On the other hand, Shin Yun-bok used the subject matter of a romance between man about town and artist-courtesan such as *Portrait of a Beauty, Painting of the Tavern* and *Woman at Yeondang*. In the late Joseon period, not only genre paintings but also folk paintings became popular. Folk painting refers to paintings for the pragmatic purpose of decorating living spaces such as a painting on folding screens or a painting of study materials and books, stationery items or craftworks. Folk painting was also included in talismans or Buddhist hanging-paintings, and the faith of the people of the times was in these paintings. Simple and humorous, folk painting is Korea's cultural heritage that makes viewers smile.

어휘와 표현 \ Words & Expression

풍속화 genre painting
민화 folk painting
후반 late
화풍 style (of painting)
서민 commoner, ordinary people
일상생활 daily lives
모습 aspect
담다 to contain, to portray
고려 시대 Goryeo period
불화 Buddhist painting
그리다 to draw, to paint
조선 시대 Joseon period
전기 early days, the former part
이상향 utopia
산수화 landscape
선비 Confucian scholar, seonbi literati
N와/과는 달리 unlike N
일상적 everyday, ordinary
소재 subject matter
크게 greatly, very

인정받다 to be appreciated, to be recognized
김홍도 Kim Hong-do
신윤복 Shin Yun-bok
화가 artist, painter
절정기를 맞다 to have one's heyday, to reach one's height
〈씨름〉 *Ssireum* (Korean wrestling)
〈빨래터〉 *Washing Place*
〈서당〉 *Seodang*
작품 work (of art)
남기다 to leave
반면 meanwhile, on the contrary
한량 man about town
기녀 artist-courtesan, *gisaeng*
연애 romance, relationship
〈미인도〉 *Portrait of a Beauty*
〈주막도〉 *Painting of the Tavern*
〈연당의 여인〉 *Woman at Yeondang*

생활 공간 living spaces
장식하다 to decorate
실용적 practical, pragmatic
목적 purpose
병풍 folding screen
책거리 painting of study materials and books
문방구 stationery item
공예품 craftwork
부적 talisman
탱화 Buddhist hanging-painting, *taenghwa*
당시 the times, then
신앙 belief, faith
담기다 to be in, to be contained
소박하다 to be simple
익살스럽다 to be humorous
웃음을 자아내다 to make someone laugh/smile
문화 유산 cultural heritage

010

전통 악기 ★
Traditional Musical Instruments

옛날부터 한국인들이 즐겼던 악기로 거문고와 가야금이 있다. 거문고는 6줄, 가야금은 12줄의 현악기인데, 가야금은 손으로 연주하지만 거문고는 작은 술대로 연주한다. 가야금은 소리가 가늘고 화려해서 여성적이고, 거문고는 굵고 깊어서 남성적이다. 서양의 피들(fiddle)과 비슷한 악기로 2줄로 된 해금도 있다. 전통 관악기로는 대금과 피리가 있다. 대금은 깊고 신비로운 음색을 가진 반면, 피리는 가늘고 경쾌한 소리를 낸다. 장고는 대표적인 타악기로 모래시계 모양이고 궁중 음악에서부터 민간의 농악, 굿, 탈춤에 다 사용된다.

문제
Questions

1 현악기로 줄이 6개인 한국 전통 악기는 무엇입니까?
What is the 6-stringed traditional Korean musical instrument called?

2 깊고 신비로운 음색을 가진 전통 관악기는 무엇입니까?
What is the traditional wind instrument that has a deep and mystic tone?

Among musical instruments enjoyed by Koreans from the old days, there are *geomungo* and *gayageum*. *Geomungo* is a 6-stringed instrument, and *gayageum* is a 12-stringed instrument. While *gayageum* is played with one's bare hands, *geomungo* is played with a pick. The former is feminine as it has a soft and glamorous sound; the latter is masculine as it has a low and deep sound. There is also an instrument similar to the Western fiddle, a 2-stringed *haegeum*. As for traditional wind instruments, there are *daegeum* 과 *piri*. While *daegeum* has a deep and mystic tone, *piri* makes a soft and cheerful sound. *Janggo* is a representative percussion instrument in an hour-glass shape, and it is used altogether for court music and for folk music. It is also used in *nong-ak*, shamanistic rituals and mask dances.

어휘와 표현 Words & Expression

전통 tradition(al)
악기 musical instrument
옛날 old days
한국인 the Korean people
즐기다 to enjoy
거문고 *geomungo*
가야금 *gayageum*
줄 string
현악기 stringed instrument
손 hand
연주하다 to perform, to play
작은 small
술대 pick, plectrum
소리 sound
가늘다 to be soft, to be faint
화려하다 to be impressive, to be glamorous

V_R아서/어서/여서 as V, because V
여성적 feminine
굵다 to be deep, to be low
깊다 to be deep
남성적 masculine
서양 Western
피들 fiddle
비슷하다 to be similar
해금 *haegeum*
관악기 wind instrument
대금 *daegeum*, traditional Korean flute
피리 *piri*, traditional Korean pipe
신비로운 mysterious, mystic
음색 timbre, tone
가지다 to have
반면 meanwhile, on the other hand, while

경쾌한 to be cheerful, to be light
내다 to make (a sound)
장고 *janggo*, *janggu*, hour-glass shaped drum
대표적 representative
타악기 percussion instrument
모래시계 hour-glass
모양 shape
궁중 음악 court music
민간 folk, among people
농악 *nong-ak*, traditional Korean music performed by farmers
굿 *gut*, shamanistic ritual
탈춤 Korean mask dance
다 altogether
사용되다 to be used

민속촌 ★★
Korean Folk Village

경기도 용인에 가면 민속촌이 있다. 민속촌은 한국 민속 문화를 소개하기 위해서 조선 시대 한옥을 복원해서 만든 전통 마을이다. 이곳에서 조상들의 생활 풍습을 직접 체험할 수 있다. 부채, 탈, 짚신이나 옹기를 만드는 공예품 아틀리에가 있고 그네뛰기, 윷놀이, 제기차기와 같은 민속놀이도 있다. 또한 줄타기와 탈춤과 같은 전통 공연도 볼 수 있고, 식당, 술집, 찻집에서 전통 음식도 맛볼 수 있다. 특히 놀이 마을에는 한국의 모든 귀신들이 모여 있는 '귀신전', 한여름에도 등이 오싹한 '전설의 고향', '4D 입체 영상관' 등이 있다. 온 가족이 아름다운 자연 속에서 전통문화를 재발견할 수 있는 전통문화 테마파크이다.

1 민속촌은 어디에 있습니까?
Where is the Korean Folk Village located?

2 민속촌에서 즐길 수 있는 민속놀이는 무엇입니까?
What are the folk games you can enjoy at the Korean Folk Village?

The Korea Folk Village is found in Yong-in, Gyeonggi-do. The Folk Village is a traditional village made by restoring Joseon's *hanok* to introduce the folk culture of Korea. Here you can experience the daily customs of ancestors firsthand. There are craft workshops where you can make a hand fan, a traditional mask, straw shoes or pottery. You can also enjoy folk games including swinging, *yunnori* and *jegichagi*. You can also see traditional performances like tightrope walking and mask dances and taste traditional food at restaurants, bars and tea houses. In the Play Village, there is the Horror of Ghost Zone where all Korean traditional ghosts are present; Korean Folk Village's Legendary Hometown that will send chills down your spine even in hot midsummer days. There is also a 4D theater. This folk village a theme park where all family members can rediscover traditional culture amid beautiful nature.

민속촌 Korean Folk Village
경기도 Gyeonggi-do/Province
용인 Yong-in
민속 문화 folk culture
조선 시대 Joseon period
복원하다 to recreate, to restore
전통 마을 traditional village
이곳 here, this place
조상 ancestor
생활 풍습 daily customs
직접 firsthand
체험하다 to experience
부채 hand fan
탈 traditional mask
짚신 straw shoes

옹기 pottery
공예품 craftwork
아틀리에 atelier, workshop
그네뛰기 swinging
윷놀이 *yunnori*, a game of *yut*, Korean traditional board game
제기차기 *jegichagi*, a game of kicking *jegi*
N와/과 같은 like/such as N
민속놀이 folk game
또한 and, in addition
줄타기 tightrope walking
탈춤 Korean mask dance
공연 performance
특히 in particular

놀이 마을 Play Village
모든 all
귀신 ghost
모여 있다 to gather, to be present
귀신전 Horror of Ghost Zone
한여름 midsummer
등 back, spine
오싹하다 to feel a chill
전설의 고향 Legendary Hometown
입체 dimensional
영상관 theater
재발견하다 to rediscover
테마파크 theme park

012

벚꽃 놀이 *
Cherry Blossom Picnic

벚꽃은 보통 3월 말부터 4월 중순까지 핀다. 벚꽃이 피면 주로 친구, 연인, 가족과 함께 벚꽃 놀이를 간다. 전국에 벚꽃으로 유명한 곳들이 많다. 서울 여의도 윤중로에는 벚나무 약 1,400그루가 장관을 이룬다. 30만 그루의 벚나무를 자랑하는 진해 벚꽃축제는 매년 4월 1일부터 10일 동안 열리는데 한국에서 가장 큰 벚꽃축제다. 그 기간 동안에는 서울시와 진해시를 연결하는 임시 열차가 운행되고, 다양한 행사가 열린다. 경상도 화개장터 벚꽃축제에는 십 리 벚꽃 마라톤 대회, 민속놀이, 전통 혼례, 가수왕 선발 대회 등의 행사가 있다. 부산 〈경포대 벚꽃축제〉, 계룡산의 〈동학사 벚꽃축제〉도 볼 만하다. 한국에서 벚꽃이 가장 늦게 피는 전라북도 마이산은 수천 그루의 하얀 벚꽃들이 정말 아름답다.

1 한국에서 가장 큰 벚꽃 축제 이름은 무엇입니까?
What is the biggest cherry blossom festival in Korea?

2 서울에서 유명한 벚꽃 거리는 무엇입니까?
What is the famous cherry blossom street in Seoul?

Cherry blossoms bloom generally from late March to mid-April. In Korea, when cherry blossoms bloom, people usually go on a cherry blossom picnic with friends, lover or family. There are many places famous for cherry blossoms across the country. On Yungjungno-road in Yeouido Island, Seoul, about 1,400 cherry trees make a magnificent sight. The Jinhae Cherry Blossom Festival, boasting 300,000 cherry trees, is held for 10 days from April 1 every year and it is the biggest cherry blossom festival in Korea. During that period, temporary trains operate to connect Seoul and Jinhae-si, and various events are held. The Hwagae Marketplace Cherry Blossom Festival offers events, such as 10-*ri* Cherry Blossom Marathon, folk games, a traditional wedding ceremony and a top singer contest. It is also worth seeing Busan's Gyeongpodae Cherry Blossom Festival and Gyeryongsan Mountain's Donghaksa Cherry Blossom Festival. At Maisan Mountain in Jeollabuk-do, where cherry blossoms bloom the latest in Korea, thousands of white cherry blossoms are truly beautiful.

벚꽃 놀이 cherry blossom picnic
–말부터 from the end of…, from late…
중순까지 to mid-
피다 to bloom
연인 lover
가족 family
N와/과 함께 with N
전국 the whole country, across the country
유명한 famous
곳 place, spot
여의도 Yeouido
윤중로 Yunjungno-road
벚나무 cherry tree
약 about
그루 stump, a unit of plant
장관을 이루다 to make a magnificent sight

자랑하다 to boast, to be proud of
축제 festival
매년 every year
동안 during, for
열리다 to be held, to open
가장 the most
큰 big
기간 period
진해시 Jinhae-si
임시 temporary
열차 train
운행되다 to be in service, to operate
다양한 diverse, various
행사 event
경상도 Gyeongsang-do/Province
화개장터 Hwagae Marketplace
십 리 10-*ri* (4km)

마라톤 marathon
대회 competition, contest
민속놀이 folk game
전통 tradition
혼례 marriage
가수왕 top singer
등 …and many more, such as…
부산 Busan
경포대 Gyeongpodae (Pavilion)
계룡산 Gyeryongsan Mountain
동학사 Donghaksa (Temple)
V_R을/ㄹ 만하다 to be worth V-ing
늦게 late
전라북도 Jeollabuk-do/Province
마이산 Maisan Mountain
수천 thousands of
하얀 white
아름답다 to be beautiful

013

부산 국제 영화제 ★★
Busan International Film Festival (BIFF)

〈부산 국제 영화제〉는 1996년에 시작된 한국 최초의 국제 영화제이다. 도쿄와 홍콩 영화제와 함께 아시아에서 가장 큰 영화제이다. 매년 10월에 해운대 '영화의 전당'과 센텀시티, 남포동 극장가에서 개최되는데 2023년에는 28회를 맞았다. 부산 국제 영화제에서는 세계 유명 감독의 신작을 빠르게 감상할 수 있고 아시아 영화감독들의 다양한 화제작도 볼 수 있다. 또한 '아시아 영화의 창', '아시아 필름 마켓', '뉴커런츠' 등 아시아의 우수한 작품을 소개하는 여러 행사가 있다. 특히 감독, 배우, 관객이 모두 함께 영화를 보고 대화할 수 있는 프로그램인 '관객과의 대화(GV)' 등도 있다. 이처럼 부산 국제 영화제는 아시아 영화인들의 네트워크를 마련하는 데 중요한 역할을 하는 영화인들의 축제다.

1 한국 최초의 국제 영화제는 무엇입니까?
What was the first international film festival of Korea?

2 〈부산 국제 영화제〉는 언제 열립니까?
When is the Busan International Film Festival held every year?

The Busan International Film Festival (BIFF) was the first international film festival in Korea that began in 1996. It is one of the biggest film festivels in Asia, along with Tokyo International Film Festival and Hong Kong International Film Festival. In October every year, BIFF is held at the Busan Cinema Center in Haeundae and at theater districts in Centum City and Nampo-dong. It has celebrated its 28th anniversary in 2023. At BIFF, you can preview new films by famous directors from the world and watch many much-talked-about films by Asian directors. Among various events of the BIFF, A Window on Asian Cinema, Asian Film Market and New Currents are connected to the background of creating BIFF, which is to introduce outstanding Asian films to the world. There is also a program like Guest Visits (GV) in which directors, actors and the audience can watch the film together and have a dialogue. Thus, BIFF is a festival of cineastes that plays an important role in preparing a network among Asian people involved in filmmaking.

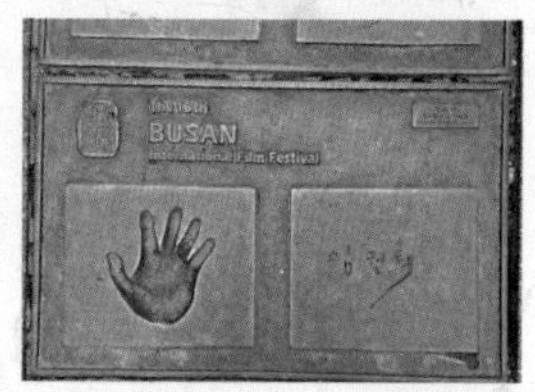

부산 Busan	극장가 theater district	배우 actor, actress
국제 international	개최되다 to be held, to be hosted	관객 audience
영화제 film festival	맞다 to celebrate, to see	대화하다 to talk, to have a dialogue with
시작되다 to begin, to start	세계 world	
최초 first	유명 famous	프로그램 program
도쿄 Tokyo	감독 director	N와/과 같은 like N
홍콩 Hong Kong	신작 new film/work	영화인 cineaste
함께 together with	아시아 Asia	네트워크 network
가장 the most	화제작 hot/much-talked-about work of art	마련하다 to offer, to prepare
매년 every year		중요하다 to be important
해운대 Haeundae	또한 in addition	역할 role
전당 center, hall	필름 마켓 film market	
남포동 Nampo-dong	행사 event	

014

전주와 전주 축제들 ★
Jeonju and Its Festivals

전주는 한식, 한옥, 한지로 잘 알려진 전통문화 도시다. 그래서 다양한 전통문화를 체험할 수 있고 축제에도 참가할 수 있다. 전통 음식으로 한정식, 콩나물국밥, 전주 막걸리, 전주비빔밥이 유명한데, 특히 전주비빔밥은 세계적으로 알려져 있다. 전주에서 한정식을 먹으면 약 30개 반찬이 한 상에 차려지기 때문에 산, 바다, 강에서 나는 모든 음식을 맛볼 수 있다. 한옥마을에서 전통 집을 체험할 수 있는 한옥 스테이가 요즘 관광객들에게 인기가 있다. 또 다양한 축제에도 참가할 수 있다. 10월에는 〈전주비빔밥축제〉와 〈전주 세계 소리축제〉가 있다. 소리축제는 판소리를 중심으로 국악과 세계 음악을 함께 소개하는 국제 음악 예술제다. 5월에는 독립 예술 영화를 중심으로 하는 〈전주 국제 영화제〉도 있다.

1 전주에서 유명한 전통 음식은 무엇입니까?
What are the famous traditional foods in Jeonju?

2 판소리 축제로 유명한 전주 축제 이름은 무엇입니까?
What is the Jeonju festival that is famous as a *pansori* festival?

Jeonju is a city of traditional culture well known for traditional Korean food, *hanok* housing and *hanji* paper. Therefore, you can experience various traditional cultures and participate in festivals. Among traditional food, Korean meal, bean sprout soup with rice, and Jeonju *makgeolli* are famous. In particular, Jeonju *bibimbap* is globally known. When you have Korean meal(set menu) in Jeonju, about 30 side dishes (*banchan*) are laid on one table; hence you can taste all foods coming from mountains, rivers and the sea. Nowadays at the Hanok Village, a hanok stay is popular among tourists as it allows them to experience the traditional Korean housing. In addition, it is possible to join various festivals. In October, there is the Jeonju Bibimbap Festival and the Jeonju World Sori Festival. The latter is an international music festival that introduces traditional Korean music *gugak* focusing on *pansori*, together with world music. In May, the Jeonju International Film Festival is held, focusing on independent and art house cinema.

전주 Jeonju
축제 festival
한식 traditional Korean food
한옥 *hanok*, traditional Korean housing
한지 *hanji*, traditional paper
N로 알려진 known as N
전통 traditional
문화 culture
도시 city
그래서 therefore
다양한 diverse, various
한정식 Korean meal/set menu
콩나물국밥 bean sprout soup with rice
막걸리 *makgeolli*

유명하다 to be famous
비빔밥 *bibimbap*
세계적으로 globally
알려져 있다 to be known
약 about
반찬 *banchan*, side dish
한 상 one table
차려지다 to be laid, to be set
N에서 나다 to come from N, to be produced at N
모든 all
맛보다 to taste
V_R을/ㄹ 수 있다 can V
마을 village
하옥 스테이 hanok stay
관광객 tourist

인기가 있다 to be popular
세계 world
소리 sound
판소리 *pansori*
N을/를 중심으로 focusing on N
국악 *gugak*, Korean traditional music
세계 음악 world music
함께 together with
소개하다 to introduce
국제 음악 예술제 international music and arts festival
독립 independent
예술 art, art house
국제 영화제 International Film Festival

015

세종문화회관, 국립 극장, 예술의 전당 ★★

Sejong Center for the Performing Arts, National Theater of Korea, Seoul Arts Center

세종문화회관, 국립 극장, 예술의 전당은 서울의 대표적인 공연장이다. 100여년 전에 지어진 세종문화회관은 서울의 중심인 광화문 광장에 있다. 총 3층의 공연장이 있는 대극장에는 3,022개의 객석이 있는데 세 공연장 중 규모가 가장 크다. 이외에도 미술관에서 미술 전시를 관람할 수 있고, 컨벤션 센터, 콘퍼런스홀, 삼청각 등 부대시설도 이용할 수 있다. 남산에 위치한 국립 극장은 주로 전통 연극이나 국악 공연을 소개한다. 관객들은 공연을 본 다음에 남산 산책로를 따라 걸으면서 공연의 감동을 나누기도 한다. 강남 서초동에 있는 예술의 전당은 한국 최대 종합 예술 센터이다. 2,300석의 오페라 하우스에서는 오페라, 발레, 뮤지컬 등이 공연된다. 또한 미술관과 서예관에서는 다양한 국내외 작품 전시회가 열린다. 야외에는 음악 분수대, 식당, 카페 등이 있어서 꼭 공연을 보지 않아도 유쾌한 시간을 보낼 수 있다.

1 세종문화회관은 어디에 있습니까?
Where is the Sejong Center for the Performing Arts?

2 한국 최대 종합 예술 센터는 무엇입니까?
What is the biggest composite arts center in Korea?

The Sejong Center for the Performing Arts, the National Theater of Korea and Seoul Arts Center are Seoul's representative theaters. Built nearly 100 years ago, the Sejong Center is located at the center of Seoul at Gwanghwamun Square. Its Grand Theater is as 3-stories with 3,022 seats, which makes the Sejong Center the largest of the three theaters. At the Sejong Center, you can see art exhibitions at the art gallery and use other facilities including its convention center, conference hall and Samcheonggak. Located at Namsan Mountain, the National Theater of Korea mainly introduces traditional plays and *gugak* traditional music performances. After watching a performance, the audience may share what they have felt from it while walking through the trails along Namsan. The Seoul Arts Center in Seocho-dong, Gangnam is the biggest composite arts center in Korea. At its 2,300 seat Opera House, works of opera, ballet and musical are performed. At its Art Museum and Calligraphy Art Museum, exhibitions are held with various domestic and international works. Since there is a music fountain, as well as restaurants and cafés outdoors, you can have a pleasant time without having to watch a performance.

세종문화회관 Sejong Center for the Performing Arts
국립 극장 National Theater of Korea
예술의 전당 Seoul Arts Center
대표적인 representative
공연장 theater
−여 about, around
지어지다 to be built
중심 center
광화문 Gwanghwamun
광장 plaza, square
총 total
석 seat
규모 size
가장 the most
남산 Namsan Mountain
위치하다 to be located

주로 mainly
전통 tradition(al)
연극 play
국악 *gugak*, Korean traditional music
관객 audience
공연 performance
산책로 trail
따라 along
걷다 to walk
V_R(으)면서 while V-ing
감동 to be moved, to be touched
나누다 to share
V_R기도 하다 may V, sometimes V
강남 Gangnam
서초동 Seocho-dong
최대 biggest, largest
종합 composite, synthetic

예술 센터 arts center
오페라 하우스 Opera House
발레 ballet
뮤지컬 musical
공연되다 to be performed
또한 in addition
미술관 art museum
서예관 calligraphy art museum
다양하다 to be diverse
국내외 domestic and international
작품 work (of art)
전시회 exhibition
열리다 to be held, to open
야외 outdoors
분수대 fountain
유쾌하다 to be cheerful, to be pleasant

016

한류★

Hallyu (The Korean Wave)

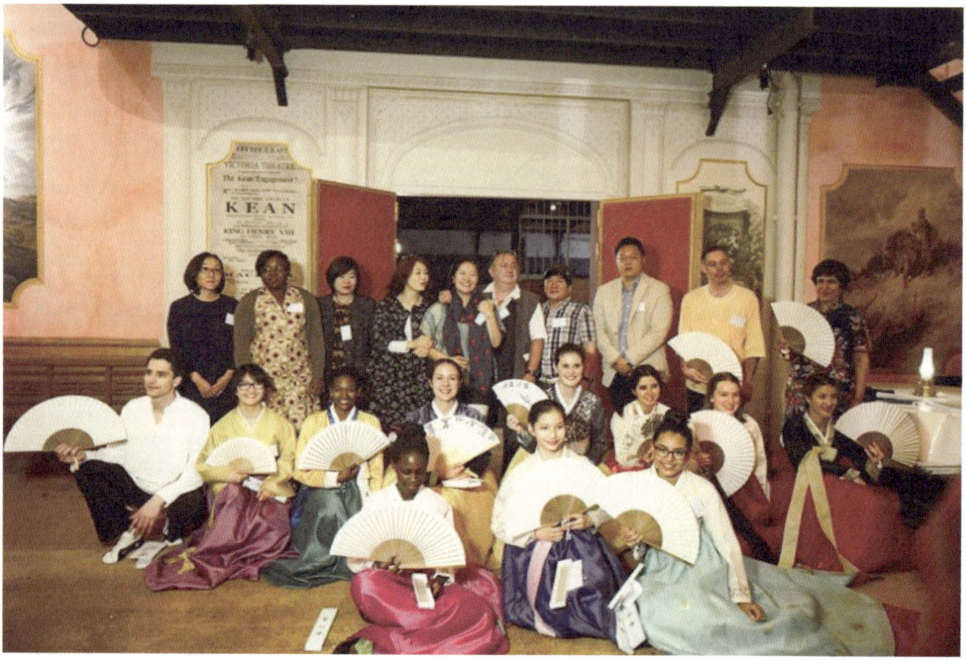

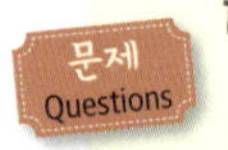

한류는 한국 대중문화가 해외에서 인기를 얻는 현상이다. 한국 드라마의 인기와 함께 1990년대 말부터 시작되었다. 한류의 영향이 이제 아시아를 넘어서 중동, 라틴 아메리카, 북아메리카, 그리고 유럽에까지 이르렀다. 블랙핑크, BTS 등이 부른 K-pop 노래에 전 세계 젊은이들이 열광한다. 한국 영화 〈기생충〉, 〈미나리〉, 〈올드보이〉나 〈봄여름가을겨울 그리고 봄〉은 국제 영화제에서 예술성과 대중성을 인정받았다. 〈해피투게더〉, 〈1박 2일〉, 〈무한도전〉, 〈런닝맨〉, 〈냉장고를 부탁해〉와 같은 텔레비전 예능 프로그램도 SNS를 통해서 넓은 한류 매니아 층을 이루고 있다. 이외에도 한국어, 한국 전통 음악, 한국 요리, 애니메이션, 웹툰, 게임 등에 대한 관심도 점점 늘어나고 있다.

문제 Questions

1 해외에서 한국 대중문화가 인기를 얻는 현상을 무엇이라고 합니까?
What is the phenomenon of Korean pop culture gaining popularity outside Korea called?

2 좋아하는 텔레비전 예능 프로그램을 써 보세요.
Please write down the titles of TV entertainment programs that you like.

Hallyu or the Korean Wave is a phenomenon of Korean pop culture gaining popularity overseas. It started in the late 1990s with the popularity of Korean TV dramas. The influence of this Korean Wave has gone beyond Asia and has reached the Middle East, Latin America, North America and Europe. Young people around the world are enthusiastic about K-pop songs sung by Black Pink or BTS. Korean films including *Parasite*, *Minari*, *Old Boy* and *Spring, Summer, Fall, Winter… And Spring* were recognized for their artistry and popular appeal at international film festivals. TV entertainment programs including *Happy Together*, *2 Days and 1 Night*, *Infinite Challenge*, *Running Man* and *Please Take Care of My Refrigerator* have formed a wide *hallyu* fan base through social networks. In addition, interests in Korean language, traditional music, food, animation, webtoons and games are gradually on the rise.

한류 *hallyu*, Korean Wave
대중문화 pop culture
해외 overseas
인기 popularity
얻다 to gain, to obtain
현상 phenomenon
드라마 TV drama
1990년대 1990s
말 late, end of
시작되다 to begin, to start
이제 now
아시아 Asia
N을/를 넘어서 beyond N
중동 the Middle East
라틴 아메리카 Latin America
북아메리카 North America
유럽 Europe
이르다 to reach
등 … and many more, such as …

부르다 to sing
전 세계 global, the whole world
젊은이 young people
열광하다 to be enthusiastic
〈기생충〉 *Parasite*
〈미나리〉 *Minari*
〈올드보이〉 *Old Boy*
〈봄여름가을겨울 그리고 봄〉 *Spring, Summer, Fall, Winter… And Spring*
국제 international
영화제 film festival
예술성 artistry
대중성 popular appeal
인정받다 to be recognized
〈해피투게더〉 *Happy Together*
〈1박 2일〉 *2 Days and 1 Night*
〈무한도전 (무도)〉 *Infinite Challenge (Muhandojeon, Mudo)*

〈런닝맨〉 *Running Man*
〈냉장고를 부탁해〉 *Please Take Care of My Refrigerator*
N와/과 같은 like N, such as N
예능 entertainment
프로그램 program, show
넓은 wide
매니아 fan, fanatic
층 base
이루고 있다 to consist of, to make
이외에 in addition to
전통 음악 traditional music
웹툰 webtoon, web comics
게임 game
N에 대한 regarding N
관심 interest
점점 gradually
늘어나다 to increase, to be on the rise

017

K-드라마 ★★
K-Drama

드라마는 텔레비전 연속극이다. 1990년대 말부터 K-pop과 함께 K-드라마는 한국의 대중문화를 세계에 알리는 '한류'에 중요한 역할을 하고 있다. K-드라마의 해외 인기는 2002년에 방송된 〈겨울연가〉부터이다. 이 드라마는 일본에서 크게 성공을 했다. 〈대장금〉도 아시아인들의 마음을 사로잡았다. 그 후 인터넷을 통해 한국 드라마를 보는 팬들이 세계적으로 늘어났고, SNS를 통해 그 영향력이 커졌다. K-드라마는 주로 〈풀하우스〉, 〈커피 프린스 1호점〉, 〈시크릿 가든〉, 〈별에서 온 그대〉, 〈태양의 후예〉 등 멜로드라마가 다양한 나라의 젊은 팬들에게 인기를 끌고 있다. 재벌가의 화려한 모습, 잘생기고 예쁜 인물들의 등장, 한국 드라마 특유의 스토리 전개 방식, 주로 행복하게 끝나는 결말 등이 시청자들에게 매력적으로 느껴지기 때문이다. 하지만 멜로 드라마만 인기가 있는 것은 아니다. 〈허준〉, 〈뿌리 깊은 나무〉와 같은 역사 드라마도 중동까지 알려졌다. 이처럼 해외 팬들이 드라마 촬영지를 찾아 한국을 방문하기도 한다. 핫한 명소는 〈도깨비〉의 강릉, 〈미스터 션샤인〉의 안동, 〈스물다섯 스물하나(2521)〉의 전주 한옥마을 등이 있다. 특히 〈오징어게임〉의 성공으로 K-드라마의 인기는 세계적이다.

1 텔레비전 연속극을 뭐라고 부릅니까?
What is the televised Korean drama series called?

2 유명한 한국 드라마 제목을 세 개 써 보세요.
Please write down the titles of 3 famous K-dramas.

Korean drama means televised drama series. Since the late 1990s, K-drama has played an important part in *hallyu* to introduce the Korean pop culture to the world together with K-pop. K-drama started to gain popularity overseas first with *Winter Sonata* in 2002. This drama had huge success in Japan. *Daejanggeum* is also a pioneer of hallyu, having captivated the heart of many Asians. Since then, fans who watch K-dramas through the Internet has been increasing worldwide, and the influence has grown through through social networks. Among K-dramas, melodramas such as *Full House*, *The First Shop of Coffee Prince*, *Secret Garden*, *My Love from Another Star* and *Descendants of the Sun* are popular among young fans from different countries. That is because the glamorous aspects of rich families, handsome and beautiful people, the storytelling manner unique to K-drama and usual happy endings are received to be attractive by the viewers. However, not only melodramas are popular; historical dramas like *Heo Jun* and *Deep Rooted Tree* were also known as far as the Middle East. Many fans from abroad also visit Korea to find drama filming locations. Hot spots include Gangneung in *The Guardian*, Andong in *Mr. Sunshine*, and Jeonju Hanok Village in *Twenty Five Twenty One*. In particular, thanks to the success of *Squid Game*, the popularity of K-drama is global.

어휘와 표현 \ Words & Expression

드라마 drama
연속극 televised drama series
1990년대 the 1990s
말부터 from the end of…, from late…
대중문화 pop culture
세계 world
알리다 to introduce
한류 *hallyu*, the Korean Wave
중요하다 to be important
역할 part, role
〈겨울연가〉 *Winter Sonata*
성공을 하다 to have success
아시아인 Asian
마음을 사로잡다 to captivate/win the heart of
〈대장금〉 *Daejanggeum*
통해 through
팬 fan
세계적 global, worldwide
늘어나다 to increase

영향력이 커지다 influence to grow, to become more influential
〈풀하우스〉 *Full House*
〈커피 프린스 1호점〉 *The First Shop of Coffee Prince*
〈시크릿 가든〉 *Secret Garden*
〈별에서 온 그대〉 *My Love from Another Star*
〈태양의 후예〉 *Descendants of the Sun*
등 …and many more, etc.
멜로드라마 melodrama
젊다 to be young
재벌가 rich family, *chaebeol* family
화려하다 to be glamorous
잘생기다 to be handsome
인물 character
특유의 unique
전개 development
결말 ending

시청자 viewer, audience
매력적이다 to be attractive
〈허준〉 *Heo Jun*
〈뿌리 깊은 나무〉 *Deep Rooted Tree*
N와/과 같은 like N, such as N
역사 history
중동 the Middle East
알려지다 to be known
촬영지 filming site
남이섬 Namiseom Island
홍대 Hongik University neighborhood (Hongdae)
부암동 Buam-dong
산모퉁이 mountain foot
인천 Incheon
시도 Sido Island
〈선덕여왕〉 *Queen Seondeok*
경주 Gyeongju
무장산 Mujangsan Mountain
다녀가나 to visit

018

K-팝 ★★
K-pop

K-pop은 한국에서 유행하는 대중 음악이다. 외국에서는 2000년대부터 아이돌 그룹의 음악들이 많이 알려지면서 한류의 열풍이 가속화되었다. 힙합, 댄스, R&B 등 영미권에서 유행하는 장르의 노래에 멋진 보이 밴드와 예쁜 걸 그룹들의 화려하고 강렬한 무대가 더해져 K-pop만의 개성을 가지게 되었다. 즉 K-pop은 뮤직 비디오나 무대 영상 등을 눈으로 보면서 즐길 수 있는 음악이라고 할 수 있다. 이러한 영상이 SNS를 통하여 전달되면서 전 세계에 많은 K-pop 팬들이 생겼다. 유명 아이돌 그룹으로 샤이니, 세븐틴, IVE, 뉴진스 등이 있다. 특히 2013년에 결성된 이후 세계 최고의 음악 그룹으로 인정받은 방탄소년단(BTS)이 있다. BTS는 팬클럽인 ≪아미(Army)≫들의 팬덤 활동으로도 유명하다. 또한 4인조 여성 그룹 블랙핑크(Blackpink)는 세계적으로 '선한 영향력'이 있는 그룹으로 긍정적인 국가 이미지 형성에 많은 기여를 하고 있다.

1 유명한 가수 그룹 이름을 써 보세요.
Please write down the names of famous K-pop singing groups.

2 2012년 세계적 스타가 된 한국 가수와 노래 제목은 무엇입니까?
What is the title of the song that made a Korean singer a global star in 2012? Who is the singer?

K-pop is a pop music form that prevails in Korea. Outside Korea, the *hallyu* fever accelerated as the music of idol groups got widely known from the 2000s. K-pop came to have a unique character as its glamorous and intense stage by cool boy bands and pretty girl groups were added to the genres popular in Britain and the United States such as hip hop, dance and R&B. Namely, K-pop is a kind of music that can be enjoyed while watching music videos and stage performance images. As the videos spread through social networks, many K-pop fans were formed worldwide. Famous idol groups include SHINee, Seventeen, IVE, and New Jeans. In particular, there is BTS, which has been recognized as the world's best music group since its formation in 2013. BTS is also famous for the fandom activities of its fan club, «Army». Additionally, the four-member female group Blackpink is a group with a 'good influence' globally and is contributing a lot to forming a positive national image.

유행하다 to be fashion, to prevail
대중 popular, public
년대 in the (decade)s
아이돌 그룹 idol group
알려지다 to be known
한류 *hallyu*, Korean Wave
열풍 fever
가속화되다 to accelerate
힙합 hip hop

멋지다 to be cool
보이 밴드 boy band
걸 그룹 girl group
화려하다 to be glamorous
강렬하다 to be intense
무대 stage
N을/를 통하여 through N
샤이니 SHINee
블랙핑크 Black Pink

방탄소년단 BTS (Bangtan Sonyeondan)
등 …and many more, etc.
싸이 Psy
〈강남스타일〉 "Gangnam Style"
스타 star

Korean Culture in 100 Keywords

외국인 학습자를 위한
한국 문화 100선

Keywords

부록
Appendix

정답
Answers

색인
Index

사진 출처
Sources of photos

I. 상징물 \ Symbolic Icons

001 한글 *Hangeul*

1 백성을 가르치기 위한 바른 소리입니다.
It means the proper sounds to teach the people.

2 백성들도 쉽게 사용할 수 있도록 만들었습니다.
He created *hangeul* so that the people can easily use it.

002 태극기 *Taegeukgi*

1 태극기입니다.
It is *Taegeukgi*.

2 빨간색, 파란색, 하얀색, 까만색이 있습니다.
There are red, blue, white and black.

003 애국가 *Aegukga*

1 애국가입니다.
It is *Aegukga*.

2 1948년부터입니다.
Since 1948

004 무궁화 *Mugunghwa*

1 무궁화입니다.
It is *mugunghwa*.

2 영원히 피는 꽃입니다.
It means a flower that blooms forever.

005 아리랑 *Arirang*

1 아리랑입니다.
It is *Arirang*.

2 정선 아리랑, 진도 아리랑, 밀양 아리랑입니다.
They are Jeongseon Arirang, Jindo Arirang, and Milyang Arirang.

006 고려청자 Goryeo Celadon

1 푸른빛이 납니다.
It has a grayish blue-green hue.

2 운학 무늬 매병입니다.
It is Celadon Prunus Vase with Inlaid Cloud, Crane Design.

007 김치 *Kimchi*

1 발효 식품입니다.
It is a fermented food.

2 김치찌개, 김치전, 김칫국 등이 있습니다.
There is *kimchi jjigae*, *kimchi jeon* and *kimchi soup*.

008 비빔밥 *Bibimbap*

1 비빔밥입니다.
It's *bibimbap*.

2 전주입니다.
It is Jeonju.

009 태권도 *Taekwondo*

1 2000년 시드니 올림픽에서입니다.
In 2000, at the Sydney Olympics.

2 하얀색 띠를 합니다.
We wear white belt.

010 첨단 과학 기술
Advanced Science and Technology

1 한국입니다.
It is South Korea.

2 삼성, 대우, 엘지가 있습니다.
There is Samsung, Daewoo and LG.

II. 의식주 \ Food, Clothing and Shelter

001 한복 *Hanbok*

1 한복입니다.
It is *hanbok*.

2 소매와 깃의 둥근 곡선입니다.
It is the curves of its sleeves and collars.

002 불고기 *Bulgogi*

1 불고기입니다.
It is *bulgogi*.

2 간장, 설탕, 참기름, 후추, 마늘, 파로 만듭니다.
It is made of soy sauce, sugar, sesame oil, pepper, garlic and scallion.

003 인삼 Gingseng

1 홍삼입니다.
It is red ginseng.

2 삼계탕입니다.
It is *samgyetang*.

004 한국의 술 Korean Liquor

1 소주와 막걸리입니다.
They are *soju* and *makgeolli*.

2 "건배!", "위하여!" 등이 있습니다.
There are such expressions as "Geonbae!" or "Uihayeo!"

005 젓갈/젓
Jeotgal/Jeot (Salted Fermented Seafood)

1 젓갈입니다.
It is *jeotgal*.

2 충청북도 강경에 있습니다.
It is in Ganggyeong, Chungcheongbuk-do.

006 김장
Gimjang (Seasonal Preparation of Kimchi)

1 십일 월 말이나 십이 월 초에 합니다.
It is done in late November or early December.

2 야채가 귀한 겨울 동안 먹으려고 합니다.
We do it to eat (*kimchi*) during the winter when vegetables are scarce.

007 장독대 *Jangdokdae* (Jar Stand)

1 간장, 된장, 고추장입니다.
They are *ganjang* (Korean soy sauce), *doenjang* (fermented soy bean paste), and *gochujang* (red pepper paste).

2 장독대입니다.
We call it *jangdokdae*.

008 다례 Tea Ceremony

1 '다례'는 신라 시대와 고려 시대에 발달했습니다.
The tea ceremony developed during the eras of Silla and Goryeo.

2 왜냐하면 몸과 마음을 수련하기 때문입니다.
Because it is about training the body and the mind

009 한옥 *Hanok*

1 한옥이라고 합니다.
We call it *hanok*.

2 북촌입니다.
It's Bukchon.

010 온돌 *Ondol*

1 온돌입니다.
It is *ondol*.

2 '따뜻한 돌'입니다.
It means 'warm stone.'

011 마당 *Madang* (Courtyard)

1 마당입니다.
We call it *madang*.

2 돗자리와 평상 위입니다.
On a mat or a low wooden bench

012 전통 정원의 아름다움
Beauty of Traditional Garden

1 자연을 존중해서 만듭니다.
It is made respecting/preserving nature.

2 창덕궁 후원입니다.
It is Huwon Garden at Changdeokgung Palace.

III. 지리와 관광 \ Geography and Tourism

001 한반도 Korean Peninsula

1 70퍼센트가 산입니다.
70 percent of the land consists of mountains.

2 제주도입니다.
It is Jejudo Island.

002 극동 아시아 속의 한국 Korea in East Asia

1 동해입니다.
It is the East Sea.

2 휴전선입니다.
It is the truce line.

003 계절과 날씨 Seasons and Weather

1 봄, 여름, 가을, 겨울 사계절이 있습니다.
It has four seasons of spring, summer, fall and winter.

2 덥고 습합니다.
It is hot and humid.

004 한강 Hangang River

1 강북과 강남으로 나눕니다.
It divides Seoul into Gangbuk ("north of river") and Gangnam ("south of river").

2 2,559m입니다.
It is 2,559m long.

005 서울의 고궁 Ancient Palaces in Seoul

1 경복궁, 창덕궁, 창경궁, 덕수궁입니다.
They are Gyeongbokgung Palace, Changdeokgung Palace, Changgyeonggung Palace, and Deoksugung Palace.

2 창덕궁입니다.
It is Changdeokgung Palace.

006 서울 남산 Namsan Mountain, Seoul

1 N서울타워입니다.
It is N Seoul Tower.

2 남산골 한옥마을입니다.
It is Namsangol Hanok Village.

007 남대문과 남대문시장
Namdaemun Gate and Namdaemun Market

1 숭례문입니다.
It is Sungnyemun Gate.

2 명동과 가깝습니다.
It is close to Myeongdong.

008 동대문과 근처 시장들
Dongdaemun and Nearby Markets

1 서울의 동쪽에 위치합니다.
It is located in the east of Seoul.

2 경동시장입니다.
It is Gyeongdong Market.

009 인사동 Insadong

1 인사동입니다.
It is Insadong.

2 실타래 엿, 붕어빵, 떡꼬치, 호떡, 계란빵입니다.
We can taste honey string taffy, crucian carp cake, rice cake skewer, Korean sweet pancake, and egg bread.

010 북촌 한옥 마을 Bukchon Hanok Village

1 북촌입니다.
It is in Bukchon.

2 불교 미술 박물관, 동양 문화 박물관, 세계 장신구 박물관 등이 있습니다.
There is the Buddhist Arts Museum, the Oriental Culture Museum, and the World Jewellery Museum.

011 홍대 앞 거리
Hongdae (Hongik University) Streets

1 홍익대학교 앞 거리입니다.
It began in the streets near (in front of) Hongik University.

2 매주 토요일 오후에 열립니다.
It is open on every Saturday afternoon.

012 강남 Gangnam

1 서울 한강 남쪽에 있습니다.
It is to the south of Seoul's Hangang River.

2 압구정동 로데오거리입니다.
It is Rodeo Street in Apgujeong-dong.

013 서울 지하철 Seoul Metropolitan Subway

1 1974년입니다.
It started service in 1974.

2 9호선까지 있습니다.
There are 9 lines.

014 제주도와 한라산
Jejudo Island and Hallasan Mountain

1 한라산입니다.
It is Hallasan Mountain.

2 한라산, 성산일출봉, 용암 동굴입니다.
They are Hallasan Mountain, Seongsan Ilchulbong and the lava tubes.

015 경주와 경주 남산
Gyeongju and Gyeongju Namsan Mountain

1 경주입니다.
It is Gyeongju.

2 절터, 불상, 불탑, 석등이 산이 여기저기에 많이 남아 있기 때문입니다.
Because Buddhist temple sites, statues of Buddha, pagodas and stone lamps remain all over the mountain

016 하회마을 Hahoe Folk Village

1 풍산 류씨 가문이 600년 동안 모여 살고 있는 씨족 마을입니다.
It is a clan village where the Ryu clan of Pungsan has gathered and lived together for 600 years.

2 하회 별신굿 탈춤입니다.
It is Hahoe Byeolsingut mask dance.

017 부여와 백제 유적
Buyeo and Baekje Historic Sites

1 부여였습니다.
It was Buyeo.

2 왕궁터, 왕릉, 부소산성, 궁남지, 낙화암 등이 있습니다.
There is the site of the royal palace, royal tombs, Busosanseong Fortress, Gungnamji Pond, Nakhwaam Rock, etc.

018 부산과 자갈치시장 Busan and Jagalchi Market

1 부산 자갈치시장입니다.
It is Jagalchi Market in Busan.

2 밀면, 곰장어와 어묵입니다.
They are wheat noodles, sea eel and fish cake.

019 동해안과 설악산 국립 공원
Donghae Coast and Seoraksan National Park

1 속초 해수욕장, 경포대 해수욕장입니다.
They are Sokcho Beach and Gyeongpodae Beach.

2 설악산은 강원도에 있습니다.
Seoraksan Mountain is in Gangwon-do.

020 다도해와 해상 국립 공원
Dadohae and Haesang (Marine Archipelago) National Park

1 섬이 많은 바다라는 뜻입니다.
It means a sea with many islands.

2 동피랑 벽화 마을, 충무 김밥, 나전칠기가 유명합니다.
It is famous for Dongpirang Mural Village, *Chungmu gimbap* and *najeon chilgi* lacquer ware.

021 보성 차밭 Boseong Tea Plantation

1 보성 다향제입니다.
It is Boseong Dahyangje (Green Tea Festival).

2 녹차 비빔밥, 녹차 아이스크림, 녹차 국수입니다
They are green tea *bibimbap*, ice cream and noodles.

IV. 사회와 일상생활 · Society & Daily Life

001 한국어 The Korean Language

1 한류의 영향으로 늘고 있습니다.
It is increasing due to the influence of *hallyu* (the Korean Wave).

2 문장 끝에 있습니다.
It is located at the end of a sentence.

002 인구 Population

1 오천만 명입니다.
It is 50 million.

2 중국인과 동남아시아인들입니다.
They are from China, Southeast Asia and the US.

003 성과 이름 Family Name and First Name

1 세 글자로 되어 있습니다.
There are three characters.

2 김입니다.
It is Kim.

004 호칭 Titles Addressing People

1 언니 또는 누나라고 부릅니다.
They call her *eonni* or *nuna*.

2 할머니 또는 할아버지라고 부릅니다.
They call the person Grandmother or Grandfather.

005 숫자 Numbers

1 열한 시 삼십 분입니다.
Yeolhan-si samsip-bun imnida.

2 공일공에 이이구공에 삼삼육팔입니다.
Gong-il-gong-eh i-i-gu-gong- -eh sam-sam-yuk-pal immnida.

006 나이 Age

1 한국 나이와 만 나이가 있습니다.
There are Korean age and age after the day you are born.

2 무슨 띠예요?
They say, "In what animal year were you born?"

007 결혼식 Wedding Ceremony

1 봄과 가을입니다.
Spring and fall are wedding seasons.

2 폐백이라고 합니다.
It is called *pyebaek*.

008 교육 제도 Educational System

1 15세까지입니다.
To age 15.

2 4년입니다.
It is 4 years.

009 대학 입학 시험 University Entrance Exam

1 수능 (수학 능력) 시험입니다.
It is called CSAT (Collage Scholastic Ability Test).

2 엿입니다.
It is *yeot*.

010 병역 의무 Duty of Military Service

1 18세부터입니다.
From age 18

2 18개월입니다.
It is 18 months.

011 설날 *Seollal* (New Year's Day)

1 세배입니다.
It is called *sebae*.

2 떡국입니다.
They eat *tteokguk*.

012 추석 *Chuseok*

1 음력 8월 15일입니다.
It is on August 15 the lunar calendar.

2 송편입니다.
It is *songpyeon*.

013 한의학 Traditional Korean Medicine

1 침, 뜸, 부황, 한약이 있습니다.
There is acupuncture, cautery, cupping and herbal medicine.

2 동의보감입니다. 저자는 허준입니다.
It is *Donguibogam*. The author is Heo Jun.

014 노래방 *Noraebang* (Singing Room)

1 노래방이라고 부릅니다.
We call it *noraebang* (singing room).

2 보통 시간당 지불합니다.
It is generally paid by the hour.

015 찜질방 *Jjimjilbang* (Korean Dry Sauna)

1 찜질방입니다.
It is *jjimjilbang*.

2 찜질방에서 잠을 잘 수도 있기 때문입니다.
They often use it because they can sleep there.

016 단풍놀이 Fall Foliage Picnic

1 단풍놀이라고 부릅니다.
We call it fall foliage picnic.

2 설악산과 내장산입니다.
They are Seoraksan Mountain and Naejangsan Mountain.

017 등산 Hiking

1 등산입니다.
It is hiking.

2 북한산 성벽길과 둘레길입니다.
They are Fortress Wall Trail and Dulle-gil Trail.

018 집들이 Housewarming

1 세제, 비누, 두루마리 휴지 등을 선물합니다.
Items like detergent, soap or toilet paper are given.

2 팥 시루떡을 돌립니다.
They deliver steamed rice cake topped with red beans to neighbors.

019 비상 시 긴급 전화 Emergency Phone Numbers

1 119입니다.
It is 119.

2 112입니다.
It is 112.

V. 역사와 종교 \ History and Religion

001 단군 신화 The Dangun Myth

1 단군입니다.
It is Dangun.

2 개천절이라고 부릅니다.
It is called *gaecheonjeol*.

002 원효대사 Great Master Wonhyo

1 원효대사입니다.
It is Great Master Wonhyo.

2 〈해골물 일화〉입니다.
It is the 'Story of Water in a Skull.'

003 세종대왕 King Sejong the Great

1 세종대왕입니다.
King Sejong the Great did.

2 만 원짜리 지폐에 세종대왕의 초상화가 있습니다.
The 10,000 won bill has the portrait of King Sejong the Great.

004 이순신 장군과 거북선
Admiral Yi Sun-sin and the *Geobukseon*

1 이순신 장군입니다.
It is Admiral Yi Sun-sin.

2 거북선입니다.
It is the *Geobukseon* (the 'turtle ship').

005 신사임당 Shin Saimdang

1 16세기 화가, 작가, 시인입니다.
She was a painter, writer and poet from the 16th century.

2 강원도 강릉 오죽헌입니다.
It is Ojukheon House in Gangneung, Gangwon-do.

006 이황 Yi Hwang

1 이황입니다.
It is Yi Hwang.

2 도산 서원입니다.
It is the *Dosanseowon*.

007 한국의 종교 Religions of Korea

1 무교입니다.
It is Shamanism.

2 삼국 시대에 들어왔습니다.
It was introduced during the period of Three Kingdoms.

008 고인돌 Dolmen

1 기원전 10세기에서 기원전 2세기 사이에 만들어 졌습니다.
They were made between the 10th century and 2nd century BCE.

2 전라도 고창, 화순과 강화도입니다.
They were discovered in Gochang and Hwasun of Jeolla-do and Gwanghwado Island.

009 무속 신앙 Shamanism

1 무당이라고 부릅니다.
We call the person '*mudang*' (shaman).

2 굿입니다.
It is *gut*.

**010 점과 사주
Fortunetelling and *Saju***

1 태어난 해, 달, 날, 시간을 말합니다.
It represents the year, month, day and time of your birth.

2 미아리에 있습니다.
It is located in Miari.

011 선 *Seon*

1 선입니다.
It is *seon*.

2 조계사입니다.
It is Jogyesa Temple.

012 절 Buddhist Temple

1 절이라고 부릅니다.
It is called *Jeol* (Buddhist Temple).

2 해인사와 통도사와 송광사입니다.
They are Haeinsa, Tongdosa and Songgwangsa.

**013 불국사와 석굴암
Bulguksa Temple and Seokguram Grotto**

1 신라 시대에 지어졌습니다.
It was built during the Silla Kingdom.

2 석굴암입니다.
It is Seokguram Grotto.

**014 팔만대장경
Tripitaka Koreana *(Palman Daejanggyeong)***

1 불교의 신앙으로 나라를 구하기 위해 만들었습니다.
They created it to save the country by Buddhist faith.

2 해인사 장경각에 보존돼 있습니다.
It is kept at Janggyeonggak, Haeinsa Temple.

015 템플 스테이 Temple Stay

1 절에서 머물면서 불교문화를 체험하는 것입니다.
It is to stay at a Buddhist temple and experience Buddhist culture.

2 예불, 선, 108배, 한국 다례를 체험할 수 있습니다.
You can experience Buddhist service, meditation, 108 bows and a Korean tea ceremony.

016 서원 *Seowon* (Confucian Academy)

1 옥산 서원과 도산 서원입니다
They are the Oksanseowon Confucian Academy and Dosanseowon Confucian Academy.

2 안동에 있습니다.
It is in Andong.

**017 장례식, 제사, 차례
Funeral, *Jesa* and *Charye* Rituals**

1 불교식 화장과 유교식 매장입니다.
They are Buddhist style cremation and Confucian style burial.

2 산에 있습니다.
They are mainly located in the mountains.

**018 천주교와 개신교
Roman Catholicism and Protestantism**

1 18세기 말에 들어왔습니다.
It came at the end of the 18th century.

2 명동 대성당입니다.
It is Myeongdong Cathedral.

019 판문점 Panmunjeom

1 판문점입니다.
It was concluded at Panmunjeom.

2 경기도 파주시에 있습니다.
It is located in Paju-si, Gyeonggi-do.

020 이산가족 Dispersed Families

1 1985년입니다.
They met again for the first time in 1985.

2 KBS 이산 가족 찾기입니다.
It is the KBS program "Finding Dispersed Families."

VI. 예술과 문화 \ Arts and Culture

001 한지 *Hanji* (Korean Paper)

1 닥나무입니다.
Paper mulberry tree is used.

2 전주, 원주, 안동입니다.
They are Jeonju, Wonju and Andong.

002 택견 *Taekkyon*

1 부드럽고 자연스럽고 율동적인 동작으로 하기 때문입니다.
They can perform it because it is performed in soft, natural and rhythmic movements.

2 택견입니다.
It is *Taekkyon*.

003 인쇄술 Printing Technology

1 《직지》입니다.
It is *Jikji*.

2 1377년에 인쇄됐습니다.
It was printed in 1377.

004 종묘 제례
Jongmyo Jerye (Royal Ancestral Memorial Rite of Joseon)

1 종묘 제례입니다.
It is called *Jongmyo Jerye*.

2 5월과 10월 첫 번째 일요일에 볼 수 있습니다.
You can see it on the first Sunday of May and October.

005 춘향전
Chunhyangjeon (The Tale of Chunyhyang)

1 춘향전입니다.
It is *Chunhyangjeon*.

2 전라도 남원 광한루입니다.
It is Gwanghallu Pavillion in Namwon, Jeolla-do.

006 판소리 *Pansori*

1 한 사람이 고수의 반주에 맞춰 긴 이야기를 노래로 하는 공연 예술입니다.
It is a performing art in which one person tells a long story using songs to the rhythms made by one drummer.

2 춘향가, 심청가, 흥보가, 적벽가, 수궁가입니다.
They are *Chunhyangga*, *Simcheongga*, *Heungboga*, *Sugungga*, and *Jeokbyeokga*.

007 시조 *Sijo* Poetry

1 '당시의 노래 곡조'라는 뜻입니다.
It means the 'tune of the times.'

2 조선 시대에 유행했습니다.
It was popular in the Joseon period.

008 탈춤 *Talchum* (Korean Mask Dance)

1 서민들이 즐기던 놀이입니다.
It is a play enjoyed by commoners.

2 하회탈춤입니다.
It is Hahoe Mask Dance.

009 풍속화와 민화 Genre Painting and Folk Painting

1 신윤복, 김홍도입니다.
They are Shin Yun-bok and Kim Hong-do.

2 민화입니다.
It is folk painting.

010 전통 악기 Traditional Musical Instruments

1 거문고입니다.
It is *geomungo*.

2 대금입니다.
It is *daegeum*.

011 민속촌 Korean Folk Village

1 경기도 용인입니다.
It is located in Yongin, Gyeonggi-do.

2 그네뛰기, 윷놀이, 제기차기입니다.
They are swinging, *yunnori* and *jegichagi*.

012 벚꽃놀이 Cherry Blossom Picnic

1 진해 벚꽃축제입니다.
It is the Jinhae Cherry Blossom Festival.

2 여의도 윤중로입니다.
It is Yunjungno in Yeouido.

013 부산 국제 영화제
Busan International Film Festival

1 〈부산 국제 영화제〉입니다.
It is the Busan International Film Festival.

2 10월입니다.
It is held in October.

014 전주와 전주 축제들 Jeonju and Its Festivals

1 전주비빔밥, 한정식, 콩나물밥, 전주 막걸리입니다.
They are Jeonju *bibimbap*, Korean meal(set menu) (*hanjeongsik*), bean sprout rice bowl and Jeonju *makgeolli*.

2 '전주 세계 소리 축제'입니다.
It is the Jeonju World Sori Festival.

015 세종문화회관, 국립 극장, 예술의 전당
Sejong Center for the Performing Arts, National Theater of Korea and Seoul Arts Center

1 광화문에 있습니다.
It is in Gwanghwamun.

2 예술의 전당입니다.
It is the Seoul Arts Center.

016 한류 *Hallyu* (The Korean Wave)

1 한류입니다.
It is called *hallyu* (the Korean Wave).

2 〈해피투게더〉, 〈1박 2일〉, 〈무한도전〉 등이 있습니다.
There are *Happy Together*, *2 Days and 1 Night*, *Infinite Challenge*, etc.

017 K–드라마 K-drama

1 드라마입니다.
It is called drama.

2 〈대장금〉, 〈별에서 온 그대〉, 〈태양의 후예〉.
*Daejanggeum, My Love from Another Star,
Descendants of the Sun.*

018 K–팝 K-pop

1 샤이니, EXO, 방탄 소년단입니다.
They are SHINee, EXO and BTS.

2 싸이의 〈강남 스타일〉입니다.
It is Psy's Gangnam Style.

ㅂ

ㅊ

ㅍ

작품 및 축제명

VI. 예술과 문화 Arts and Culture

참고 문헌 및 사이트 Ouvrages et sites consultés

- **외국인을 위한 한국어 문법 1 & 2** (국립국어원, 커뮤니케이션 북스, 2005)

- *Histoire de la littérature coréenne des origines à 1919* (Cho Dong-il & Daniel Bouchez, Fayard, 2001)

- *Histoire de la Corée* (André Fabre, L'Asiathèque Langues du monde, 2001)

- *La Corée du Chosŏn* (Francis Macouin, Les Belles Lettres, 2009)

- **한국 민속 대백과 사전**
http://folkency.nfm.go.kr/main/main.jsp

- **네이버 국어 사전**
http://krdic.naver.com/

- **국립국어원 표준 국어대사전**
http://stdweb2.korean.go.kr/main.jsp

- **누리 세종학당**
http://www.sejonghakdang.org/opencourse/grammar/grammar/list.do